To Wendy —

Cherished
Co-conspirator,
dear colleague,
best of friends.

— Rick

Henry Fielding and the Narration of Providence

Henry Fielding and the Narration of Providence ∾

Divine Design and the Incursions of Evil

Richard A. Rosengarten

palgrave

First published 2000 by
PALGRAVE™
175 Fifth Avenue, New York, N.Y. 10010 and
Houndmills, Basingstoke, Hampshire, England RG21 6XS.
Companies and representatives throughout the world.

PALGRAVE™ is the new global publishing imprint of St. Martin's
Press LLC Scholarly and Reference Division and Palgrave Publishers
Ltd (formerly Macmillan Press Ltd).

ISBN 0-312-23245-4

Library of Congress Cataloging-in-Publication Data
Rosengarten, Richard A.
   Henry Fielding and the narration of providence : divine design and the
incursions of evil / Richard A. Rosengarten.
      p. cm.
   Includes bibliographical references and index.
   ISBN 0-312-23245-4
   1. Fielding, Henry, 1707–1754—Religion.   2. Religious fiction,
English—History and
criticism.   3. Didactic fiction, English—History and criticism. 4.
Providence and
government of god in literature.   5. Fielding, Henry, 1707–1754—Ethics.
6. Narration
(Rhetoric)   7. Evil in literature.   I. Title.
PR3458.R4 R67   2000
823'.5—dc21

                                                                00–044628
                                                                       CIP

A catalogue record for this book is available from the British Library.

Design by Letra Libre

First edition: December 2000
10   9   8   7   6   5   4   3   2   1

Printed in the United States of America

Mary D. Rosengarten
H. Richard Rosengarten

Contents

Acknowledgments   ix
Preface   xi

Chapter 1   Principled Diffidence:
             Religion, the Narrating of Providence,
             and the Novels of Henry Fielding   1

Chapter 2   From This World to the Next:
             Poetic Justice and Deism   21

Chapter 3   Providence Victorious:
             Narrative Viewpoint in
             Joseph Andrews and *Tom Jones*   51

Chapter 4   Providence Displaced:
             The Recourse to the Final Judgment in *Amelia*   91

Chapter 5   The Binding of Providential Narrative:
             Fielding, Genesis 22, and the
             Eighteenth-Century Religious Sensibility   117

Notes   129
Bibliography   157
Index   165

Acknowledgments

I began to write this study about Fielding and divine providence just less than a decade ago, and have benefited tremendously from the concerted attention and good counsel of a number of readers whom I am very pleased to thank publicly. Anthony C. Yu, estimable advisor and dear friend, favored me on several crucial occasions with his perfect pitch in the delineation and assessment of a scholarly argument, and has been a steady and much appreciated source of both encouragement and expectation. Langdon Gilkey's seminar on Augustine first suggested to me the possibilities of thinking about narrative, history, and providence; my work on Fielding owes much to his exposition in that setting of the *Confessions*. I am not sure whether J. Paul Hunter's graciousness exceeded his generosity or vice versa, but this project has been the grateful beneficiary of each. Lynn Poland and John Barbour offered incisive questions and encouragement at the outset that shaped the direction of the project. John Ward first introduced me to *Tom Jones* some twenty years ago at Kenyon College; his spirited, principled pedagogy remains for me the ideal for the discussion of Fielding.

All or parts of the manuscript benefited from the thoughtful reactions and commentary of a set of readers whose care and generosity makes a pleasure of duty: Paul Duff, Gary Ebersole, Paul Griffiths, W. Clark Gilpin, Jennifer Jesse, Elizabeth Kowaleski-Wallace, Kevin Madigan, John Mahoney, Margaret M. Mitchell, Kyle Pasewark, Stephanie Paulsell, Kathryn Tanner, and Eric Ziolkowski. My research assistant, Jeremy Biles, has been ready, willing, and able to assist in myriad ways with the process of revision. I am also grateful to two anonymous readers who played their roles to the hilt.

Kristi Long of St. Martin's Press has been, in her encouragement, efficiency, and general acumen, the Platonic ideal of an editor. My thanks as well to Ella Pearce, Jen Simington, and the production department for patient assistance with the maze of issues involved in getting the volume from my computer program to theirs, and from theirs into production.

To Margaret M. Mitchell I owe thanks for unceasing support and encouragement, and for maintaining in exquisite balance uxorial partiality and truly excellent editorial judgment. Our daughters Nora and Katie arrived x Henry Fielding and the Narration of Providence

during the writing to introduce a new excitement and novelty into our lives; they have, happily, had little to do with this project, and I sincerely hope that it will not deter them from someday reading Fielding.

My mother and father raised me in a home that encouraged not only reading, but talking about what one had read. Over time I have learned that what I then took for granted was truly a great gift. So it is my privilege to dedicate this study to them, with my gratitude and my love.

Preface

In *The History of Tom Jones,* Henry Fielding creates a series of debates between the two tutors engaged by Squire Allworthy to instruct Paradise Hall's younger inhabitants, the rascal Tom Jones and his prudent counterpart, Master Blifil. These tutors—a quasi-Aristotelian philosopher named Square and a Church of England prelate with a penchant for discipline, Parson Thwackum—attend more to each other's opinions than to the education of their young charges. At one point their debate settles on the meanings of the words "honor" and "religion." Square remarks that, considered philosophically, such words inevitably foster debate, but what is indubitably clear is that the idea of virtue—with its true, natural beauty—exists independently of all religion. Indeed, Square notes, Christianity's chief failure, one shared by its fellow monotheistic traditions Judaism and Islam, has been precisely its inattention to this transcendent natural good. Thwackum's legendary temper takes unusual offense on this occasion:

> Thwackum replied, This was arguing with the usual Malice of all the Enemies to the true Church. He said, he doubted not but that all the Infidels and Hereticks in the World would, if they could, confine Honour to their own absurd Errors, and damnable Deceptions; "But Honour," says He, "is not therefore manifold, because there are various Sects and Heresies in the World. When I mention Religion, I mean the Christian Religion; and not only the Christian Religion, but the Protestant Religion; and not only the Protestant Religion, but the Church of England. And when I mention Honour, I mean that Mode of divine Grace which is not only consistent with, but dependent upon, this Religion; and is consistent with, and dependent upon, no other. Now to say that the Honour I here mean, and which was, I thought, all the Honour I could be supposed to mean, will uphold, much less dictate, an Untruth, is to assert an Absurdity too shocking to be conceived."

Beginning one's preface with Parson Thwackum provides a pointed reminder of the pitfalls of mincing one's point to extinction, but it also places at the forefront the most literal reminder in Fielding's fiction of this book's animating theme: namely, that the fundamental formative influence on Fielding's major works of fiction was religion.

To argue for this claim demands address to three distinct audiences, each of whose work too rarely intersects with what can only be regarded, on this topic at least, as its appropriate counterparts. I list them alphabetically to underscore their equal importance: historians of eighteenth-century religious and philosophical thought; literary critics of the early English novel; and theologians with special interests in narrative. This book is written for all three of these audiences, and draws significantly on work from each. At the same time, the resulting argument is of necessity eclectic, and each particular audience may find itself in what follows on familiar terrain at certain points and in uncharted territory elsewhere. Hence this preface, which aims to make explicit a set of assumptions or understandings that may not be commonly shared among its intended readership.

In the mid-eighteenth century when Fielding wrote, the relationship of religion to the created world, and to the places of human nature and morality within that world, were hotly debated. Contemporaries who addressed these topics included philosophers such as Mandeville and Hume and theologians as different as William Law and John Wesley. Fielding self-consciously entered this arena with the creation of his novels, and I contend that the complexity of his thought on these matters either has been rendered null, or dismissed because it is not, in fact, easily categorized. Yet Fielding was a genuinely independent religious thinker who chose the novel to explore theological questions otherwise handled through more traditional forms such as polemical tracts and sermons. Critics who seek to align Fielding for or against religion, or for or against some particular religious party, inevitably skim over the complexity of this approach and its fruits.

This complexity is best captured through the elucidation of a central idea that Fielding deploys complementarily as both narrative device and theological claim: this is the idea of retrospection. The keystone of Fielding's dovetailing literary and theological interest is his fascination with the ways in which human plans, calculations, and designs are diverted or confirmed by accident, or unintended consequences of independent human decisions, or unanticipated external developments. Yet recognition of such reversals and redirections only reveal themselves after the fact. Such local but signal factors inevitably raise questions about the roles chance, design, and fate play in our experience of the world. Really to understand the world, then, requires the privileged viewpoint of retrospection; and as narrative device, Fielding brings to life retrospection in the forms of his narrators, self-proclaimed "historians" who report the results of their investigations into such (now concluded) chains of circumstance. These reports are framed by an ongoing authorial commentary whose relative degrees of confidence and detail outline the development of Fielding's thinking on these themes. More systematic in *Tom Jones,* but present and unmistakably central in the earlier *Joseph Andrews* and the later *Amelia,* the retrospective commentary of Fielding's narrators is the cardinal interpretive fact of his fiction. Its renowned Palladian structure is rendered meaningless without it. The different degrees of authority claimed by these narrators, discussed briefly below and at length in chapters three and four, are variations on this great, enduring theme of his fictional narrative practice.

By speaking retrospectively, Fielding's narrators assume a didactic role that readers today might term "controlling." The end this device serves is Fielding's direction of the reader's considered attention to what can be claimed for our understanding and discernment of events in the world. It is here that the theological claim enters, and its substance is that most retrospective of theological doctrines—divine providence. To engage seriously the work done by Fielding's retrospective narrators is, I argue, to engage Fielding's attitude about providence. This is the heart and soul of his narrative art. A brief rehearsal of the theological tradition of the doctrine of providence prior to Fielding may, then, be useful.

Christian theologians who have sought to characterize the course of divine activity as it can be partially understood by humans have classically done so through the articulation of a three-part structure of creation, providence, and eschatology. Providence describes God's role in the created world we inhabit, a world which will be concluded at the time of the eschaton or final judgment. As the middle term, providence bears explicit relation to the other two: it is an extension of the order implied by the creation, and an anticipation of the forthcoming kingdom of God. An understanding of providence thus always implies understandings of the nature of the creation, and of the values that will mark the fully realized reign of God. As the discussion of the deism controversy and the debate about poetic justice in chapter two demonstrates, these relationships were absolutely crucial in late seventeenth- and eighteenth-century England. There the crux of disagreement turns precisely on whether providence is encompassed by creation, or absorbed into the eschaton.

This tendency to relegate providence to either the creation or the eschaton was the result of the classic philosophical conundrum raised by the idea of providence, namely the extent to which the deity's alleged government of the world qualifies or compromises the free activity of its human agents. Systematic theology literally embodies this tension in the centuries prior to the Enlightenment. The classic formulation is offered by Aquinas: God causes not only our will but our willing, and humans act for the good in cooperation with divine grace. In the sixteenth century, this claim and its ramifications prove acutely vexing for the reformers. Molina and his followers demur from Aquinas, arguing that God's cooperation or concurrence with human action does not compromise human freedom because it does not influence the individual human will. Calvin and his followers affirm the direct involvement of the deity in the world's government through the doctrine of double predestination, while also claiming—at least rhetorically—that the fact that humans are elected by God either to salvation or damnation does not actually compromise their creaturely freedom. Arminius takes issue with the Calvinists, repudiating the notion that God damns individuals and claiming that Christ's death and resurrection, with its atonement and offer of salvation, is available to all who will accept it.

There is much to be said for the observation that this particular theological debate is perennial, and it is possible to trace its influences directly into the eighteenth century—Wesley, for example, was deeply informed by Arminian theology. But this account of providence as it contextualizes the reading of Fielding would be incomplete without mention of a further, equally crucial, tradition that I term "narrating providence." For this tradition the originating figure is Augustine, whose *Confessions* provides the classic testimony both to its form as retrospective narrative, and to the inevitable way that retrospective narrative raises questions about fate, chance, and design. The crucial consideration Augustine's narrative raises for the reading of Fielding is this: the post-conversion, faithful Augustine can no more readily identify God's providential ways in the world than could his pre-conversion self. While he knows beyond doubt that God is in fact leading him, Augustine also recognizes that the specifics of providence are a matter of faith only to be recognized after the fact. The problematic relationship of divine government and free will thus remains, but rather than affirming one over the other the narrative seeks to maintain the integrity of each within a framework of faithful affirmation. Fielding took recourse to the novel to maintain, as it were, a delicate balance that more classical forms of discussion on this theme struggled without success to achieve.

Yet in doing so Fielding—as has inevitably been the case for both the systematic theologian elucidating doctrine and the narrator telling a story of the retrospective discovery of divine design—thereby faced the classic challenge to any idea of providence: the fact of human evil, and how to make sense of its presence in a world understood to be providentially ordered. What I term "the incursions of evil" in Fielding's novels refers to this problem, and requires clarification both because Christian theology has elucidated two major alternative responses, and because Fielding's engagement is considerably subtler, and in a sense more mundane, than our post-Holocaust sensibility might understandably lead us to anticipate. The crucial point is that the attempts of the Christian tradition to construct a theodicy—to reconcile the fact of evil

with the central tenets of God's goodness and beneficence—are not understood to be outside the realm of providence. Augustine will argue that only
out of evil can result a yet greater good; Calvin will speak of secondary causes
that create evil as a fact of human life; and, in this century, John Hick has
constructed an important argument for a tradition that regards evil as "soul-
making" for humanity.

Fielding knew that by taking providence as his theme he raised this set of
questions, and his fiction represents and queries these options, particularly
as presented in Calvin and Hick. The privileged retrospection of the narrator documents the full vagaries of the uncertain course of events, including
secondary causes both that conduce to and deter from the desired end.
Readers of Fielding cannot but emerge from his novels with an acutely in-
stantiated sense of his observation, most explicit in *Tom Jones* but informing
his entire fictional corpus, that fortune always works by halves. Within this
broader context, Fielding marshals his powers of plotting and characterization to create two prominent proponents of the argument for the world as
the vale of soul-making. Parson Adams in *Joseph Andrews* and Dr. Harrison
in *Amelia* each counsel their respective novels' titular heroes to have patience
and bear up under their privations in the confidence that all must, in the
end, turn out for the best. As I argue in chapters three and four, the most
salient dimension of these two counselors is precisely their tendency to invoke the perspective delineated by Hick. Yet in Fielding's hands it is, I argue,
presented as possessing a central aspect that can only be characterized as sin-
ister: potentially so in the case of Adams, and to an uncomfortable degree
really so in the case of Harrison.

In narrating providence, then, the question of "the incursions of evil" is
inevitably raised. In Fielding's novels we see three kinds of evil. The first is
blunt malfeasance, which presents itself most ominously in scenes that in-
volve the potential for rape: each of the major heroines faces this, and I
strongly contend that Fielding consistently makes the threat more real than
those who describe him as a comic novelist tend to credit. Second, the novels document a plethora of instances in which characters, whether from self-
interest or heedlessness, mar the progress of the narrative toward its
manifestly preferable destiny. In these cases Fielding often suggests that the
source of the problem is not intent (or lack thereof), but a flaw in character.
The incorrigible tendency of Tom's companion Partridge to gossip betrays
Tom's own genuine delicacy with the name of Sophia Western; where Tom
is discreet, Partridge is blatant, a juxtaposition that leads Sophia to the incorrect (but, Fielding's narrator dutifully notes, entirely understandable)
conclusion that the wide badinage of her name on the road is due to the indiscretion of her lover, when it is in fact due to the loose lips of someone she
has never met.

The third kind of evil is perhaps the most interesting: this is the case where evil is revealed in the grand retrospection of the denouement. It is also the rarest. The outstanding, and probably the sole fully realized instance of it may be found in the character of Blifil in *Tom Jones*. In the character of Blifil, Fielding comes as close as he can to presenting the distillation of evil in his moral universe: he combines supremely both malfeasance and intentional, even cunning, marring. And it is telling that, however much those around him recognize his fundamentally maleficent nature, Blifil survives. We are told in conclusion that he is running for Parliament, and while the satiric swipe at politics is surely intentional it is also beyond question the case that Fielding sought here to underscore his permanence to the otherwise happy landscape. (The city of London, I shall argue, performs a parallel function in *Amelia*.) The function of "the incursions of evil" in Fielding's fiction works to honor the distaff side of the narration of providence by fully incorporating into the account the most severe challenge to its central claim.

Fielding's decision to describe his novels as "histories" and to establish as their central value the realization of family comity and security became the frame through which he developed these themes. His singularity as a thinker on these questions—and, I maintain, his greatness as an artist—resides in his complexification of these values and his thoughtful scrutiny of how they do and do not inform us concerning the providential order. Much as the theme of conversion functions in Augustine, in Fielding the ideal of family life is the fulcrum around which everything is understood, and around which, the reader comes to recognize, understanding is not everything we hoped.

If Fielding's invocation of family parallels Augustine's deployment of conversion within the narrative, it results in the artistic vision of this greatest eighteenth-century novelist in the expression of a sensibility that is both Augustinian in its faith that providence must exist, and quasi-Faulknerian in its acknowledgment of the seeming fatefulness of human affairs. In that particular sensibility, with its deeply nuanced integrity both familiar and alien, resides Fielding's perennial interest as a practitioner of the narrative arts. And it is to the location and articulation of that sensibility that this study is dedicated.

The structure of this attempt at location and articulation bears brief rehearsal. Chapters one and two are primarily concerned with issues of location. Chapter one considers Fielding's status among literary critics and narrative theologians to the end of clarifying the assumptions articulated above in the context of previous work; the goal there is to clarify both what is at stake in my claim, and to outline more fully the meaning of "principled diffidence." Chapter two offers a historical analysis of the debate about poetic justice and the deism controversy in eighteenth-century England, arguing that in the end they addressed a common issue and that they provide the appropriate direct historical context for thinking about Fielding's novels.

Chapters three and four turn to articulation of Fielding's principled diffidence through the artistic vision of his novels; these include analysis of the function of narrative viewpoint as refracted through parallels of theme and characterization. Chapter five sketches the implications of this reading of Fielding for the study of providential narrative and our understanding of the eighteenth-century religious sensibility.

Henry Fielding and the
Narration of Providence

Chapter 1 ∾

Principled Diffidence: Religion, the Narrating of Providence, and the Novels of Henry Fielding

Augustine narrates providence in his *Confessions*. Setting out the way in which God led him unknowingly, that he might eventually be led knowingly, Augustine's retrospective narrative uncovers manifold instances of the divinely providential hand interposing to direct his ultimate course. Here God truly resides in the details, rendering a fabric so tightly woven that in the end the reader is hard pressed to sort the large from the small. Monica's death is and can only be momentous, and the narrative gives us reason to think so; yet a phrase can be as telling—"Give me chastity, but not yet." Each helps to chart the course of the providential plan. This has its effect: to the degree that it generates suspense, Augustine's autobiography does so in terms of when and how, rather than whether, he will accept God's plan for his life and convert to the one, true religion. The reader's attention and consideration are directed not to the outcome, but to the process and those telling details. In these we are meant to see clearly, inevitably, decisively, the hand of God at work in the world. While books 10 to 13 shift abruptly from narration to speculation—from the providentially structured events of Augustine's own life to general questions of memory, time and eternity, and creation—Augustine clearly intends these concluding chapters to be an extension of the narrative of his life. They provide a coda for the activity of the reflective believer who, having faith, now can truly seek understanding. The questions may not be substantially different from those of the pagan teacher of rhetoric, but the context is in unmistakable counterpoint: no longer does the asking index a restless shifting among Manichean and Platonic worldviews. The frame of the cosmos has been settled and, however recalcitrant the topic, it can now be addressed in the confidence that the answer resides with God, whatever lack of headway we make toward an answer. Knowing or unknowing, Augustine—and by extension the believing Christian—thinks and acts out of the security of participating in the providential plan for the world.

William Faulkner narrates fate in *Absalom, Absalom*. It is not Faulkner, but Quentin Compson, Shreve McCannon, and anyone or anything that might contribute to the historical record they seek to establish, who tell various versions of what turns out to be the quest for the historical Sutpen. The overall effect is dramatically different, indeed directly at odds with the *Confessions*. Quentin and Shreve are not led; they commence their journey unknowing and they conclude it embroiled in ongoing, bewitched speculation about the truth and significance of the random details they encountered. No sacred text orients their quest or affords stability for their endeavor. The narrative effect is one not of suspended disbelief, but of literal suspension: will they, indeed can they, learn the truth about the past? The reader closes Faulkner's novel with the clear sense that they cannot. Quentin has no God in whom he can confidently deposit the mystery and enigma he discovers at the heart of his experience. He and Shreve address each other, the night, the silence, sometimes the reader—never God. Their unanswered queries do not bespeak some larger perspective in which they can be confident of an answer. Readers of Faulkner's wider corpus are left as well with the troubling implication of Quentin Compson's suicide, an ending of his time to which *Absalom, Absalom* surely provides the coda. The self-imposed end to Quentin's search for understanding leaves the reader with no sense that the world is providentially ordered, or indeed that there is an eternity that provides the basis for meaning in time as we know it.

An autobiography from late fourth-century Hippo and a novel from the early twentieth-century American South may seem—in some respects unquestionably are—unlikely partners. I juxtapose them at the outset not to propose a brief against such distinctions, but to invoke through them a common but perhaps often overlooked narrative practice, and to situate the novels of another writer who stands, chronologically and thematically, between them. The narrative practice in question is retrospection. Augustine and Faulkner each produces a narrative that is decisively retrospective in viewpoint. In its elementary sense this means that the narrative tries to explain what happened in the past. By definition most narratives do this, but when such a narrative becomes self-conscious and reflective about what it does, it ups the ante: it makes central to that telling an interrogation of the larger purpose, structure, or pattern of what is told. For all their differences, Augustine and Quentin Compson share an obsession with the "why" of the past, and with what conclusions we can draw from it. From their common question and their different circumstances arise vastly different answers. Augustine finds that his life has happened this way because God so ordained it—"Providence." The exchanges between Quentin and his roommate Shreve in their Harvard dormitory that form the conclusion of *Absalom, Absalom* do not answer but speculate, with increasing despair, about the void at the center of their query—"Fate." In its self-conscious form retrospective narrative literally reads the world by staking a claim about not just the sequence of events, but their character. What is the quality of the circumstantial chain? The reader of these narratives closes these volumes with the sense that the question has been asked and answered.

Henry Fielding's novels are just such self-consciously retrospective narratives, and the reader also closes them with the sense that the same question has been asked and answered. The quality of the answer, however, proves less sweeping and unqualified than the answers Augustine and Faulkner provide. *Joseph Andrews* (1742), *Tom Jones* (1749), and *Amelia* (1751) each concerns itself with "how events fell out," but what is most interesting about the novels is not the mere fact of retrospection but the self-conscious way in which Fielding employs an intrusive narrative voice to articulate and indeed sustain diffidence about whether providence or fate (Fortune in Fielding's parlance) holds sway in the world. In genre and chronology closer to Faulkner, in religious commitment closer to Augustine, Fielding the novelist occupies a midpoint on the thematic spectrum for self-consciously retrospective narratives whose span can be measured by the Bishop of Hippo and the Count of No Account. Neither so confident as Augustine nor so ultimately desperate as Faulkner's Compson, Fielding's narrators actively query the circumstantial chain. Their diffidence consists in their uncertainty about what can be claimed for the hand of God in the world. Where Augustine sees God's hand everywhere and Faulkner nowhere, Fielding is simply less sure, in specific instances, whether it can be said that God has interposed.

In Fielding's novels, however, the asking raises a further question: is the narrator's diffidence about whether the world runs on providence or fate mere diffidence, or is it principled? Is Fielding in the end neither more nor less than unsure, an agnostic on the matter? Or is his diffidence thought and felt through to its core, so that it becomes the necessary principle behind any answer to the question of what we can know about what Fielding's contemporary, William Congreve, called "the way of the world?" The worlds of Fielding's novels, and their ways, have at their center Fielding's vision of happiness, the marital union. Complexly plotted and studded with intrusive narrative commentary, Fielding's real story examines the way that events surrounding the happy couple (fail to) conduce to the life they manifestly deserve. There is no diffidence about the fact that Joseph and Fanny, Tom and

Sophie, and Booth and Amelia really love and deserve each other, and there is no doubt that, in the end, they will achieve the desired condition. Like conversion in the *Confessions,* the reader's attention comes to focus less on this and more on what they encounter, and must endure, to arrive there.

Fielding intends what we see to give us pause, at least about the degree to which we discern the providential hand interposing on the behalf of manifestly good people. Virtue is rewarded, but vice usually goes unpunished and Fielding gives his reader the sense in ending that things falling out happily was a closer call, that events have resulted in a less secure condition for the hero and heroine, than we might wish. He means to unsettle: it is unclear that the hand of God's providence can be found at work in the lives of good people. The worthies themselves are made to feel keenly that their fate is precarious. The reader not only feels but knows this unmistakably, to a degree that the characters cannot, thanks to the narrator and his retrospection.

That the narrative itself raises the question of what can be claimed for providence testifies to diffidence, and a distinguished school of Fielding's interpreters holds the view that in the final accounting this is in fact the full story. Debit and credit cancel each other out, and render a bottom line that is absent any remainder of positive religious conviction. On this reading, Fielding wrote in a period of massive intellectual upheaval and shifting paradigms that simply did not in the end afford him the structure, much less the foundation, to sustain the assured didactic tone that was his natural metier.[1] I demur from this view, and propose to present a case for the principled diffidence of Fielding's novels. I shall argue as follows. Fielding shared with his immediate predecessors and contemporaries the inherited orthodox Christian view that the activity of God encompasses a temporal sequence of creation, providence, and eschatology. In this context it is possible to specify the upheaval he did indeed face: an increasing skepticism, due either to reservations about the extent of human sagacity or the fact of evil, about positing active providential interposition in the world. The upheaval was not felt solely by Fielding, and the immediate historical context for his novels are the literary and theological controversies that surrounded him: the debate about poetic justice and the deism controversy. I examine these in chapter two, arguing that they fully complement and indeed parallel each other in their fundamental question: what claim can be made for God's providential interposition in this world? The answers offered both underscore the very close relation at this time between literature and religion, and demonstrate that in addressing the question himself, Fielding's context was ample and informed what he wrote. That context has as its unmistakable consensus the idea that providence is no longer a matter of easy, or at least ready, attribution. Actually at issue—and hotly debated from the late seventeenth century through and well beyond Fielding's own life—was whether the (unquestioned) integrity of the general providential design for the world was safely ensconced in the creation, or required the eschatological final judgment.

In what follows I work chronologically up to Fielding's novels, devoting chapters three and four to their interpretation. Here one encounters directly, and I shall challenge, the claim for what I call Fielding's mere diffidence, an inability to transcend debate that amounts to paralysis. This claim rests heavily on the assertion that Fielding's final novel, *Amelia,* is decisively anticlimactic: a betrayal of narrative voice that serves in the end to underscore the ultimate untenability of the tonal assurance of its predecessors. I shall argue that, while a lesser literary accomplishment than *Joseph Andrews* or *Tom Jones,* *Amelia* employs a similar theological paradigm and constitutes in the end not a departure from its predecessors, but a new variation on an old theme.

Fielding's diffidence, then, takes quite literally the narrative form of an attempt to characterize the ways of the world when the viability of direct providential interposition is no longer apparent. His principle is his fealty to the framing structure of divine activity, and a corresponding conviction that, to whatever degree direct interposition was curbed, there was in fact a broader providential plan mandated by the assurances of the creation and the final judgment. Fielding must be understood within the religious context and preoccupations of his time, in which he was enmeshed and indeed to which his novels contribute. In arguing for principled diffidence I claim the existence in Fielding's novels of warrants for both ambiguity and affirmation. This is the great theme of his fiction, through which individual novels play out variations: in this is its abiding interest.

Fielding's novels always end "happily"—at least to the degree that virtue is rewarded. Perhaps their chief delight resides in their capacity to effect happy resolutions as the outcome of labyrinthine plots. Coleridge's judgment that *Tom Jones* ranks with Sophocles's *Oedipus* and Ben Jonson's *Alchemist* as the three most perfect plots ever planned remains the oustanding tribute to Fielding's widely acknowledged virtuosity. These superbly realized happy endings, however, can only be the starting point of interpretation. Like Augustine, in Fielding it is not so much the ending we read to discover as it is the process that we seek to discern, for the ending of *Tom Jones* underscores that happiness has been purchased not by the elimination of evil, but by its (momentary?) displacement. Resolution quickly gives rise to review, and the attentive reader is thrown back to what J. Paul Hunter has called "the chains of circumstance" on which that resolution depends. However happy the final moment of the narrative, the resolution discovers little to make the reader particularly sanguine that the future will continue in kind. Oscar Wilde's Miss Prism, who remarks in *The Importance of Being Earnest* that "[t]he good ended happily, and the bad unhappily. That is what fiction means," either had not read Fielding, or (what is more likely) read him glancingly.

My thesis is situated at the nexus of three crucial questions in study of the eighteenth century, each of which constitutes a building block of the present argument. The first concerns the history of the interpretation of *Amelia* and its decisive impact upon the critical reception of Fielding's major novels. Second is the past valorizations and denials of the place of religion in Fielding's novels. The third is the debate over the "rise of the novel" in eighteenth-century England, and how Fielding has been perennially (mis)placed in that discussion. As will become apparent, each of these issues addresses dimensions of the other two. Together they show how Fielding's interpreters cannot avoid, sometimes explicitly and at others implicitly, the religious dimension of his fiction.

The state of these questions raises the enormous and central issue of how to speak constructively about the role religion plays in the eighteenth century. Scholarly vexation on this point extends far beyond Fielding, but he himself, and work about him, certainly exemplify this challenge. I address this topic through consideration of recent work on narrative theology. Always central to religious belief and practice, the human impulse to tell stories has emerged in the last two decades as a central heuristic in the study of religion.[2] Like "deconstruction" in literary theory, the term "narrative" in the study of religion carries a too wide range of connotations and defies easy summary. But to think about Fielding as a narrative theologian usefully focuses the full value of his novels because it makes genuinely complementary their literary and religious dimensions. To distinguish these is, at least in Fielding's case, a signal instance of murdering to dissect. I seek to avoid such criminal behavior to the end of clearing space for Fielding as a literary novelist who wrote to express his belief. Through this focus on Fielding and the eighteenth century, I seek as well to discipline to some degree the at times unruly use of narrative as a category in the study of religion.

The Reception of Fielding's Novels: A Critical Wheel of Fortune

Even a cursory review of the more recent work on Fielding's novels underscores the pivotal role played by the critical evaluation—whether positive or negative—of *Amelia*, Fielding's last novel. Earlier critics regarded *Amelia* as a betrayal of Fielding's artistic greatness.[3] Gone was the magisterial narrator and his authoritative, if at times problematically intrusive, commentary. Lost were the assurances of tone and characterization that propelled the earlier novels. Bad as these diminishments seemed to be, what appeared in their stead proved yet more problematic: an at times unsteady emphasis on individual culpability and helplessness, juxtaposed with a brute depiction of life in the world as marked by cruelty and meanness. A strong verdict of betrayal results. The happy end-

ing of *Amelia,* unlike those of *Joseph Andrews* and *Tom Jones,* really fails to engage the reader and is entirely unearned. These critics consider *Amelia* a problem, to be bracketed off from the earlier novels or, in some cases, ignored.

Some recent work makes more positive claims.[4] These critics see in *Amelia*
an understandable, even admirable turn to a new social realism because Fielding exhibits an unexpected willingness to experiment with new structures of
characterization and psychology. *Amelia* picks up on and elaborates intimations of the earlier novels. This is particularly true in relation to Fielding's female characters: Fielding's final word on heroic behavior, Amelia is an
amplification of Sophia Western, who displaces Joseph Andrews and Tom
Jones. Fielding's decision to focus his last novel on his leading female character stands for these critics not as a confused departure from established, successful practice, but as a positive outgrowth of Fielding's newly adopted
interest in illustrating the plight of the socially marginalized or disempowered.

Despite the fact that these two interpretive approaches present contradictory valuations of the Fielding canon, they present nonetheless an important canonical consensus. Each places Fielding's fiction on a critical
wheel of fortune, with *Tom Jones* and *Amelia* occupying opposite points, so
that one cannot be up without the other being down. Their respective spins
have opposite results but the same effect. For the earlier generation, *Tom
Jones* is up and *Amelia* is down; for the later *Amelia* is up, and *Tom Jones* is
down. This becomes an enshrined canonical principle, of ineluctable choice:
either *Tom Jones* or *Amelia,* but not both.

Those who wish to claim critical pride of place for both *Tom Jones* and
Amelia require a point of reference outside any individual novel.[5] One striking fact of this fortune's wheel is that, regardless of which end is up, religion
is regarded as playing a crucial negative role in the interpretation of *Amelia.*
Robert Alter speaks for the earlier generation in his assessment that the character of Booth constitutes Fielding's sole attempt to fashion a Christian hero.
His failure extends the Renaissance's inability to fashion a character who can
"live a Christian life in a pagan world."[6] Alter judges that the conventions of
form and the resulting realism of depiction render such a presentation at best
implausible. When he decided to write explicitly as a Christian, Fielding thus
fell prey to an insoluble literary dilemma that only highlighted the increasingly enfeebled place of Christian faith in the modern world. An important
reason that *Tom Jones* is up and *Amelia* down, on this view, has to do with
Fielding's decision to express in fictional form an explicit religious interest.

Dubiety about religion as a positive force in Fielding's fiction also informs,
from the opposite perspective, the view of the more recent generation of critics. Here the challenge resides in the claim that Amelia's integrity of character,
so sympathetically rendered by Fielding, focuses attention on the grim realities
of her situation to a degree that entirely discredits the pronouncements of Dr.

Harrison, Amelia's clergyman and the novel's proponent for the Christian providential worldview.[7] Readers cannot avoid the facts of Amelia's case: penniless, ever faithful to an untrue husband, the object of schemes on her virtue. The world is hardly friendly to Amelia, and even her stalwart faith is not immune to despair. The facts utterly eclipse Harrison's reassurances about the providence of the world and his references to a future state. Belief in providence buckles under the weight of the experience of evil. Here social realism and providence are seen as entirely incompatible: emphasis on one precludes the other, and Fielding's newfound commitment to social realism mandated that he abandon his earlier commitment to providence. The basis of these critics' judgment for *Amelia* at the expense of *Tom Jones* is their approval of what they judge to be Fielding's abandonment, rather than his promulgation, of the expression of his religious commitments in fictional form.

Whether Fielding erred by attempting to be explicitly Christian, or triumphed by abandoning Christianity, the signal dimension of the understanding of *Amelia,* and of the construction of an either/or proposition about the Fielding canon, is the influence of Fielding's Christianity. It must be said that this is an odd consensus that leads to opposite results: one side has to be wrong. In the end it begs at least two questions: did Fielding really write in the throes of a kind of schizophrenic conflict between his literary and religious interests? Was his Christianity so brittle that the demands of realism, whether formally literary or social, respectively precluded or overwhelmed it? I shall argue that the answers to these questions are, respectively, that there was not such a conflict and that in his novels Fielding presents a view of Christian belief that acknowledges the challenges of realism and compromises in response, but is by no means brittle in its overarching commitment. If the emergent wheel of fortune does not present a coherent or compelling view of the Fielding canon, it does underscore the critical if sometimes only implicitly acknowledged role the religious question of his day plays in how we think about Fielding. Other interpreters of Fielding have addressed this explicitly.

Religion in Fielding's Fiction:
Valorization, or Stigmatization and Denial

When scholars have explicitly addressed religion in Fielding, they have presented their own either/or option, with valorization or denial as the only possibilities. The powerful champion for valorization has been Fielding's biographer, Martin Battestin. Battestin argues that Fielding wrote out of an explicitly religious concern for ethics. Influenced deeply and directly by the latitudinarian tradition, Fielding grounded his moral teaching in a view of the world as a fully realized theater of divine providence. Prudence becomes the hallmark human virtue in this account, because when we act prudently we act in accord with the overarching divine design for the world and ourselves. The human being who acts prudently acts in accord with the divine plan.[8]

The claim for ethics resonates deeply with the general tenor of the narrative commentary and the detailed attention Fielding lavishes on the predilections and peccadilloes of even minor characters. *Tom Jones* announces its theme to be human nature, and without question its narrator follows through on this declaration. Battestin's argument that Fielding located his theme in a broader claim about the fundamental orientation of the cosmos—and that he saw this as complementary—is also insightful. He takes seriously the proposition that Fielding was a novelist of ideas, and his work attends to the narrative commentary itself to a degree that was previously unknown. Valorization of religion in Fielding yields ripe critical fruit.

The pitfall of valorization, however, is also illustrated in Battestin's work. That Fielding knew and admired Tillotson, South, and Barrow does not demonstrate that Fielding was therefore simply antagonistic to the claims of deism. In Battestin's rendering, however, latitudinarianism straightforwardly excludes deism. Battestin mentions "Fielding's own early flirtation with the alluring doctrines of deism" but maintains that his fiction demonstrates his outright rejection of it in his mature years.[9] The endgame conversions of the philosopher Square in *Tom Jones* and of Billy Booth in *Amelia* allegedly underscore this rejection; but the former is a minor moment in the complex conclusion of an elaborately plotted work, and the latter, while more prominent, conveys a tone of retreat, not affirmation. Each is a textbook case of how Fielding calls into question the stability of conventional "happy" resolutions. No evidence, in fact, suggests that Fielding felt such an explicit moral animus for deism. Indeed, his context argues strongly against such a distinction. The complexity of eighteenth-century Christianity in England turned precisely on a series of fast-dissolving antonyms: natural and revealed, reason and revelation, heresy and orthodoxy, deist and Christian. Fielding was no such reactionary. Battestin's does not acknowledge Fielding's inherent diffidence about providence. Fielding's novels include the recognition in both their structure and their narrative rhetoric that the idea of the providential plan could be implausible, and that human certitude about such things is at best uncertain.[10]

If Battestin valorizes religion in Fielding, a long tradition of predecessors and successors have stigmatized it.[11] Leo Braudy reacts against Battestin's emphasis on providence by analyzing the term "History" as a governing narrative concept in eighteenth-century writing.[12] Braudy gives explicit attention to the narrative conventions common to history and fiction in the eighteenth century, resulting in the helpful hypothesis that Fielding developed in his novels an informed interest in the ways that causality and factual

detail inform the literary problem of presenting human character in time
and history. This highlights the privileged perspective of Fielding's narrator,
his didactic purposes, and the extended role the narrator bestows upon the
reader in *Tom Jones*. Here, Braudy argues, Fielding addresses the question of
whether chance or providence governs the world. In his rendering, the
choice is without remainder: either chance or providence. Braudy chooses
chance and rejects providence. Thus the narrator's famous statement that
Tom Jones is not a system, but a history, axiomatically means that "the providential view in *Tom Jones* is at best supererogatory and at worst ignorantly
or meretriciously self-serving."[13] Bestowing any narrative role on providence
systematizes history, and this violates Braudy's assumption that history and
its writing finally demonstrate not order, but chance.

A virtue of Braudy's approach, in addition to its construction of important dimensions of *Tom Jones* as "History," is the integrity he brings to
his argument. Stigmatization shows its true colors: it is ultimately the denial of any possible intersection of religion and literature in Fielding's fiction. Where Battestin looks for religion and finds everything, Braudy's
search yields precisely nothing: a dead end, or at best a once captivating
cul-de-sac of now deserted residences that we—following Fielding, Hume,
and Gibbon—need to exit quickly. While Fielding clearly felt the power of
the question, he was not decisive in answering it and he certainly did not
treat it as an either/or conundrum.[14]

While Battestin elides Fielding's diffidence, Braudy eliminates his principle: Fielding was not post-Christian, indeed he wrote out of an explicitly
Christian religious framework. Here reservation reflects not abandonment
but engagement. What Braudy identifies as the narrator's rejections of the
Christian view of providence in the name of historical causation are in fact
the hedgings and qualifications of a believer who seeks to make his doctrine
accord with his world. Fielding's engagement with religion was thoughtful,
even critical, and his world may well have been in flux, but his theological
alternatives were not so stark as Braudy's formulation suggests. In the end
Fielding's theology, and his expression of it in narrative form, was amenable
to neither all-encompassing systematization nor outright rejection. These
questions of tradition and innovation have an even more explicit context in
discussions of the rise of the novel in England.

Religion and the Rise of the English Novel

Criticism focused on Fielding himself has tended to construct one of two ei-
ther/or dilemmas: in terms of the canon, either *Joseph Andrews* and *Tom Jones*
or *Amelia*, but not both; in terms of explicit religious interest, narratives of
either providence or chance, but not both. A third, more broadly-based crit-

ical approach—and one that has arguably exerted more lasting influence on Fielding's reception than either of these—is studies of the rise of the novel that place Fielding in the context of other early English novelists. My review of these studies focuses on Fielding's place in them, from which two conclusions emerge. First, these theorists always work from a set of assumptions, more often implicit than explicit but absolutely decisive for their judgments, about the role of religion in the early novel. Second, whatever the approach, Fielding's relation to the tradition tends to be that of the problem child, the awkward fit, not quite the outcast but perilously close: as one figure in the tradition of the early English novel, he himself parallels almost eerily the role *Amelia* has played in the earlier interpretive tradition of his own novels. Why one of its undeniably great practitioners occupies such an odd and uneasy place in stories of the early novel in England has to do finally with a set of assumptions about how religion influenced, and by implication did not influence, the emergent literary form.

The story of these stories begins with Ian Watt, and in important respects Watt is in fact the whole story.[15] Seeking to account for the literary and social forces that gave birth to the novels of Defoe, Richardson, and Fielding, Watt predicated the unifying concern of "formal realism," "a set of narrative procedures which are so commonly found together in the novel, and so rarely in other literary genres, that they may be regarded as typical of the form itself." Watt highlights "individuality," "details," and "a more largely referential use of language" than is common in other literary forms. The novel lives up to its name when it distinguishes itself from other literary genres, and does so through its emphases on the particularities of character and on telling its story in language that is straightforwardly referential.

Fielding provides the negative counterpoint to the exemplary practices of Defoe and Richardson. With regard to characterization, for example, it is Richardson who presents "the usual treatment of these matters in the novel"; Fielding appears to learn slowly, and finally grasps the standard technique in *Amelia*. When Watt turns to *Tom Jones*, it is apparent that he measures Fielding's artistry with a Richardsonian yardstick. Without question Watt was cognizant of the emerging distinction—he refers to it as a "curious antinomy"[16]—but the reader emerges with little doubt that it is Fielding rather than the category "formal realism" that merits revision. There is longstanding critical consensus that *The Rise of the Novel* raises exactly the right social and historical questions for the emergence of the genre and offers particularly insightful readings of Defoe and Richardson, but falls notably short of this standard of excellence in its discussion of Fielding.[17]

While I share this judgment, in Watt's defense I note that the consensus, while indisputable, has not advanced beyond the assertion to specify why this is the case. I propose that Watt falls short in his discussion of Fielding because his concept of formal realism manifestly will not permit, indeed discounts, the narrative conjunction of historical verisimilitude with a sense of providential design. Watt dismisses such a conjunction, and in the process eliminates from consideration the essence of Fielding's narrative art.[18] Like Leo Braudy, Watt assumes that a narrative cannot be both historically grounded and seriously engaged with the representation of providence. He assumes that history precludes providence. Yet a narrative that is simultaneously historically grounded and providential—or, in Watt's terms, verisimilar and marvelous—is precisely what Fielding's novels seek to be.

Thus, for Watt, the chains of circumstance that keep Tom Jones and Sophia Western apart are nothing more than comic-heightening conventions. They intensify our pleasure in their ultimate union, but with the lamentable consequence that Sophia's frustration with her father is not real anguish, and the corresponding (unfortunate) recognition that Fielding aims to eliminate "any unnecessary expenditure of tears on our part." This cannot but diminish regard for Fielding's stature as a novelist. Crucial here is Watt's rendition of Fielding's narrator, whom he simply collapses into Fielding, to the effect of flattening the narrator's range of commentary.[19] Distinguishing narratives of fact (Fielding's) from narratives of causes or emotions (Defoe's, Richardson's) reveals in the case of the former not a different set of priorities, but a lacuna. The result is that Fielding must continually manufacture deception and surprise to maintain the reader's interest in a narrative that is not about personal relationships, and *Tom Jones* becomes a feat of literary legerdemain whose author succeeds (to the degree that he does) in spite of himself, against impossible odds.

Michael McKeon offers the most significant revisionary consideration of "formal realism," not incidentally focusing the problem of the early novel in terms of Fielding's, rather than Defoe's and Richardson's, work.[20] He objects to "formal realism" because it establishes an artificial disjunction between the novel and its predecessor tradition, the romance. Historically untenable, he argues, this finally distorts the genre by placing it in a naive evolutionary paradigm. McKeon proposes instead a dialectical theory characterized by the tension between the rise of democratic institutions and the demise of the traditional economic structure. These tensions have to do with "questions of truth" and "questions of virtue," the former addressing epistemological, and the latter social, issues. Seventeenth-century predecessor genres of the novel—spiritual autobiography, travel narrative, criminal biography—reveal a history of reversal and negation in both categories that bespeaks epistemological confusion and crisis. Questions of truth center on the possibilities of objective knowledge and the description of reality. McKeon locates in these earlier narratives a series of abstractions that address such questions: romance, empiricism, and skepticism. In good dialectical fashion empiricism critiques romance, and skepticism in turn critiques empiricism. What is striking, however, is that in its critique of sensory evidence, skepticism opens the door to a return of the romance sensibility, because its attack affirms a reality with dimensions beyond, or unverifiable by, sensory perception.

McKeon's revision of formal realism argues that it deprives the novel of its legitimate range of representational options. In this respect, he honors the premise that Fielding's efforts to yoke verisimilitude and the marvelous may in principle be characteristic of the novel. Fielding stands firmly in the canon and any account of the early novel must embrace his distinctive practice.

By implication this would appear to provide a helpful basis from which to place religion in Fielding's novels. Yet what McKeon offers with one hand, he takes away with the other. He places explicit limits on the role of the marvelous in a time of epistemological crisis, and he specifically discounts any affirmative potential for providence in eighteenth-century narrative form.[21] The warrants he offers to justify this bracketing come from history, and from an assumption about what providence means in this context. The historical warrant is McKeon's claim that it is only with the Reformation that Christian writers attempt a correlation of everyday worldly contingency with divine providence. The assumption about providence is McKeon's rough equation of the marvelous with the deus ex machina of the romance tradition. The old Christian conviction that God's providence can be found in the details becomes an anxious affirmation whose fervor testifies not to faith, but to the emergent felt uncertainty about it.

McKeon's warrants bespeak partial truths that he presents as absolute. The Reformers and their successors produced providential narratives in unprecedented numbers, but they had their antecedents, such as Augustine's autobiographical handbook for the Christian believer. Fielding's narrators distance their self-proclaimed new genre from the romance tradition; in *Tom Jones* the narrator explicitly asserts that any happy turns of circumstance should not be understood as instances of the "machines" of romance. This does not discount uncertainty, but it does suggest that other options are at least more forcefully invoked than McKeon's outright dismissal allows. McKeon discovers only instances of language working against Christian belief. The ironic result is that, despite his self-conscious revision of Watt via explicit attention to Fielding, McKeon's Fielding can in fact still only write narratives of human verisimilitude. Fielding's theological options were essentially null and void. In my judgment this deprives Fielding's novels of their most singular dimension, and surprisingly it also seems to deprive McKeon's dialectic of half its luster and all its drama. While McKeon proposes to revise "formal realism," his revision has the same effect as Watt's category: it discounts the possibility that the religious idea of providence mattered integrally to the newly emergent genre of the English novel.

Hans Frei, Fielding, and
the Sense of the Story

If Watt and McKeon stint religion in their accounts of the novel, scholars of religion who appropriate narrative in their work have stinted its history. Work done in narrative theology affords an excellent example. A range of scholars has sought in narrative a connection between the fundamental human impulse to tell stories and the ways religious traditions express their beliefs, organization, and codes of conduct. Yet in such work actual engagement of a text is not inevitable, and when it occurs the selection is telling: the chosen one is usually either biblical, modern (twentieth century), or post-modern (late twentieth century). This canonical leapfrog effect tends to valorize the narrative, or the agenda for which it is chosen, without remainder: the text cannot talk back, as it were, to the purpose which it has been chosen to serve. Indeed it all too easily becomes a proof text in the service of a particular theological position.[22] In such cases the appropriation of literature in the study of religion is not well served.

The most interesting example of narrative theology is Hans Frei's *The Eclipse of Biblical Narrative*.[23] Frei writes the history of the theory of biblical interpretation in the eighteenth and nineteenth centuries in England and Germany. At this time, he argues, the literal and figural approaches to reading biblical narrative broke down under the pressure of historical investigation. Distinguishing the "precritical" predecessors from the "critical" onslaught, the period under scrutiny saw a loss of the sense of the biblical text as realistic.

Before the late seventeenth century, Frei argues, the Bible was received as a realistic narrative, at once literal and historical. The events related were understood not only to have taken place as related, but were also taken as having occurred in past historical time. As a result, the Bible came to be the text by which Christians understood the world. Indeed, the Biblical text *was* the world. The Christian's Bible elucidated the world because it contained the world's history, past, present, and future. Such books as Genesis and the Synoptic Gospels (Frei's favored texts) are singular not only for their narrative shape and claims for chronological sequence, but as "realistic narrative" in which character and circumstance "fitly render each other," so that "[n]either . . . separately, nor yet their interaction, is a shadow of something else more real or more significant. Nor is the one more important than the other in the story."[24] Subject is inseparable from rendering, social context and character are literal—the realism Frei describes is precisely analogous in these ways to any conventional historical account.

There are, however, significant differences between biblical and modern historical accounts. Frei focuses here upon the miraculous: in a modern his-

torical account, supernatural agency is unsatisfactory, while the Bible min-
gles the natural and the supernatural. Frei argues that this does not detract
from the realism of the scriptural account, given his definition of realism as
essentially non-symbolic. So long as the depicted action proves, without excess and without recourse to figural strategy, to elucidate a divine or human
character, the account remains, on Frei's terms, realistic. Biblical miracles,
for example, are strikingly non-symbolic.[25] The key to Frei's definition of realism would appear to be this: does the narrative in question completely in-
tertwine narrative shape and meaning, to the exclusion of the necessity for
symbolic, allegorical, or mythical interpretation?

Everything in Frei's account hinges on this definition of narrative realism, and the conclusions he draws from it are highly significant. First,
realism in story and history had always been identical, but modern critical
history changed the terms of the relation by leading us to distinguish fiction from veracity ascertained through natural causality and analogy. This
implication is bluntly but effectively illustrated by saying that the
antonym of a realistic narrative is not a romance but an allegory or a myth,
in which the meaning, Frei argues, is not a direct function of the sequence
of events and of characterization.

In effect, then, the rise of historical criticism fashioned a false dichotomy
which nonetheless came quickly to rule biblical hermeneutics: if the biblical
narratives cannot sustain tests for historical veracity, then they cannot be understood as realistic. The consequence, in Frei's account, is catastrophic. The
precritical realism which guided biblical exegesis and interpretation for sev-
enteen centuries is lost.

The Eclipse of Biblical Narrative thus documents what Frei judges should
not have happened in the eighteenth and nineteenth centuries, and it is in
this context of regret that he specifically discusses the early English novelists.
The discussion emerges via a grand historical irony: the two homes of these
debates, England and Germany, actually halved the solution to the dilemma.
With the novel, England developed a new narrative tradition with complete
affinity to the precritical realism of earlier biblical hermeneutics, while Germany developed an extensive tradition of biblical commentary. Thus in England the new literary tradition was not applied to the task of biblical
interpretation, and in Germany the task of biblical interpretation lacked
such an ongoing literary tradition, with the result that it veered toward the
now urgent question of the facticity of the biblical accounts.

Fielding's novels reflect, in Frei's judgment, an appreciation of the precritical realist sensibility and afford a link with that tradition of narrative.
They self-consciously aim to maintain verisimilitude to historical fact.
While Frei also collapses Fielding and the narrator, he heeds the commentary of *Tom Jones* and makes much of its lengthy discussion of possibility

and probability as the grace notes of a narrative "History." As a contemporary historian rather than a chronicler or a newspaper editor, Fielding aims to describe recognizable sequences of events involving credible human characters with convincing motives for acting in ways that reveal their virtues and their vices. All this occurs within a specific time frame, and within a social and economic structure, which helps especially to focus characterization. Most crucial for Frei, however, is that Fielding "deliberately reminded the reader at regular intervals that he, the reader, is not confronting reality immediately but only under the controlled guidance of the author, who remains a distinct and significant presence external to the narrative he holds before the reader as the image of reality."[26] This is crucial because it leaves open the possibility of events necessarily unsupportable by modern historical investigation. The startling and extraordinary, so long as it does not appear contrived, in no way compromises the realism of the narrative.

Frei's account stands in direct counterpoint to the concept of "formal realism" and its revision. It offers a constructive case for how Fielding's narrative art was fundamentally informed by an inherited theological sensibility, and it does so in terms of a realism that bears at least a family resemblance to that articulated by Watt. The claim that realism paradoxically requires extension into the realm of the marvelous to maintain its historical credibility effectively stands Watt's theory on its head. Frei's argument also usefully counters McKeon's restriction of the influence of religion to a retreat from traditional affirmation. The implication of Frei's approach is that neither Watt nor McKeon allows us to take Fielding seriously as a religious thinker for whose narrative art the issue is nothing less than whether the world really encompasses providential activity. *The Eclipse of Biblical Narrative* argues for a place for the marvelous in eighteenth-century narrative on religious grounds. Frei's emphasis on eighteenth-century religious and hermeneutical thought alerts him to Fielding's intention to yoke verisimilitude with the marvelous. His assumption that such thought and Fielding's novels mutually inform each other on the issue of narrative construction and interpretation—both activities of his novels—is salutary. Frei makes the strongest case for the principled substance of Fielding's narrative art.

At the same time, Frei's discussion of Fielding is brief and absent any sustained analysis of his narrative art. As a proof text it stands as a splendidly informed and suggestive hermeneutical hunch. It is also the case, however, that Frei brings to his analysis a theological perspective that owes a great deal to Karl Barth. Barth famously regarded the eighteenth century as an arrogant era in which "absolute man" trumpeted his human capacities at the expense of any acknowledgment of the fall, sin, and the necessity of God. Frei's Fielding emerges as a beacon against the eclipse, a light in religion's dark Enlightenment hour.

This view of Fielding, however, renders less than full justice to that other prominent strain in Fielding's narrative art—what I term his diffidence and what Frei identifies as the Germanic tendency to insist upon critical historical realism. Frei associates Fielding's narratives with the cherished precritical interpretative assumptions that were dashed against the rocks of historical-critical scrutiny. Whatever one's judgment about Frei's sense of regret about this development,[27] it is questionable whether the Fielding of *Tom Jones* and *Amelia* shared it. In these novels the narrators provide ample evidence of their concern with critical attestation: references to eyewitnesses, to the limits of understanding, and to retrospectively revealed causal explanations of what the reader might mistakenly identify as providential interposition. Fielding's novels demonstrate real anxiety about just these issues and exhibit a restiveness about the persuasion that merely telling will muster. To a lesser degree than Martin Battestin, but in the same vein, Frei's articulation of Fielding's Christian principle has as its price the evisceration of his equally real diffidence.

Summary

In this study I pursue the proposition that Fielding, too, narrated providence, but that he did so with principled diffidence. In his novels he explores the degree to which experience supports the idea of a directly interposing providence. His narratives demonstrate both a confident belief in the divine creation and the final judgment, and an uncertainty about what claims might be made for providence within those framing events of the divine activity. What Frank Kermode has helpfully described as "the sense of the ending" applies well to Fielding's novels, which conclude happily but without the sense either that the happiness results from specific divine intervention, or that it is due only to random circumstance. This generates an attendant anxiety about the durability of happiness in this life. The result is a most complexly felt rendering of what can be believed, and what can be known, about God's activity in the world.

Each of the three topics reviewed above presents a dilemma which suggests that the discussion of religion in relation to Fielding's novels is unavoidable. The critical wheel of fortune spins in such a way that what is up has as its (negative) criterion the judgement of where Fielding's Christian convictions intruded on his writing. Robert Alter defines *Amelia* as anticlimactic precisely because in it Fielding attempts the impossible by trying to construct a Christian hero. Feminist appropriations of Fielding applaud *Amelia* precisely because, in its move to social realism, it rejects the theological interests of the earlier novels. The canonical assessments contradict, but the claim that religion was detrimental to Fielding's narrative art is a point not of contradiction but of agreement. In the case of the explicit discussion of religion in Fielding's novels, Martin Battestin and Leo Braudy agree about Fielding's question even as they directly disagree about his answer. Their direct contradiction suggests an important consensus: Fielding's novels addressed questions of "how things turn out," and the implications of such accounts for what can be said about divine design in the world. They disagree about Fielding's answer, but agree about his question. Charting the broader literary practice to which Fielding contributed, Ian Watt and Michael McKeon each predicates a principle of realism for the novel that explicitly excludes recourse to providence. For Watt, Fielding is odd because he struggled against the grain; for McKeon, Fielding's grain was the inevitable horizon of secularization, to which he succumbed. Religion is the keynote of controversy in the study of Fielding.

This study constructs a case that Fielding's principled diffidence about providence was the central genius of his narrative art. I shall make this case through interpretations of his novels that mitigate at least to some extent the disagreements of the critical heritage. My conclusive aim can be expressed in several declarative and complementary statements: that, far from being at odds, *Tom Jones* and *Amelia* are variations on Fielding's great narrative theme; that providence and fate each plays a prominent role in Fielding's fiction; and that Fielding was a brilliant, central practitioner of the nascent genre of the novel in England, who sought to write narratives that honored the canon of realistic depiction yet reserved a place for a sense of divine interest in the world.

My goal is not to effect the absolute conciliation of all parties to these debates; the disagreements outlined above are, in some measure, beyond mediation. I seek rather to argue that Fielding's central question was, in fact, religious, and that he wrote continually, perhaps even obsessively, in response to it. His question is Augustine's, and Faulkner's: can we discover God's action in the world? If we can, how much can we depend upon it? To the degree that this question is understood to inform, at the most fundamental level, his novels, I hope to demonstrate the important respect in which Fielding's justly famous literary resolutions also resolve them.

What follows focuses largely on Fielding and his eighteenth-century context, but I would offer the corollary claim for a wider application. Here again, the invocation of Augustine and Faulkner, with whom we started, matters. The tendency to collapse providence into either creation or eschatology was decidedly an eighteenth-century habit of mind. Whether it was only that, restricted only to that time and place, is dubious. Augustine saw God's hand retrospectively, and the implications of retrospection are not that we see God's hand in the here and now but that, having seen God's hand, we can believe that it must be there all the time. Fielding's novels aim for precisely this assurance, but stumble over the fact of human evil. Evil in Fielding's novels works against the happy resolution, sometimes in terms of sheer meanness but often by occluding instances that, we learn retrospec- tively, could themselves have been providential. Faulkner's sense of evil, born of the experience of slavery and its aftermath, is perhaps more blunt than Fielding's and renders even more urgent the need to know, and the despair that not knowing raises the specter of repetition. Again, Fielding stands pre- cisely between these figures, succeeding Augustine and anticipating Faulkner: in his novels the Augustinian retrospective effect is compromised by a partial version of the Faulknerian sense of the human state as fallen from grace.

Fielding believed that he lived in the theater, if not of God's glory, then of God's broadly encompassing activity. He was less certain, however, about the degree to which confidence in God's broad embrace of the world could rest firmly on the events of daily life. Over the span of his life as a novelist, Fielding took increasing recourse, in facing this question, to the invocation of the final judgment. As such he was a kind of working narrative theologian who stood within a very long tradition in the West, seeking artistic form to express a felt religious conundrum that perhaps defied doctrinal or dogmatic formulation, but manifestly warranted and required narrative expression.

Chapter 2 ~

From This World to the Next: Poetic Justice and Deism

In February and March of 1750, London had experienced earthquake tremors, and a third was prophesied for April. Seizing upon these omens of impending natural disaster and their propensity to fuel popular hysteria, Thomas Sherlock, Bishop of London, issued a pastoral letter attributing the tremors to the vice of London and its citizens. Calling for reform, the bishop, in good ecclesial fashion, listed exemplars. Among other histories and romances condemned for their "execrable Scenes of Lewdness"— and by implication for their part in causing the tremors—the Bishop listed Fielding's *Tom Jones,* characterizing its hero as a "Male Prostitute." "Eubulus," writing in *Old England* shortly following the appearance of Sherlock's missive, appropriated the theme and elaborated: "Of the grand Hero *Tom Jones,* may be also said what the just-mentioned Mr. *Collier* applies to another scandalous Character: 'He would gladly blanch this foul Character: But, alas! 'tis no Purpose to wash and rub: The Spots are not *Dirt* but *Complexion,*' p. 81. Which will be found equally true of the infamous *Jones,* whose Character is laid down by Mr. *F.* in such Terms, as *are sufficient,* as the Examiner observes, p. 29, *to nip him in the Bud.*"[1]

Like the playwright Congreve, whose stimulation of Mr. Collier's moral sense we shall soon examine, Fielding was no stranger to a formula of critical opprobrium that suggested a causal link between artistic production, morality, and the disposition of the deity toward the world. The willingness to attribute very specific acts of natural history to the divine government, and to draw from it explicit conclusions about God's disposition toward the world (and its artistic production), was of course not uncommon in Fielding's age. What is of interest, however, is that Fielding himself, just two years after Bishop Sherlock's missive, produced a similar pamphlet. "Examples of the Interposition of Providence in the Detection and Punishment of

Murder" lacks the striking tonal combustibility of Sherlock, Eubulus, and Jeremy Collier, but its overarching equation is strikingly parallel. In it Fielding aims to demonstrate, by enumerating cases from the annals of murder in eighteenth-century London, that evil is in fact punished by providence. The discussion is straightforward. Murder has increased in recent years. Why? The answer is lack of religious faith. To remind humanity of the heinous nature of murder, Fielding writes that God "hath been pleased to distinguish the atrociousness of the Murderer's guilt, by dwelling his Thunder directly at his head, in this world. The Divine providence hath been pleased to interpose in a more immediate manner in the detection of this crime than of any other."[2]

At the time he wrote this pamphlet, Fielding was a harassed and perplexed judge seeking ways to stem the tide of crime that appeared before his bench. (It is noteworthy that the pamphlet appeared after his final novel, *Amelia,* in which the narrative depiction of providence shades most closely to its full realization only in the final judgment—outside the events of this world.) Fielding himself both elicited and produced writing that sought to forge explicit links between specific worldly events and a providentially interposing deity. If his novels present his most nuanced—and, I would argue, his most profound—thinking on this theme, it remains the case that the arena in which these issues were discussed, debated, indeed deployed embraced a broad array of literary critical and theological writing that was unabashedly polemical. Fielding's novels have as their background, sometimes explicitly and always implicitly, this broad arena, and the present chapter is devoted to establishing this crucial context of his narrative art.

The question of what might be claimed for divine providence in a world marked by the fact of evil had special explicit resonance in England at least from the late seventeenth century through the middle of the eighteenth. No better testimony to the presence—indeed, the tenacity—of the question exists than the fact that two controversies, spanning roughly the sixty years just prior to the publication of *Joseph Andrews* and engaging a notable range of writers, turned on precisely this issue. Differences in ostensible topic, realm of discourse, and actual interlocutors has completely obscured the striking confluence of the debate about poetic justice on the one hand, and the deism controversy on the other.

Words such as "debate" and "controversy" imply disagreement, and the writers who contribute their wisdom on these matters at this time certainly judge themselves to be in substantial disagreement with one another. Yet whether literary critics arguing the use of poetic justice in the drama (Joseph Addison and John Dennis) or natural philosophers (John Toland and Matthew Tindal) and theologians (William Law and Joseph Butler) debating the true knowledge Christianity affords, these writers in fact share a crucial, and unacknowledged, initial assumption. It is this: given Christianity's triadic structure of divine activity—creation, providence, eschatology—each displaces providence, effectively collapsing it into one of the two framing activities. The majority collapses providence into eschatology (Addison, Dennis, Law, and Butler) in acknowledgment of the pressures of theodicy; the minority collapses providence into creation (Toland and Tindal) to underscore the perfection of God and the decisive goodness of the created order and our rational capacities. Whatever the direction, the effect underscores a general reluctance—a reluctance no less firm in the theologians than in their literary or philosophical counterparts—to posit providential interposition in the events of the present time.

From this shared assumption emerges in turn a set of common questions around which thought and debate circle. Absent a providentially interposing deity, it is not surprising that these focus on the nature of the world in which we live. What is the character of evil? To what degree does it exist, what is its power and extent, and what can we do about it? What is the character of our own knowledge of the world? How much power do we get from the knowledge that we have? Their answers tell us where these writers turn for assurance of God's decisive activity, given their certainty that they will not find that activity here and now. Whether they look back to the perfection of the creation or forward to the final judgment turns precisely on the degree to which they find evil a potent force in the world.

These questions, I shall argue in chapters three and four, reside at the heart of Fielding's enterprise as a novelist. All of the positions discussed in this chapter can be found in them, as well as discussions of their relative merits.[3]

Poetic Justice:
"Either Here or Hereafter"

Micheal McKeon has argued that poetic justice arises as a "special method . . . of compensating for the deficiencies of providential justice" that replaces the Christian orthodox belief in the afterlife with the construct of the stage. McKeon writes that "there is good reason to see these years as a critical period in which the orthodox spirituality of an equitable afterlife was being replaced by the aesthetic spirituality of an equitable denouement."[4] The concept of poetic justice in late-seventeenth-and eighteenth-century England becomes, in McKeon's account, an early example of Matthew Arnold's famous claim for literary art's occupation of the throne once occupied by religious belief.

An examination of early eighteenth-century discussions of the theory of poetic justice, and of one case of its application to a work of drama, suggest, however, that the Christian belief in providence directly informed the nascent formulations of poetic justice. Thomas Rymer's influential formulation of the term was subsequently appropriated by Jeremy Collier, who linked poetic justice directly with divine providence. Nahum Tate justified his revision of *King Lear* on the grounds of its superior rendering of poetic justice, and his version enjoyed both unanimous popular success and the critical imprimatur of Samuel Johnson. The controversy of 1711 involving Joseph Addison and John Dennis began from a disagreement about the merit of Tate's version and quickly evolved into a discussion of the idea of poetic justice. In each case poetic justice takes its theoretical or practical substance to be the Christian view of providence, and this theological doctrine constitutes the substantive claim which the drama addresses in its resolution. Disagreement focuses not on any displacement of providence by human artifice, but on whether providence is rightly depicted as a force in this world or the next. All regard poetic justice as an expression of the deity's providential influence over events. Indeed, there—for Joseph Addison at least—is precisely the rub!

"Poetic justice"[5] has its genesis in England in the writings of the late seventeenth-century critic Thomas Rymer. Both the term and Rymer's discussion of it have been understood "to signify the need to distribute earthly rewards and punishments at the close of a literary work in proportion to the virtue or vice of the various characters.[6] Rymer's explanation, while not falsifying this characterization, does complicate it:

> They [Sophocles and Euripides, as opposed to Aeschylus] were for teaching by *examples,* in a graver way, yet extremely *pleasant* and *delightful.* And, finding in History, the same *end* happy to the *righteous* and to the *unjust, vertue* often opprest, and *wickedness* on the throne, they saw these particular *yesterday-truths* were imperfect and unproper to illustrate the *universal* and *eternal truths* by them intended. Finding also that this *unequal* distribution of rewards and punishments did perplex the *wisest,* and by the *Atheist* was made a scandal to the *Divine Providence,* they concluded, that a *Poet* must of necessity see *justice* exactly administred, if he intended to please. For, said they, if the world can scarce be satisfied with God Almighty, whose holy will and purposes are not to be *comprehended;* a *Poet* (in these matters) shall never be pardon'd, who (they are sure) is not *incomprehensible;* whose *ways* and *walks* may, without *impiety,* be penetrated and examin'd. They knew indeed, that many things naturally unpleasant to the World in *themselves,* yet gave *delight* when well *imitated.*[7]

The world according to Rymer distributes rewards and punishments disproportionately, heedless of the virtue or vice of the recipients. Yet we know (and Sophocles and Euripides knew!) that a divine providence in fact governs events yet stands beyond the mundane limits of our human comprehension.[8] Historical representations of the natural world prove deficient when they fail to illustrate "the *universal* and *eternal truths*" which are beyond immediate reality yet undeniably, finally, most real indeed. History betrays drama and the higher purpose of dramatic art: Sophocles and Euripides "found that *History*, grosly taken, was neither proper to *instruct*, nor apt to *please*; and therefore they would not trust History for their examples, but refin'd upon the History; and thence contriv'd something more *philosophical*, and more *accurate* than *History*."[9] That higher purpose is nothing less than the affirmation of divine providence, and divine providence is the source of the idea of poetic justice. Dramatic poetic justice affirms the divinely provident deity we can otherwise know only fleetingly.

Rymer's assertions would prove themselves a harbinger of eighteenth-century sensibilities. Jeremy Collier attacked popular drama, most notably Congreve's, on grounds always derived from religious belief.[10] Poetic justice affirms divine providence, especially in its punishment of the wicked at the final judgment.[11] In a section titled "The Immodesty of the Stage," Collier asserts that the playwrights of the English stage engage in "*making* their *Top Characters Libertines,* and giving them *Success* in their *Debauchery*."[12] Invoking Plato's banishment of the poets for immorality, and citing early church fathers who described the drama as "*Vinum Demonum,*" Collier contrasts the standards that applied to the "Heathen" dramas with those that must apply to the Christian: "That which might pass for Raillery, and Entertainment in Heathenism, is detestable in Christianity. The Restraint of the Precept, and the Quality of the Deity, and the Expectations of Futurity quite alter the Case."[13]

The cursing and swearing in much of the dialogue amounts—especially and most grievously when combined with a failure to punish such behavior in the denouement—to an abuse of religion and the Holy Scriptures. It makes a mockery of the final judgment and the doctrine of providence. Closely linked staples of Collier's Christianity, the final judgment serves as the culminating and cumulative providential act. Invocations of providence on the stage juxtapose religious doctrine with wit and repartee to the inevitable diminishment of the former.[14] This juxtaposition is the source of the immorality of the stage. Collier finds occasional dialogue about the future state to be of a piece. Extracting a bit of dialogue that appears to call into question the mind-body distinction, Collier extrapolates: "The meaning is, he suspects our Souls are nothing but Organiz'd Matter. Or in plain English, our *Souls* are nothing but our Bodies. And then when the Body dies you may guess what becomes of them! Thus the Authorities of Religion are weaken'd, and the prospect of the other World almost shut up. And is this a likely Supposition for Sincerity and good Nature?"[15]

Making the arresting claim that "The Lines of Virtue and Vice are Struck out by Nature in very Legible Distinctions,"[16] Collier accosts the stage for blurring these natural delineations and thus complicating their straightforward human recognition. Appeals to classical precedent no longer avail because the context is now Christian. Revelation has advanced our understanding well beyond Plautus and Terence. Playwrights should instead heed Horace's dictum by aiming to instruct their audiences. The source of that instruction is, unmistakably, Collier's Christianity. This means moral instruction, and moral instruction can take no form superior to the Christian poetic justice such as that which Shakespeare visits upon Falstaff. Collier disputes the notion that the chief end of comedy is to delight or divert its audience. Diversion proves decidedly unwise:

> It may not be improper to consider in a word or two, what a frightfull Idea the *Holy Scriptures* give us of Hell. 'Tis describ'd by all the Circumstances of Terror, by every Thing dreadful to Sense, and amazing to Thought. The Place, the Company, the Duration, are all Considerations of Astonishment. And why has God given us this solemn warning? Is it not to awaken our Fears, and guard our Happiness; To restrain the disorders of Appetite, and to keep us within Reason, and Duty?[17]

Like the Scriptures, the stage must constantly remind its audience of the chief end of life, and of the clear preference of the heavenly state to its alternative. To promote immorality mocks what we know to be the end of such behavior. Inattention to poetic justice flies full in the face of the divinely providential scheme which governs the world.[18] Collier's backhanded tribute to Aristotle offers perhaps the final word concerning his estimate of late seventeenth-century playwrights: "Aristotle was a bold Man: However, this is to be said for him; he was no *Stage Poet*."[19]

While his attack consists of little more than vitriol and diatribe, Collier's emphatic connection of providential affirmation with poetic justice proved to be a key consideration in dramatic practice and theory in eighteenth-century England.[20] Perhaps the best representation of this sensibility is Nahum Tate's *The History of King Lear,* which first appeared in 1681 and would enjoy immense popularity on the English stage well into the nineteenth century. The magnitude of the revision bears rehearsal. Tate cut fully one-quarter (827 of 3,201) of Shakespeare's lines[21] and rearranged many scenes to effect a metamorphosis of the denouement, from tragedy to comedy. Cordelia and Lear survive and endure, Cordelia as the wife of Edgar and Queen, Lear in happy retirement with Kent and Gloucester. Tate achieves this resolution through basic revisions of the action. Lear and Cordelia face death in prison onstage rather than off, and Lear defends Cordelia by slaying two men and forestalling a veritable army of reserves until Edgar and Albany appear and quell the disturbance. Tate also introduces a love story between Cordelia and Edgar.[22] One of Cordelia's suitors, Edgar eventually wins her affection by proving true even after Lear disinherits her. Tate entirely removes the Fool and renders the blinded Gloucester a revolutionary orator who speaks out against "the new regime" and inspires the revolt that restores Lear to the throne.

Tate's revision of the denouement extends beyond replotting to utter alteration of its tenor. Edgar, Cordelia, Lear, Kent, and Gloucester stand onstage. Edgar announces the deaths of Edmund, Goneril, and Regan. Lear responds with two lines lamenting "their wretched fall" before urging Edgar to marry Cordelia and enlisting Gloucester's support for this. Edgar becomes the bashful benefactor ("the gift strikes merit dumb"), Cordelia the grateful maiden and ready accomplice to her husband's every wish as she could never be to her father's ("Nor do I blush to own myself o'erpaid / For all my sufferings past"). Gloucester asks to die, but Lear summons him to retirement in "some cool cell" where the two benighted fathers and loyal Kent may "gently pass our short reserves of time . . . Enjoy the present hour, nor fear the. last." Tate systematically eliminates the ambiguities of Shakespeare's characterizations: Lear commandeers Gloucester's death wish; Edgar's ambition is ordered by his devotion to the virtuous and unambiguously grateful Cordelia; and Lear regards his imminent death with an irenic spirit. Tate then has Edgar conclude the play:

> Our drooping country now erects her head,
> Peace spreads her balmy wings, and Plenty blooms.
> Divine Cordelia, all the gods can witness
> How much thy love to empire I prefer!
> Thy bright example shall convince the world
> (Whatever storms of Fortune are decreed)
> That truth and virtue shall at last succeed.[23]

Compare Tate's Edgar-in-closing with Shakespeare's:

> The weight of this sad time we must obey;
> Speak what we feel, not what we ought to say.
> The oldest hath bourne most; we that are young
> Shall never see so much nor live so long.[24]

Shakespeare's "sad time" becomes through Tate a time which demonstrates "That truth and virtue shall at last succeed"; there remains no remnant of the "gor'd state" that Edgar and Albany (its sole survivors in Shakespeare's version) must sustain.

Tate's *King Lear* enjoyed monumental success on the eighteenth-century English stage.[25] It eclipsed its source: Shakespeare's *Lear* disappeared from the stage for approximately 150 years, while Tate's was acted in all but 9 of the years comprising the eighteenth century. Some productions, notably those of Garrick in the 1750s, made minor restorations of Shakespeare's language and some of the scenes excised by Tate.[26] Every production, however, retained the Cordelia-Edgar love story and the triumphant, poetically just denouement. It was 1838 before Shakespeare's *Lear* reappeared.[27] It effected a metamorphosis: arguably the most formidably tragic denouement in Western dramatic history became through Tate's revisionary genius the happy resolution of a politically divided nation.[28]

Some eighty years into its run on the stage, Tate's version garnered the imprimatur of the eighteenth century's foremost critic, Samuel Johnson. Johnson defends Shakespeare against charges that his *Lear* is too savagely and shockingly cruel in its depiction of Goneril and Regan, but he cannot do the same for the Bard's decision to present onstage the gouging of Gloucester. Yet more disturbing to Johnson is Shakespeare's chosen fate for Cordelia, whose virtue he allows "to perish in a just cause, contrary to the natural ideas of justice, to the hope of the reader, and, what is yet more strange, to the faith of chronicles." Johnson then engages in uneasy equivocation. A play in which the wicked prosper and the virtuous miscarry can indeed constitute a just representation of the ways of the world. Yet "all reasonable beings naturally love justice," and all other things being equal an audience is in the end better pleased when virtue finally triumphs. Johnson never says that Tate's version is actually better than Shakespeare's, but the final verdict is unmistakable, and sealed by personal anecdote: "In the present case the publick has decided. Cordelia, from the time of Tate, has always retired with victory and felicity. And, if my sensations could add any thing to the general suffrage, I might relate, that I was many years ago so shocked by Cordelia's death, that I know not whether I ever endured to read again the last scenes of the play till I undertook to revise them as an editor."[29]

Johnson's equivocation concerning Shakespeare's denouement parallels Rymer's general ambivalence on how to judge any tragedy's denouement. Johnson can excuse Shakespeare's presentation of the behavior of Lear's daughters on the grounds of historical accuracy, but when he turns first to Gloucester's blinding and then particularly to the death of Cordelia, he finds no warrant for what flies in the face of general expectation and notions of justice.[30] So it is with Rymer in more general terms: the world may indeed be an awful place to the degree that we apprehend it, but dramatic works must not entirely imitate that apprehension. Instead they should affirm our general sense of justice, and ultimately our belief that the world is providentially ordered. Johnson's pain arises not only from actually witnessing the blinding of Gloucester, or the felt anguish of Cordelia's death; it is also a function of his sense of the violation of the justice of nature. Relatively bad things happening to bad people are tolerable while decisively bad things happening to the virtuous are not.

Historians of English drama analyze Tate's work as the adaptation of a Renaissance play for a Restoration audience. They explain its success with reference to the appeal of the love story of Edgar and Cordelia, and Tate's elimination of the Fool as a character inappropriate to a tragedy—both revisions which reflect Restoration sensibilities.[31] This, however, accounts only in part for this remarkable concord of revision, approbation, and affirmation. Tate, Johnson, and eighteenth-century audiences manifestly regarded Shakespeare's *Lear* as too painful to bear,[32] and the conventions of Restoration comedy constitute a species of that regard but not its genus. Tate spoke of his work as aiming to rectify the problems in Shakespeare's rendering, and Johnson endorses Tate's version because Shakespeare's does such violence to "the natural ideas of justice."

The denouement of Tate's *Lear*, and specifically its superiority or inferiority to Shakespeare's, stood at the heart of a controversy in 1711 between Joseph Addison and John Dennis. Addison—who "stood almost alone in preferring the play as Shakespeare wrote it"[33]—discussed in *The Spectator* no. 40 (April 16, 1711) the concept of "poetical Justice." This "ridiculous Doctrine in modern Criticism," Addison writes, in fact defeats the classic rationale for tragedy: "Whatever Crosses and Disappointments a good Man suffers in the Body of the Tragedy, they will make but small Impression on our Minds, when we know that in the last Act he is to arrive at the End of his Wishes and Desires."[34] Addison's defense of the ancients is based on the notion (contrary, as we have seen, to Rymer and Johnson) that the drama has its basis in mimesis: by imitation, dramatists show us the world as it is. That world is decidedly one "on this Side of the Grave," where good and evil alike happen to all, heedless of justice. To alter this in the drama—to abandon mimesis—is, in the case of tragedy, to eliminate the genuine cathartic effect. The depth of affliction the hero faces can never evoke genuine pity and fear when we know that this essentially good person will emerge unscathed from the fray. Addison's prime example of this flawed notion is Tate's *Lear*: "*King Lear* is an admirable Tragedy of the same Kind, as *Shakespear* [sic] wrote it; but as it is reformed according to the chymerical Notion of poetical Justice, in my humble Opinion it has lost half its Beauty."[35]

Addison's objections to Tate's editing, and to the prevailing approval of Tate's *Lear*, elicited an immediate, angry rejoinder from John Dennis. In "To the Spectator, Upon His Paper on the 16th of April [On Poetical Justice],"[36] Dennis responds directly to Addison's assertions about the world, the drama, and the proper mimetic function. Dennis grants Addison's claim that affliction is as much a fact of life as happiness. He moves immediately, however, to the fact of human immortality, "a Compensation in Futurity for any seeming Inequality in his Destiny here." Stage characters enjoy no such eternal dispensation. Rather they exist only so long as the fable that surrounds them, and this requires the "temporal to represent eternal Punishments." Dennis suggests that the lesson has to do with the final fact of providence, whether in this world or the next: "therefore when we shew a Man unfortunate in Tragedy, for not restraining his Passions, we mean that every one will for such Neglect, unless he timely repents, be infallibly punish'd by Infinite Justice either here or hereafter."[37] Either here or hereafter: Dennis differs from Addison not about the disposition of events in the world but about what the drama imitates. For Dennis, the drama must imitate, not the earthly and at times unsatisfactory justice we witness daily, but the divine and always excellent justice that must eventually hold sway, if not in this then in the future world. Addison's criticism that poetic justice misrepresents events in this world is, in Dennis's view, misplaced because providence's purview extends to the hereafter. And while the temporal scope of the drama is circumscribed, its theological scope cannot be.

The exchange did not end there. *The Spectator* no. 548, given over wholly to an unsigned letter to Mr. Spectator, proposes to strengthen the opinion presented in no. 40 against objections raised by "some eminent Criticks." Addison invokes humanity's fallen condition. We can always discover sufficient vice "to justifie Providence in regard any Miseries that might befal" a tragic hero. Happiness and triumph render moot this fact and its very real consequences in daily life. In contrast, a genuinely tragic resolution "corrects the Insolence of Human Nature, softens the Mind of the Beholder with the Sentiments of Pity and Compassion, comforts him under his own private Affliction, and teaches him not to judge of Mens Virtues by their Successes."[38] Addison proceeds to note that the earlier discussion in no. 40 did not preclude the punishment of vice, but only promoted the notion that good men may meet with tragedy. Here he turns the tables: "The best of Men may deserve Punishment, but the worst of Men cannot deserve Happiness."[39]

Addison's debate with Dennis hinges on two questions: the real condition of the world, and the proper artistic representation of the world on the stage.[40] For Addison, evil is an undeniable fact of existence. Our sufferings in this world, and its imminent yet unpredictable end, are genuine sources of gloom and terror. Our only antidote to despair is faith, not only in the existence of God but in a deity whose providential plan guarantees some order to this apparent chaos, and some ultimate righting of its wrongs. In this, and in this alone, can we find the comfort of our days.[41] Addison spent Good Fridays contemplating tombs in a cemetery, and wrote about his habit in no. 26. This sense of human mortality fuels Addison's disgust with Tate's

Lear as one example of the general English proclivity for emending a tragic denouement to fit present notions of poetic justice.

Addison did share Dennis's belief in a future state, and in the completion of the providential dispensation.[42] They differ in that Addison believes that tragedy properly understood must imitate the world as it is, and the world as it is cannot be construed as the complete dispensation of the deity's design. Further, the point of tragedy can only be to reconcile us to this world's ways because our knowledge of the providential order itself is of necessity inexact.[43] To fashion any emblem of it, whether situated in this world or the next, must therefore be the stuff of folly.

For Dennis, happiness is "the chief End and Design of Man," in which providence is the most singular means. "It had indeed, been an Inconsistency in Providence, to have made a Thinking and Reasoning Creature, that had been indifferent as to Misery and Happiness; for God had made such a one only to disturb the rest, and, consequently, had acted against his own Design."[44] We turn to religion, according to Dennis, not as consolation against the distressing facts of existence, but because it is "the only Way to be solidly and lastingly Happy, even in this Life . . . the best christian being always the happiest man."[45]

A formula underlines the importance of drama to Dennis's outlook. Happiness is a state of pleasure, and to be in a state of pleasure is to be moved in a manner reason will allow. It is the peculiar capacity of tragedy to move us, and so to please us and make us happy. The stakes of the drama are thus, for Dennis, quite high[46]: in poetic justice we have, potentially, an exact image of that divine governance that guarantees our ultimate happiness. There exists an important analogy between art and religion: " . . . as the end of every Religion must be the Happiness of those who embrace it, so the Design of every Art must be the very same. . . ."[47] The limits of dramatic characterization mandate what we might term ultra-mimetic presentation. Failure in this regard denies the scope of the providential government. In contrast to Addison's vision of corrected human insolence, Dennis argues that the drama offers instead affirmation of particular providence and the divine dispensation.

For Dennis, the drama exists to call our attention to a future state, which will in turn lead us to amend our behavior in the present. In an almost quixotic observance of Johnson's three unities, Dennis argues that because the drama is emphatically prescribed in space, time, and action it must provide a mirror of the resolution of the Christian life in its denouement. Dennis's at best passing acknowledgment of Addison's point—that the world in which we live is not like this—underlines his very different mimetic basis for the drama. It is about the hereafter even though it is here. To Addison, the particular providence and the divine dispensation are at best uncertainly evidenced by the circumstances of this world.

The true tragic catharsis, therefore, must be the unhappy denouement which faithfully renders the present, worldly situation. This may, in turn, lead the devout Christian to thoughts of a happier recourse to the general dispensation of providence and its completion in a future state. But for the drama to do otherwise would make a charade of its claim to represent human experience in this world.

Addison represents the minority opinion.[48] Collier, Tate, Johnson, and Dennis write for the majority that the drama has an ethical imperative of the highest order to ensure that its denouement directly witnesses the deity's providence. Addison's demurrer hinges in the end, not on a different estimate of the state of life in the world, but on a difference of opinion about whether the drama should replicate our condition now, or our condition in the future. Addison shares the belief in the future state, but he also displays an insistent stoicism about our being in the world that at least these four contemporaries—and, apparently, audiences for another 125 years—lacked.

The Deism Controversy

In its focus on the idea of the appropriate dramatic denouement and its application to the staging of *King Lear*, poetic justice lends itself to fairly declarative historical exegesis. Not so deism.[49] In the case of England, the difficulty is one of vigorous polemical and controversial declarations in a context of ultimate agreement. Critics of Christian revelation ultimately have more in common with its foremost apologists than their rhetoric implies. Apologists for Christianity finally prove quite willing to concede—indeed, already to have conceded—considerable doctrinal ground on the point of, for example, special providential acts. While Matthew Tindal and William Law are hardly cozy bedfellows, their respective polemics—Tindal's attacks on revelation, Law's dismissal of the claim for reasonable religion—obscure important family resemblances. As in the debate between Addison and Dennis, discerning the nub of disagreement requires prior recognition of substantial concord. Unlike that debate, however, the grounds of ultimate disagreement are less clear.

This section offers a case for generalization via consideration of four important and representative controversialists. Robert Sullivan has well described the dilemma in terms of John Toland[50]: generalizations about the deists—opposition to superstition, a desire to establish a basis for morality apart from revelation—are in fact bedrock principles for some of deism's opponents. Sullivan clarifies much about Toland that is in fact murky in the surveys, and no one can return to past generalizations with the sense that they are as easily earned. One cannot but also conclude simultaneously that Toland himself was genuinely part of a larger phenomenon, one that in the end demonstrates the old saw that the historical total is greater than the sum of its individual parts. The recent studies by Byrne and Harrison confirm the real advantages of clarifying common assumptions.

My aim in what follows is, then, twofold and, I shall argue, genuinely complementary. First, I hope to capture the texture of how four individual participants in what was undeniably the theological controversy of eighteenth-century England thought about religion, and how the thought of each immediately turns, willy-nilly, to questions about providence. Second, while myself suspicious of synthetic arguments, I do think a case can be made on the basis of these readings for consensus on important points. Whatever their differences, all these writers collapse two-thirds of the traditional theological structure of the divine activity. Creation, providence, and eschatology comprise for these writers, if not an eternal golden braid, then certainly a continuous account of the deity's actions in which the pressures of the facts of life force the middle term—providence—toward either the initial creative or the conclusive eschatological moment. In this they afford a striking parallel to their fellow controversialists on the matter of poetic justice, and thus go some distance toward suggesting that the collapse of providence into eschatology was in fact a hallmark of eighteenth-century thought about God—so decisively so, in fact, that even its self-proclaimed antagonists share it.

John Toland

John Toland's notorious *Christianity Not Mysterious*[51] (1696) appeared on the heels of John Locke's *Reasonableness of Christianity* (1695). Whether Toland sought to establish a connection, Bishop Stillingfleet thought he perceived one, and Locke himself was drawn into a debate in which he veered dangerously close to protesting too much his innocence of agreement.[52] Toland's successor Matthew Tindal explicitly claimed Locke as a fellow traveler down the path of enlightened rationality. Tindal's claim reflects a preoccupation with respectability (a consideration perhaps even more dear to Toland) and, behind this, the sense that a critique of traditional Christianity would engender controversy. Underlining its affinity with Locke's position could only enhance its respectability.[53] The dilemma of pinpointing the genuine differences which mark the participants in the deism controversy is nicely limned by the fact that its first major contribution managed at one and the same time to foment considerable notoriety, and to establish a credible connection with the age's most respected philosopher.

As with so many contributions to the deism controversy, Toland's title encapsulates his argument: *Christianity Not Mysterious: Or, a Treatise shewing, That there is nothing in the Gospel Contrary to Reason, Nor Above it; And that no Christian Doctrine can be properly call'd A Mystery.* An epigraph from no less an authority than Archbishop John Tillotson extols the testimony of reason to the rightness of any opinion. This invocation is all the more remarkable because not only Toland's title but much of his argument's impetus develops as a self-conscious antithesis to a sermon delivered two years earlier by Tillotson's fellow divine, Robert South.[54] Published at the peak of Tillotson's influence, *Christianity Not Mysterious* invokes favorably at the outset one of the most famous Restoration divines and then proceeds to attack, systematically if obliquely, a fellow divine whose theology was, if not indistinguishable, then very nearly so.

From the outset Toland styles himself a moderate, standing between "the only Dispensers of the Favours and Oracles of Heaven" and "the declar'd Antagonists of Religion." In other words, he says, he speaks for the truth. His divinely endowed reason guides him: "God was pleas'd to make my own Reason, and such as made use of theirs, the happy Instruments of my Conversion."[55] The truth about Christianity—as about anything—must be intelligible to reason. Christianity is not the business only of clerics to proclaim (authorization from Tillotson, presumably, notwithstanding); it is, rather, the position of all reasonable people who stand between clerical authority and antagonism to religion. This series of declarations concludes with a final assertion of identity: "The only religious Title therefore that I shall ever own, for my part, is that most glorious one of being a Christian."[56]

Toland launches *Christianity Not Mysterious* with the Lockean pronouncement that true Christianity follows the Scriptures, of which "there is nothing more true if rightly understood."[57] A quasi-syllogistic proposition follows: right understanding is a matter of reason; Christianity is the religion of reason; so there can be nothing in the repository of divine revelation that runs counter to reason. We know, writes Toland, in four ways: through our experiences of sense and of mind, and through human and divine revelation. It is nonetheless the case that "*God,* the wise Creator of all . . . has also endu'd us with the Power of *suspending our Judgments about whatever is uncertain, and of never assenting but to clear Perceptions.*"[58] God is a source of truth, and therefore anything that is false in the world can only be the result of the human failure to subject it to scrutiny and the light of evidence. The quartet of sources of knowledge are in fact a solo act: experiences of sense and mind and human revelation all fall under the rubric of reason, and divine revelation is rendered unnecessary.

The consequent hermeneutic of suspicion cuts a wide swath through much classical Christian doctrine: these "*Absurdities* that ever were seriously vented among *Christians*" include transubstantiation (chief among the many "ridiculous Fables of the Church of *Rome*"), the many corruptions of Eastern Christianity, the Lutheran Implantation, the Arian creature-God, and the widespread belief in the Trinity. Toland names *credo quia absurdum* as the basis of subsequent defenses of such traditional teachings, indeed as the essence of much of what passes for divine revelation. "Respect for the *Scripture*," Toland maintains, "does not require us to grant any [seeming Contradiction] in it, but rather to conclude, that we are ignorant of the right Meaning when a Difficulty occurs; and so to suspend our Judgments concerning it, till with suitable Helps and Industry we discover the Truth."[59] Those "Helps" and all that industry are, in fact, the substance of reason for Toland.

Revelation functions, then, not to command the believer's assent, but to provide a basis for obtaining accurate information.[60] This, for Toland, is the heart of the matter: "Whoever reveals any thing, that is, whoever tells us something we did not know before, *his Words must be intelligible, and the Matter possible.* This Rule holds good, let *God* or *Man* be the Revealer."[61] Anticipating the later position of Conyers Middleton in *Free Inquiry into the Miraculous Powers* (1749), Toland argues that for any proposition to be accepted as true by a rational creature, it must be fully intelligible and possible. "We are then to expect the same degree of *Perspicuity* from God as from Man, tho' more of *Certitude* from the first than the last."[62] As illustration Toland cites Luke 1:26–38:

The Virgin *Mary,* tho of that Sex that's least Proof against Flattery and Superstition, did not implicitly believe *she should bear a Child that was to be called the Son of the most High, and of whose Kingdom there should be no end,* till the *Angel* gave her a satisfactory Answer to the strongest Objection that could be made: Nor did she then conclude (so unlike was she to her present Worshippers) it should unavoidably come to pass; but humbly acknowledging the Possibility, and her own Unworthiness, she quietly wish'd and expected the event.[63]

Even the appearance of an angel of the Lord and her innate feminine gullibility did not inhibit Mary from using her rational faculties to make Gabriel's revelation intelligible. Once understood, Mary then strictly assessed the possibility of the angel's declaration. This resulted in her hope that it might be so, but a hope tempered by an innate disinterested historical sagacity that awaited confirmation. Having gained perspicuity, Mary awaited certitude. Toland neglects to specify at what point Mary achieved certitude: whether at her son's birth, or his miracle at Cana, or the events of his death and resurrection.

In fact, all the events of Christ's life—properly understood—make intelligible the rational truth of Christianity. Scripture, the vehicle of this truth, evinces it in the miracles it reports, and in its very method and style of reporting them. In these documents we find, Toland writes, "the most il-lustrious Examples of close and perspicuous Ratiocination conceivable."[64] The overarching principle, itself identified by Toland as a manifest act of providence, is the New Testament fulfillment of Old Testament prophecy. Christ's miracles do not shock or surprise or puzzle, given the testimony that preceded his arrival. The parables prove genuinely incomprehensible for the briefest of moments, "*mysterious* to them only to whom they were not unfolded . . . Nor is there anything more easy, than the Explication which *Christ* gave of these Parables at the Request of his Disciples."[65] The fulfillment of prophecy and the explanations provided by Jesus Christ with his pronouncements are blessings the New Testament provides for human perspicacity: these are, respectively, "Promises of Light and Assistance from above" and "the Privilege of Reason in common."[66] These argue strongly against any place for "the Vulgar Notion of *Mystery*" in the biblical record.

Toland's reasonable Christianity reverses the traditional conception of *credo ut intelligam:* understanding becomes the basis for faith. Faith is ratio-nal and helped in its rationality by the revelation of a God who takes care to present information in a form that is readily comprehensible to the reason-able creatures who comprise the centerpiece of the created order. Revelation is entirely reasonable, or else it is not—and cannot be—revelation. Sure and certain are both the light from God and the reason from within, so that er-rors, when they occur, result from one of two human failings: either blind-ness to the proffered light without, or heedlessness to the gift of reason within. These are the sources of heresy: not the opacity of revelation, not the ambiguities which play before the interpreter of revelation, but the simple failure to heed the reason in ourselves and in revelation that tells us every-thing we need to know.

As he approaches the conclusion of *Christianity Not Mysterious,* Toland anticipates objections by considering another biblical example:

> But to all this will be objected that remarkable Instance of *Abraham*'s Faith, who was ready to sacrifice his only Son, notwithstanding God had promis'd that Kings should descend of him, and his Seed be numerous as the Stars of Heaven, or the Sand upon the Seashore. Did *Abraham* blindly obey then, without reconciling the apparent Contradiction between God's present Com-mand and his former Promises? Far from it: for 'tis expressly recorded, that *he that receiv'd the Promises offer'd up his only begotten, of whom it was said, that in Isaac shall thy Seed be blessed; Reasoning that God was able to raise him again from the Dead, from whence also he had receiv'd him in a Figure.* He rightly con-cluded that God was able to revive *Isaac* by a Miracle, as he was miraculously born, according to another Promise, after his Parents were past having Chil-dren, and so *as good as dead;* therefore it is elsewhere written of *Abraham,* that *being not weak in Faith, he consider'd not his own Body now dead, when he was*

about an hundred Years old, neither yet the Deadness of Sarah's Womb; nor stag-
ger'd at God's Promise through Unbelief; but being strong in Faith he gave Glory
to God, and was fully perswaded that what he had promis'd he was able also to
perform.

Now what is there in all this, but very strict Reasoning from Experience,
from the Possibility of the thing, and from the Power, Justice and Immutability of him that promis'd it?[67]

As in his earlier analysis of Mary's "discussion" with Gabriel, Toland's exegesis of Abraham's response to the ordered sacrifice of Isaac postulates (through
the closest thing to midrashic exposition in deism, which owes much to Ro-
mans 4) a theory of Abraham's state of mind when he received Yahweh's revelation. Unlike Mary, however, Abraham—like the apostles and disciples in
the New Testament—had experiences of the miraculous acts of God with
which to justify his obedience to a command that only appears to be beyond
reason. That Abraham obeys and proceeds with thorough preparation for
parricide, Toland explains, only appears to contradict his reason; for if we recall the past acts of God in making parents of Abraham and Sarah at advanced ages (when they were "good as dead"), Abraham would be able to see
that God would recall Isaac to life.[68]

Toland beats a quick retreat from such elaborate eisegesis, however, arguing for the exceptional nature of the biblical accounts and, as a consequence, for a limit to what can be understood as God's miraculous activity.
These limits are spelled out in the conclusion. The world of the biblical accounts is replaced in our day—and indeed in all days subsequent to those
of the biblical accounts—with the order of nature, which takes precedence
over Christian belief in providential intervention. God is not prodigal of
miracles, and interposes rarely, for singularly remarkable ends, and only
when the interposition is introduced by divine declaration. A doctrine of
providence, like all postulates concerning historical experience, must be
subject to the canons of evidence, attestation, and corroboration. Acts of
providence change the course of nature and thus constitute disruptions of
our reasoned apprehension of the world; it follows that they must be rare
and readily marked. Toland rains contempt on those who speak of goblins,
fairies, witches, and conjurers, for these lack historical attestation and lie
beneath the dignity of the attention of the divine providence. He iterates
this heavily qualified affirmation of providence in his concluding, even
more vigorous restatement of his original assertion of the misunderstandings foisted upon traditional Christianity: " . . . it is visible to everyone that
they are the *Contradictions* and *Mysteries* unjustly charg'd upon *Religion*,
which occasion many to become *Deists* and *Atheists.*"[69] With this concluding flourish Toland aims completely to turn the tables: it is the Christian

tradition's own self-misunderstanding that leads inevitably to deism and atheism, while Toland here promotes the correct Christianity that eliminates all need for such recourse.[70]

Matthew Tindal

In *Christianity As Old As the Creation*[71] (1730), Matthew Tindal extends Toland's argument for the complete congruence of reason and revelation in order to make more sweeping declarations concerning correct Christian belief.[72] Taken with its subtitle— *. . . or, the Gospel, a Republication of the Religion of Nature*—the direction of those declarations is clear: Tindal will assert a complete congruence between natural religion and true Christianity, with the former providing the standard of adjudication for the latter. Tindal, however, will go farther: it follows that to the degree that Christianity accords with natural religion, its adherents will recognize that "their Duty and Happiness are inseparable."[73] Where Toland's essential concern was to establish that reason and Christianity—rightly understood—could coexist, Tindal claims that this coexistence guarantees our happiness in this life.

Implanted in us by God as part of the creation, our duty as humans is to recognize, believe in, and act upon the common religious truth that reason affords.[74] Tindal pays lip service to a distinction between the manner of communication of natural and revealed religious truth, but it becomes unmistakably clear that what is natural sets the standard for what is revealed. Truth's common, indeed its only, denominator is our naturally endowed reason: " . . . I freely declare, that the Use of *those Faculties,* by which Men are distinguish'd from Brutes, is the Only means they have to discern whether there is a God; and whether he concerns himself with human Affairs . . . God will judge Mankind as they are accountable, that is, as they are rational . . ."[75] In principle Tindal permits a basis for religion in the natural or the revealed, but the revealed religion that is Christianity can be neither more nor less than the naturally apprehended faith of rational humans. He effectively preempts the permission. Reason, he declares, indisputably teaches us that God exists, is perfect, and is creator of the world. It also instructs us that this knowledge has implications for our behavior. True Christianity thus is effectively as old as the creation—or (what amounts for Tindal to the same thing) as old as the human rational capacity.

Nature's handmaiden, reason is the human virtue that corresponds to the natural order. This correspondence implies for Tindal a direct connection between the created order and human happiness. Tindal anticipates Adam Smith: the Divine Law promotes "the common Interest" of all rational creatures, and this rule is absolute. The capacities of the deity take their terms from human life and value: God can only require us to do what conduces to our happiness and avoids our harm. The "invisible hand" emerges: " . . . it being impossible for God, in governing the World, to propose to himself any other End than the Good of the governed . . . consequently, whoever acts what is best for himself both in a publick, and private Capacity, does all that either God or Man can require."[76] It follows that the most rational people are the happiest, and God emerges as the reasonable, happy creature par excellence. For Tindal the *imago Dei* consists in our capacity to imitate the divine rationality, which in turn permits us to enjoy happiness to the greatest possible extent: " . . . we do what God himself wou'd do was he in our Place . . . and if our Happiness is limited, 'tis because our Reason is so: 'Tis God alone, who has an unlimited Reason and Happiness."[77]

Providence denominates the deity's wonderful creation of a world in which reason orders life, and humanity enjoys and benefits from that order to the degree that it employs its own parallel rational endowment. As with the category of revealed truth, Tindal nods at the problem of evil when he acknowledges that happiness in this life can be neither perfect nor complete, but his qualification is in fact unabashedly modest: "if we act according to the Dictates of right Reason, we shall receive, even here, true inward Comfort and Satisfaction."[78] To the extent that evil exists in the world according to Tindal, it is an expression of unrealized human fulfillment, and we discover its source is the individual rather than in external events. The limitations that curb or compromise fulfillment appear to be material: the only sure road to unhappiness in mind and body is the failure to follow fully one's reason. Irrational conduct can bring (unspecified) misery, pain, and anguish. To follow our reason, however, virtually ensures humans against the onslaught of unhappiness because "God's Will is so clearly, and fully manifested in the Book of Nature, that he who runs may read it."[79]

Undergirding this confidence is the constancy of "the Divine Precepts," which cannot vary. Whether as judge or legislator, the fundamental fact is that God always "acts alike for our Good." And while "There are few so gross as to imagine, we can direct infinite Wisdom in the Dispensation of Providence, or persuade him to alter those Laws he contriv'd before the Foundation of the World for putting Things in a regular Course,"[80] Tindal manifestly regards providence as precisely this "regular Course," "those Laws" ordained from the creation which are constant and unchangeable. This immutability consoles and assures us; it is the bedrock of human happiness. It also stands not incidentally as the bedrock of Tindal's idea of natural religion; and all existing particular systems must be judged by this particular standard: "if [the Truth of any instituted Religion whatever] varies from the Religion of Nature and Reason in any one Particular, nay, in the minutest Circumstance, That alone is an Argument, which makes all Things else that can be said for its Support totally ineffectual."[81]

Tindal thus locates providence explicitly and fully in the divine act of creation, eliminating the necessity of a complementary special providential activity in the world. Humans do on Tindal's account act providentially when they use their reason to benefit or enhance the natural order, but this is clearly an extension of the creation and far removed from anything like divine interposition or government. At the same time, it is a signal extension because it expresses the proper union of human reason with divine creation. In contrast, organized religion can and often does work to the contrary, hindering "the Reason of Things" by cultivating in the devout uncertainty, perplexity, doubt, and difficulty. It relies on punishment, invoked eternally and imposed temporally, and has the effect of shackling divinely ordained human liberty. Those who equate natural and revealed religion avoid such symptoms of anxiety and panic, in direct contradiction to those who elevate revelation above nature (and thus subject themselves to superstition). Superstition smacks of special providential intervention; for Tindal, the perfection of the created order argues for a world in which providence is merely the witness to the perfection of the creation, expressed in its rational extension and enhancement.

This critique of superstition and its proffered alternative underscores the basis and true value of religion: morality. Reason, Tindal writes, teaches that the Indian who insists on dying with a cow's tail in his hands and the "Papist" who insists on "rubbing a dying Man with Oil" are equally deluded. It follows that "was there any Thing but Morality necessary to constitute true Religion, we might be certain that the Goodness of God wou'd give us a Demonstration for it, equal to that he has given us for Morality."[82] This encompasses doctrine, which he understands can only command our belief to the degree that it has its bases in reason and appeal to our innate goodness. Tindal's razor applies even to Scripturally-based doctrinal formulations, which are an affront to reason and thus to the dignity of the human rational capacity. Doctrines such as the Trinity, and modes of interpretation such as the allegorical, arouse Tindal's deepest suspicions and even his contempt. He queries these "external marks" of revelation:

Is it not incumbent on those, who make any external Revelation so necessary to the Happiness of all Mankind, to shew, how it is consistent with the Notion of God's being universally benevolent, not to have reveal'd it to all his Children, when all had equal Need of it? Was it not as easy for him to have communicated it to all Nations, as to any one Nation, or Person? Or in all Languages, as in any One? Nay, was it not as easy for him to have made all Men, for the sake of this noble End, speak in one, and the same Language; as it was at first, to multiply Languages, to prevent their building a Tower up to Heaven? Nay, I see not how God can have any Need at all of Language, to let

Mankind know his Will; since he has at all Times communicated his Mind to them without it."[83]

The truly religious person focuses not on such "external marks" of Christ's particular example and the subsequent doctrinal beliefs and liturgical practices he inspired, but rather on the "internal marks" of Christ's example—the reasonableness and naturalness that anyone might discover without Christ (and did, in fact, before his time). Language is an external mark, and Tindal's invocation of the tower of Babel (and corresponding silence about Pentecost) forms the basis of a critique of the appeal to Scriptural authority that provides a remarkably concrete expression of his understanding of the nature and extent of religious morality and, in turn, of the decisive role played by the consideration of personal happiness in his account.

On the matter of Scriptural authority, Tindal again trumps Toland: rather than reinterpreting Scripture to support his position, he interrogates it and finds it wanting. The Old Testament prophecies are incomprehensible; and the apostles, indeed even Paul, anticipated the Second Coming in their lifetimes. Even if we grant that Scripture and the tradition it spawned faithfully convey the teachings of Jesus, interpretive problems vex the reader and force recourse to the extrinsic but universal authority of reason: "yet since most Texts have vastly vary'd, and sometimes contrary interpretations, and the literal Sense very often *kills,* how can they be confident they do not mistake their Meaning, except the Reason of Things makes it evident?"[84] Reason alone, then, stands constant through the vagaries of translation and tradition, and alone can be the sure foundation of faith.

The exception that ought to prove the rule of Tindal's hermeneutic of scriptural suspicion is Jesus's moral teachings. Reason will not abide obscurity in moral precept. However clear in their meaning, Tindal discovers difficulty:

> These, no doubt, are the plainest; yet even These, generally speaking, are not to be taken in their obvious and literal Meaning: As for Instance, *Lend, hoping for nothing again. He that takes away thy Coat, let him have they Cloak also. Of him, who takes thy Goods, ask them not again.* And shou'd we not, without having Recourse to the Reason of Things, be apt to think, that the Poor, as such, were the only Favourites of Heaven . . . And shou'd we not likewise be apt to imagine, that the Gospel was an Enemy to the Rich as such; and consequently, to all those Methods which make a Nation rich . . . This Precept is impracticable in a Christian State, because there cou'd be no Buyers where all were to be Sellers; and so is a Community of Goods, tho' in Use among the *Essenes,* and the Christians at first."[85]

Tindal arrives finally at a Scripture-less Christianity in which the governing idea is the sense that religion serves reason (and reason reflects the status quo that has emerged from the "natural" order of the world). Tindal invokes Confucius to clarify the obscurities of Jesus,[86] and the idea that all religion redounds to the end of human happiness renders Tindal's final pronouncements on morality devoid of substantive relation to religion or morality. Actions that promote human happiness are always good, and vice versa: "the only innate Principle in Man is the Desire of his own Happiness; and the Goodness of God requires no more than a right cultivating this Principle . . ."[87] Humans who do not see that the world is so ordered, and that it conduces to their happiness, are simply blind.[88] Tindal christens this truth providence, and denotes by it the deity's benevolence in planning and the world's benevolence in then accommodating our satisfaction. This very human desire is itself as old as the creation, and it is the standard to which Tindal's Christianity must comply.

William Law

Christianity as Old as the Creation provoked an immediate rejoinder from William Law: *The Case of Reason, or Natural Religion, Fairly and Fully Stated. In answer to a Book, entitled, Christianity as Old as the Creation.*[89] While Tindal serves as his stated antagonist, however, Law formulates his critique to apply to any advocacy of reason as the basis for natural religion. Law's stated thesis invokes the classic question of theodicy: "The origin of *sin* and *evil,* or how it entered into the world consistently with the infinite wisdom of god, is a mystery of *natural* religion, which reason cannot unfold."[90] The natural order of the world, and the fitness of its parts do not cover over or redeem the urgent problem of maleficence. Those who are naturally religious, that is, those who believe in a god of infinite wisdom, and who recognize this fact of life, must take recourse to something other than reason to understand what is manifestly a contradiction. Faith has no choice but to bow before this incomprehensible dilemma, which is simply a mystery.

Law presents a case for divine revelation as a recognition on the part of the believer that the significance of the Christian message is not encompassed by reason. It is, he argues, as much a matter of vision and imagination as it is of reason and philosophy.[91] Revelation predicates the Christian's knowledge that extends beyond the rational capacity. Law's example is the atonement. Natural religion and reason may afford a recognition of sinfulness, and of the way that Jesus's life and death respond to that fact. It may also, however, distort the atonement's implication by suggesting that the death and resurrection of Jesus settles the matter. By contrast, what the atonement inspires in the genuine believer—what is revealed by it—is a more severely repentant response that acknowledges our ongoing sinfulness. Reason appears not to encompass such insights, yet they are, Law maintains, utterly essential to the import of the doctrine.

Law disputes Tindal's celebration of the power of reason, arguing that experience asks us to seek more than reason can offer. By definition the supernatural is not open to natural, reasonable comprehension. Like Toland, Law discusses Genesis 22, but to strikingly different effect. Rather than considering Abraham's state of mind and his awareness of the prospects for divine intervention against so unreasonable a decree, Law moves into the subjunctive, considering what would be the consequences of the sacrifice: " . . . it was as lawful for *Abraham* to kill his son, as it was lawful for God to require any man's life, either by *sickness,* or *any other means* he should please to appoint. And it had been as unlawful for *Abraham* to have disobeyed God in this extraordinary command, as to have cursed God at any *ordinary calamity* of providence."[92]

Two claims distinguish Law's account from Toland's, and highlight dimensions of his critique of rational religion. First, he stresses the character of the divine command. It is beyond rational expectation and constitutes a fact that is straightforward (if admittedly obdurate[93]). It requires from Abraham the same response as any other divine, and thus inherently providential, directive: obedience. Unflinching even at parricide, Law treats divine commands as imperatives regardless of their content, and seriously contemplates the prospect that Abraham would have killed his son had God not intervened a second time. This subjunctive mood is utterly alien to Toland's perspective. It leads in turn to Law's second claim: despite the sensational quality of parricide, the passage in fact differs not an iota from the most mundane examples of divine intercession. God requires the handing over of human life in a variety of ways. Ours is not to question why. Extremities of circumstance do not mitigate, positively or negatively, this principle. Moral obligation has its basis, and its justification, not in human reason but in the divine will.[94]

It follows that reason cannot be in the natures of both God and human in equal measure. Not incidentally, the analogy of power becomes relevant. Divine power is to some degree like human power yet it is infinitely greater; so, too, divine reason is in some degree like human reason yet infinitely greater. It follows—decisively so in Law's judgment—that human reason cannot possibly judge competently "the fitness and reasonableness of God's proceedings with mankind." Contrary to the deists, the divine providence is anything but immediately comprehensible to human reason: indeed, it is literally beyond its scope. What marks the human apprehension of the deity is precisely incomprehensibility; there is a huge gap between "an *eternally foreknowing creator* and *governor*" and "his free creatures." What is genuinely fitting and natural is that we cannot know the ways of God.

To question particular providential acts is therefore the ultimate act of hubris: "to ask why God *only* does that which is *fit* for him to do" leads to the conundrum that "[w]e will not allow a Providence to be *right,* unless we can comprehend and explain the reasonableness of all its steps; and yet it could not *possibly* be right, unless its proceedings were as much *above* our comprehension, as our wisdom is *below* that which is infinite."[95] To claim knowledge of providence on the basis of our reason is in fact to render it something other than truly divine providence. Law can find nothing in all of Christianity that is more genuinely mysterious (*contra* Toland), and he hints darkly that this particular doctrine has often drawn the dividing line between atheism and belief.

In concluding, *The Case of Reason* assesses and finds wanting the deists' assumptions about anthropology. Two assertions inform the critique. Law acknowledges reason to be the way humans think, regardless of religious persuasion, but he disputes the idea that we reason to virtue and vice. This, he argues, is simply incorrect. In fact, we have virtue and/or vice inculcated in us from birth. Education, authority, and social norms instruct us. So it is with God: we make this discovery too not by reason alone. Again Law takes recourse to analogy: just as bodily strength is enhanced by food, so natural reason is enhanced by education. The precedence the deists place on reason as the road to virtue is, then, entirely unwarranted by the facts of life. Second, reason is by no means so easily dissociated from our emotions, passions, tempers, imaginations, and other sources to which the deists attribute our contradictions and absurdities. As desire and inclination are in fact components of, rather than distinct from, the will, so passion is a component of, rather than distinct from, reason. The weakness and foolishness of human passion are also the weakness and foolishness of human reason: "For reason governs as fully, when our actions and tempers are ever so bad, as it does when our actions and tempers are sound and good. And the only difference is, that reason acting well governs in the one case, and reason acting ill governs in the other."[96] Law thus ends on what we today might term a Dostoevskian note: to say that reason is always right reason is as absurd as to say that love is always pure love, or hatred pure hatred.

Joseph Butler

Two themes animate Joseph Butler's *The Analogy of Religion, Natural and Revealed, to the Constitution and Course of Nature* (1737)[97]: the deity's possession of an exact sense of poetic justice, and the incapacity of either human reason or humanly received revelation to divine the deity's plan. *The Analogy* distinguishes itself from *The Case of Reason* in the way it by turns recognizes, insists upon, and acknowledges its declaration that the discrepancy between the divine plan and the human capacity to discern that plan is a source of tension, and can exert a force toward anxiety on the believer's mind. Butler divides *The Analogy* into two parts, "Of Natural Religion" and "Of Revealed Religion," and his opening chapter addresses the issue (not the question) "Of a Future Life." Reluctant to find the vindication of the divine providence in this world, Butler turns to the next to articulate the prospect of divine justice. That credibility of such a future state, he argues, strongly recommends to the thoughtful mind the acceptance of religious belief, which it holds as a fundamental doctrine. Butler immediately shifts the discussion of these issues—and by implication their resolution—beyond this world.

The ensuing argument makes evident the reason for this shift. The ways of the natural world encourage us to recognize that actions have consequences. Yet it is undeniable that those who live virtuous lives may only enjoy qualified happiness, although Butler is prepared to claim (but only after he has stated the qualification) that in the majority of cases the virtuous individual lives more happily than does the maleficent counterpart. To contend that nature reflects a moral order is not fictitious but natural, Butler argues, but this is clearly not the easiest of affirmations: it is qualified, and based on carefully accurate observation and assessment of the natural world. We might best understand this world as a state of probation in which individuals experience the conflict of reason with temptation. To act upon reason is the natural and prudent course, and our probation should be successful to the degree that we obey our reason by choosing virtue and refusing to succumb to temptation's trickery. That we know this to be the case in the natural world allows us, by analogy, to posit reason and its consequences as a quality of all God's creation, temporal or otherwise.

The idea that human existence in this world prepares us for the next is a commonplace of Christian piety. It serves, in Butler's theology, to underline the analogy between the dispensation of events in the natural world (which *tends* to reward virtue with happiness and vice with misery) and the dispensation of events in the future state (which *must* reward virtue with happiness and vice with misery). Butler sees in the natural world direct attestation of a providential disposition, but he points to a future state that will perfectly realize what is only intimated in the natural state.

The actual measure of Butler's confidence in the natural world emerges most clearly in his ensuing discussion of necessity. Butler affirms human free will against natural necessity to avoid endorsing fatalism. Happiness and misery describe the various fates of human beings only as the consequences of their behavior. The only distinction on this point between Butler's *Analogy* and Toland or Tindal is its qualifications: "upon the whole" there is a correspondence, "in the upshot" happiness and misery follow virtue and vice respectively. This distinction signifies Butler's particular sort of reliance upon analogy: while it does not allow us to comprehend the incomprehensible, it makes allowance for a discrepancy between the present and future states.

Butler further develops this analogy in his subsequent insistence that we cannot, in fact, precisely identify the providence of God in the natural world. We are, to be sure, strongly disposed to infer it—so much so that Butler views it as a mandate for religious belief. Nonetheless, consideration of God's providence leads finally not to perfect knowledge but to an awareness of uncertainty. Analogy from this world to the next tells us that there is a providential deity, but that is all it tells us. Speculation about particular acts of providence is therefore pointless. On this note Butler concludes his discussion of natural religion and turns to a discussion of revealed religion in general, and Christianity in particular.

The importance of Christianity is twofold. The Scriptural texts of the Old and New Testaments confirm the religion of nature by proving both the general providence of God and the particular dispensation of providence toward sinful creatures. This dual testimony provided by Law and Gospel extends the natural awareness of God the Father to include a complementary revealed awareness of Son and Holy Spirit—the latter being knowledge we assuredly would not otherwise possess.[98]

While such complementarity marks the relationship between the natural and the revealed, Butler nonetheless continues to insist that the knowledge we gain from this is not all-encompassing. God does not dispense favor with reference to its advantage or consequence to humans in the world. This is at least in part because we are apt to judge providence by its immediate fruits, whereas judicious consideration counsels a longer view of the issue; all "at length and on the whole" receive their just desserts, and virtue "finally" prevails over vice. We need constantly to recall that our capacity to recognize providence, despite the suggestiveness of the general analogical framework, is significantly limited. Recognitions of providential interposition are of necessity inexact, uncertain, and inconclusive.

Butler's hierarchical ordering, in which providence is a general plan of which the Christian scheme is but a subset, ought not, however, to hinder us from ascribing to God's providence such acts of the natural world and order which seem to reward virtue with happiness and vice with misery. The general constitution of the world so counsels us. Extravagance ruins fortune, excess brings disease, crime leads to punishment; all such necessary relations testify to the role of the created natural government in the providential disposition of the world.

We learn by revelation of a future state, beyond the natural order, in which there is an exact correspondence of virtue with happiness and vice with misery. The particular benefit of Christianity is the decisive interposition of a Mediator who assures us that redemption, even to those guilty of unpunished transgressions, is not impossible. Christianity's special revelation of redemption in the mediating Son allows us to know what the natural order alone cannot disclose: that there is such a future state; that it is marked by such an order; and—most important for Butler—that transgressions unpunished in the natural world need not plunge us into unending fear of retribution, so long as we embrace the message of forgiveness revealed in the Christian scriptures.

Butler yokes reason and happiness. We are motivated to comprehend the world's design out of a desire to ensure our own happiness. Thus a calculation very similar to that of Toland and Tindal resides at the heart of Butler's analogy: the world must exist for our happiness, and the question then becomes how we can most readily secure happiness. Butler only disputes with Toland and Tindal over how best to navigate the terrain of the world: revelation is for Butler a card which enhances our odds. It is, however, a card that always will be trumped by the ace of reason. Butler does dispute the claim that we can and do comprehend the world fully through a reasonable understanding of the order of nature; he also takes the position that our existence here and the design we seek to comprehend have ultimately to do with how we might best ensure our own happiness. He invokes in the end reason over revelation, and affirms a necessary connection between virtue and happiness.

Conclusion

Consensus about the inappropriate attribution to the deity of providence raised for each of these writers questions about the character of the world in which they lived. The fulcrum, or point at which opinions diverge, was the problem of evil. Addison insists upon evil as a fundamental reality of life, and Dennis acknowledges it, so that their disagreement about poetic justice hinges not on the character of the world but on whether the drama should imitate faithfully that world, or remind viewers of the consolation that awaits them. Happiness is decisively not our *telos* in the world, and only in the final judgment will the deity's just desserts emerge. Neither Toland nor Tindal, keen to emphasize the perfection of God's creation and the complementarity of human reason, afford evil any sway in the world. The creation itself is providential, and the human who acts reasonably discovers accord with nature and, thus, happiness. Law demonstrates great skepticism about the capacity of reason to negotiate the world without the assistance of revelation, implying in the process that the world is decidedly a less ordered and straightforward experience than Tindal particularly, and Toland by implication, assert. Butler is dubious on the same score, and rolls theological dice to discern the degree to which virtue is rewarded and vice punished in the world. On the whole, this is more often than not the case, but it occurs as an expression of the natural order and the final judgment is the quickly invoked recourse to ensure ultimate justice.

The account offered in this chapter presents the genesis and development of a debate Fielding knew well. It did not, of course, conclude with Butler in the late 1730s. It continued at least through the following decade—the most intense period of Fielding's creativity as a novelist. It is impossible to pinpoint with exactitude a specific influence on an author, but it is worth-while to mention briefly two writers whose work underscores the ongoing currency of the questions discussed here. The first is Thomas Morgan.[99] Morgan published *The Moral Philosopher*, his most interesting, sustained, and provocative theological treatise, in 1737. It appeared in a second edition, as did two later volumes of the same title, which responded to such critics as John Leland. Morgan followed *The Moral Philosopher* in 1740 with *Physico-Theology: Or, A Philosophico-Moral Disquisition concerning Human Nature, Free Agency, Moral Government, and Divine Providence.* The rhetoric of these volumes, particularly this last, replicates directly the rhetoric of deist-divine disputation. As noted in the discussions of Toland and Tindal, Morgan's dialogue displays specific affinities with his predecessors: its insistence upon the limitations of miraculous activity, and the appropriate use of reason in response; the claim that deism provides a crucial friend to Christianity in its battle with its true enemy, atheism; and the invocation of a providential "unseen Hand" that serves as a metaphor not for an interposing deity, but for a creation perfectly ordained to benefit those prepared to exploit it for their own happiness. Morgan's text is particularly concerned to sort the Jewish background out of Christianity (it is a trove of anti-Jewish and anti-Catholic sentiment), and to discern the essence of true Christianity and (what amounts to the same thing) true religion. Much of this aims to eliminate superstition not only from worship but from our understanding of how the world works; and, like Toland and Tindal, Morgan regards the idea of necessary providential intervention as weak reason. Unlike Toland and Tindal, however, Morgan's rejection of providential interposition results in a distinctive emphasis on both framing moments of the divine activity. He propounds not only a perfect creation, but a robust final judgment when God "will Reward or punish Men according to the Deeds done in the Body, or as their Actions have been agreeable or disagreeable to the eternal, immutable Law or Rule of Moral Truth and Righteousness."[100] There is an at least implicit acknowledgment here of the problem of evil, and of the uneasiness of any claim that virtue is consistently rewarded, and vice punished, in the world.

The second is David Hume.[101] Hume's *Dialogues Concerning Natural Religion* appeared posthumously in 1779 (although he almost undoubtedly wrote it in the late 1740s), but *An Enquiry Concerning Human Understanding,* with its notorious Sections X, "Of Miracles," and XI, "Of a Particular Providence and of a Future State," appeared in 1748. While beyond the rhetoric of the controversialists discussed above both in chronology and in quality of philosophical deliberation, the *Enquiry* firmly underscores the enduring power of these questions during Fielding's decade of novelistic fecundity. With his focus on natural theology and the argument from design, Hume raises and famously responds to the central questions of the debate about poetic justice and the deism controversy. Can we view the world rationally and credit reports of miraculous intervention? If we cannot, and if we acknowledge the existence of evil in the world, we discover significant arguments against the existence of an interposing providence. Section XI of the *Enquiry* takes the implication yet further, asserting that the same analysis argues against some future state that rectifies the imperfections of the present.

The displacement of providence ultimately raised questions for these writers about the prospects for human happiness in this world. To what degree can we expect it, and how do we account for it? Absent a deity who providentially interposes on behalf of the good, Christian believers must trust in the created order and the final judgment for confirmation that life's rewards and punishments are, and will be, justly rendered. The displacement of providence—the tendency to collapse it into either creation or eschatology—reflects the anxiety that its complete departure will eliminate any expectation that the deity is concerned with our happiness in this world. The debate about poetic justice and the deism controversy present an expressive set of variations on that fundamental worry: from Addison's grim stoicism to Butler's theological odds-playing, from Tindal's confidence in the preeminent reassurance of reason to Law's insistence that there is more to life than the natural world of our senses. The anxiety is fundamental, and in his novels Henry Fielding spoke to the full range of its expression in eighteenth-century England.

Chapter 3 ∼

Providence Victorious: Narrative Viewpoint in *Joseph Andrews* and *Tom Jones*

Whether there is a providential disposition to events, and how to account for the fact of human evil if there is: this question animates *Joseph Andrews* (1742), *Tom Jones* (1749), and *Amelia* (1751). Brought to the fore in the debates at the turn of the century about poetic justice, and carried on into the late 1730s in the deism controversy, the question receives further play (to an at least partly different and more expansive audience) in Fielding's great fictional works.[1] As his 1752 pamphlet, "Examples of the Interposition of Providence in the Detection and Punishment of Murder," demonstrates, Fielding also wrote in a controversialist manner about the question. Earlier, however, it served as the central trope in his major novels. The fact that Fielding's fictional treatment of the question changes, and is itself marked by a diffidence of assertion at least partially removed from that of the pamphlet, serves in the end only to underscore its abiding presence in his imaginative creations.

In brief, the change and the source of diffidence may be described as an ongoing tension, finally unresolved, between claiming decisive divine action in this world or the next: in special providential interpositions here and now, or in a decisive final judgment. Always Fielding assumes that the deity's worldly interest consists in rewarding the virtuous and punishing the vicious. At issue—and with an urgency that did not recede in Fielding's mature creative years—is precisely when that interest achieves decisive realization. In his narrative art Fielding vacillates on precisely the point of what claims can be made for providence in this world. No doubt exists about the future state; but such is his acute appreciation for the precarious state of goodness in the world that providential manifestations in the here and now become the pressing question of his fiction. Much depends, I argue in this and in the following chapter, on the reader's sense of the ending. The substance of my argument is the claim that in neither *Tom Jones* nor *Amelia* can the ending be discussed usefully by invoking such hackneyed phrases as "all's right with the world." Fielding may not, in the end, have been able to handle his chosen question with finality, but his inability resides close to the source of his artistic greatness. Its appreciation requires nuanced attention.

The organization of the following discussion of Fielding's novels perpetuates the traditional division by pairing *Joseph Andrews* and *Tom Jones* in this chapter, and discussing *Amelia* separately in the next. I do so both to signal no wish to deny their differences, but also to highlight what I regard as the genuine thematic continuity of Fielding's last novel with its more celebrated predecessors. They are, I hope to demonstrate, thematically more "of a piece" than we tend to recognize. At the same time, there is no mistaking the changes of tone and assurance the chronological reader encounters in moving those two seemingly short years from 1749 to 1751.

In *Joseph Andrews* and *Tom Jones,* Fielding directly engages the question of providence and evil through his narrator's intrusive, frequently didactic commentary on the action. As self-styled historians,[2] these narrators write retrospectively: they recall what has happened and highlight for readers that what they report is the result of recollection and research. They are interested in the facts, but they move quickly to questions of cause and effect, and in turn to questions of pattern. Through his narrators, Fielding created in *Joseph Andrews* and *Tom Jones* a retrospective approach to narrative telling, which directly implicates that most retrospective of theological doctrines: divine providence. In this respect, Fielding's first two major novels point to earlier narratives that told classical providential stories: Augustine's *Confessions,* in which Augustine announces the retrospective theme that he was led unknowingly, that he might knowingly be led; and Milton's *Paradise Lost,* in which the recounting of the fall of humanity becomes understood retrospectively as a *feleas culpa.* Just as these earlier narratives operate from a retrospective viewpoint to establish ideas about divine providence, so Fielding uses his narrators in *Joseph Andrews* and *Tom Jones* to raise the same set of considerations.

Determined as they are to establish their retrospection, however, Fielding's narrators do not finally offer a blanket affirmation of providence or a comprehensive justification of the ways of God. What emerges is not a Miltonic affirmation of "eternal providence," but a qualified claim for a general providential design that is both essential to human happiness and beyond the human capacity to identify with complete confidence.[3] These narrators' historical investigations always lead them to document the pervasive and disruptive intrusion of evil in human affairs. Evil proves an eminently resourceful and enduring antagonist to the implied providential design.[4]

While evil never triumphs in Fielding's novels, it also is not defeated. The ability of good people to control its impact on their lives is precarious, momentary, and decidedly an ongoing proposition at the closings of both *Joseph Andrews* and *Tom Jones*. The historian concludes these tales by providing no definitive assurance that the marriages of Joseph and Fanny and Tom and Sophia will prove impregnable to the same kinds of attacks that threatened their original prospects for union. Much can be, and is, done over the course of these novels to accomplish these devoutly wished consummations; none of it, whether human, circumstantial, or divine, fully guarantees their future security.

The resulting view of providence is thus not one of grand, overarching design, but precisely of special interposition: of moments when the narrative, however realistic and historically accountable, nonetheless defies complete realistic explanation. The diffidence of these novels about the deity's providence is only underscored by the fact that at these moments Fielding's narrator becomes coy, oblique, utterly undeclarative, and noncommittal. General invocation, rather than specific assertion, is his preferred mode of address on such extraordinary occasions. "The great, useful, and uncommon Doctrine," the inculcation of which encapsulates "the whole Purpose" of *Tom Jones*, proves, for good reason, elusive to Fielding's readers.

Comparison with Voltaire's *Candide* helps to capture Fielding's distinctive approach in *Joseph Andrews* and *Tom Jones*. Relating the theme of providence to the function of the narrator in Fielding's novels can risk the misunderstanding that Fielding's narrators function like more omniscient Panglosses, with a comic twist. Things happen in *Candide* and in *Tom Jones*, and while in Voltaire the commentary comes from a character and in Fielding from a narrator, in each case it suggests that whatever the immediate effect of what happens—good or ill—it is part of the divine plan and so ultimately contributes to the good. My claim for Fielding's narrators aims for a very different, contrasting comparison. In Voltaire, the juxtaposition of increasingly terrible evils with Pangloss's monotonic reassurances renders a satiric effect far afield from the aim and result of the commentary of Fielding's narrator. The reader of *Candide* views with mounting dismay and incredulity Pangloss's uniform invocations of providence in the face of a wealth of counterevidence. Voltaire achieves a satiric distance between Pangloss and the reader which results ultimately in the reader's outrage. Behind this reaction is an issue which Panglossian exegesis only begs: the problem of evil as the test (not the affirmation!) of any notion of divine providential activity. This is far afield from the intimacy the narrator of *Tom Jones* cultivates with the reader, because in *Tom Jones* the narrator's commentary has its basis in evidence rather than dogma. Trust in *Tom Jones* results from a narrator who aims not to beg questions but to tell things as they happened and only then to offer meditation. Fitting events to a preconceived explanation is emphatically not this narrator's modus operandi.[5] The price may be qualification and diffidence, but Fielding was no cynic and he cherished the value of verisimilitude too much to do otherwise.

Two animadversions merit rehearsal. Narrators need readers, and any discussion of how Fielding makes his narrators function must account as well for the reader. The announced readerly virtues of "judgment" and "sagacity" in *Joseph Andrews* and *Tom Jones* underline the narrator's desire for a controlling interest in that experience. The art of reading Fielding's novels is the negotiation of these claims for autonomy between narrator and reader. I claim here a stronger, more heavily didactic role for Fielding's narrator than reader-response approaches tend to allow. Fielding's narrators openly recognize the role of the reader's judgment, but the terms on which such judgment may be exercised prove to be explicitly (some might say narrowly) articulated. The readers of *Tom Jones* who fail to recognize the narrator's definition of love are boldly dismissed on the grounds that they already have read more than they can understand. This is not the statement of a narrator who lacks confidence about the appropriate readerly response to his tale. Fielding is after very specific effects in *Joseph Andrews* and *Tom Jones,* and he succeeds to a remarkable degree in stating those and imposing, not to say forcing, them on the reader. Reader-response critics tend to render Fielding's narrators less didactic, and the reader more free, than seems to me to be the case. How readers construe events and circumstances in these novels is ultimately and decisively dependent on how the narrator presents them. Those who chafe as they read Fielding probably find little consolation that there is also in these narrators the implicit recognition that reader-response criticism has a point: works are as much the product of the reader as of the author.

Second, by stressing the manner in which Fielding's narrators depict events and circumstances, I may appear to underestimate what is commonly regarded as the focus of his depiction in the novels: human nature. Discussions of Fielding's concern with verisimilitude almost always focus on characterization. The narrators themselves provide supporting evidence for this focus, nowhere more immediately than in *Tom Jones,* with its epigraph from Horace's translation of *The Odyssey*—*Mores hominum multorum vidit*—and its opening assertion that "The Provision then which we have here made is no other than HUMAN NATURE."[6] Fielding's brilliant characterizations are of course central to his narrative art and its delight, but focus on these to the exclusion of their surroundings distorts his larger enterprise. Human nature and especially human psychology are crucial inter-

ests for Fielding, but the present study seeks to locate them within epistemological questions concerning human knowledge about the ways of the
world. *Joseph Andrews, Tom Jones,* and even *Amelia* each suggests that the
world, and human experience, is greater than the sum of its characters' perspectives and actions—and even, finally, of their retrospectively privileged
narrators. Judgments about character, while indispensable, fail to provide
the full vantage Fielding seeks to cultivate in his "sagacious" reader. Fielding's concerns, then, are located not solely in character—however broadly
construed, and however brilliantly depicted—but in the relationship between human character and divine disposition.[7] In this, I would argue, resides Fielding's true connection to his predecessors in classical epic.
Through his narrator, concerns about the activity of the Christian deity
parallel the fascination in Homer and Virgil with the ways in which divinity exerts its force in human life.[8]

What follows in this chapter is an analysis of the role played by Fielding's
narrators in *Joseph Andrews* and *Tom Jones,* each of which is told by a narrator who writes retrospectively, and whose sophistication rests precisely in his
nuanced juxtaposition of a desired end, strongly implied and even endorsed
from the outset, with a series of events that by turns do and do not conduce
to that end. This retrospection develops into an ongoing meditation on the
inherently retrospective idea of divine providence. It is this that sustains the
narrative lines of these novels, and each raises in the process questions about
evil actions and the role they play in compromising the devoutly wished
consummations of the narratives.

The Adventures of Joseph Andrews

A rhetoric of historical documentation pervades *Joseph Andrews.* Its regularity and insistence underscore that the narrative record of these adventures is based on interview and personal experience, and that it is
retrospective: that its parts are selected and organized from the viewpoint
of one who has made some effort to know the whole story. Claims to historical veracity dot the narrative, often through allusions to sources. Both
its flavor and its presence throughout tend to be ignored or even dismissed,
but it merits note:

> When he came back to the Inn, he found *Joseph* and *Fanny* sitting together.
> They were so far from thinking his Absence long, as he had feared they would,
> that they never once miss'd or thought of him. Indeed, I have often been as-
> sured by both, that they spent these Hours in a most delightful Conversation:
> but as I never could prevail on either to relate it, so I cannot communicate it
> to the Reader.[9]

This was all of Mr. *Joseph Andrews*'s Speech which I could get him to recollect, which I have delivered as near as was possible in his own Words, with a very small Embellishment.[10]

Mr. *Adams,* from whom we had most of this Relation, could not recollect all the Jests of this kind practised on him, which the inoffensive Disposition of his own Heart made him slow in discovering; and indeed, had it not been for the Information which we received from a Servant of the Family, this Part of our History, which we take to be none of the least curious, must have been deplorably imperfect; tho' we must own it probable, that some more Jokes were (as they call it) *cracked* during their Dinner; but we have by no means been able to come at the Knowledge of them.[11]

The Morning after her Arrival being *Sunday,* she went to Church, to the great Surprize of every body, who wondered to see her Ladyship, being no very constant Churchwoman, there so suddenly upon her Journey. *Joseph* was likewise there: and I have heard it was remarked, that she fixed her Eyes on him much more than on the Parson: but this I believe to be only a malicious Rumour.[12]

"Why, there it is in Peaper," answered the Justice, shewing him a Deposition, which in the Absence of his clerk he had writ himself, of which we have with great difficulty procured an authentick Copy . . . [13]

Mr. *Booby* hath with unprecedented Generosity given *Fanny* a fortune of two thousand Pound, which *Joseph* hath laid out in a little Estate in the same Parish with his Father, which he now occupies, (his Father having stock'd it for him;) and *Fanny* presides, with most excellent Management in his Dairy; where, however, she is not at present very able to bustle much, being, as Mr. *Wilson* informs me in his last Letter, extremely big with her first Child.[14]

On other occasions the narrator remarks the limits of his research:

She was a poor Girl, who had been formerly bred up in Sir *John's* Family; whence a little before the Journey to *London,* she had been discarded by Mrs. *Slipslop* on account of her extraordinary Beauty; for I never could find any other reason.[15]

Adams was pleased with so perfect a Confirmation that he had not the least Fever: but advised him to a lighter Diet, for that Evening. He accordingly eat either a Rabbit of a Fowl, I never could with any tolerable Certainty discover which . . . [16]

. . . the Servant (whose Appetite for Revenge is soon satisfied) being sufficiently contented with the Drubbing which *Joseph* had inflincted on him, and which was indeed of no very moderate kind, had suffered him to go off, which he did, threatening a severe Revenge against *Joseph,* which I have never heard he thought proper to take.[17]

It would be unnecessary, if I was able, which indeed I am not, to relate the Conversation between these two Gentlemen, which rolled, as I have been informed, entirely on the subject of Horse-racing.[18]

These passages represent quite thoroughly the complete action of the novel, and in each the narrator bothers to attest the reliability of his account. Motives for actions have been pursued, and the best available explanation is proffered. Principals have been queried about their states of mind. The vagaries of recollection are documented and, when they compromise the accuracy of an account, duly noted. When lacking information or judging what he has to be untrustworthy, the narrator notes that he will neither include it, nor fabricate something in its place.[19] However intrusive or obvious, such oaths of allegiance to historical accuracy underline the narrator's claim to reliability: what happened really occurred, and the individuals involved really exist. This commentary constantly reminds the reader that the narrator writes retrospectively and that his method is historical: it has its basis in fact and human documentation, and its authority is the authority of the actual.

The rhetoric of historical documentation in *Joseph Andrews* is real, but it is not alone. Standing in regular juxtaposition to it, at times subverting it, is a rhetoric of embellishment. At the same time that the narrator stresses the historical veracity of his narrative, he undermines it. We read, for example, Joseph Andrews's speech with the implication of a high degree of verisimilitude, only to be informed at its conclusion that it exists "with a very small embellishment." The reported rumor that Lady Booby attends Sunday service to admire Joseph rather than to praise God gains good historical credence from the narrator's note that she rarely attended church prior to Joseph's arrival, at which time she became quite faithful; in a subsequent passage the narrator discards this as "malicious" rumor. The status of the narrator's embellishments of the facts can be positive or negative—most readers will be inclined to take literally the comment about Joseph's speech, and to take otherwise that concerning Lady Booby—but the point is that such qualifications inevitably modify the self-proclaimed historical reliability of the narrative. It serves to remind us that what we read cannot be literal, historical description without remainder, but must consist in judgments about the facts. Together Fielding's double-edged rhetorical gambit goes to a claim for a verisimilitude based on the facts, but more complex than the facts taken alone can provide.[20]

In *Joseph Andrews,* then, the claim is twofold and aims for complementarity. First, the *action itself* (inclusive of, but not limited to, its character portraits) possesses a verisimilitude for daily life that the reader should recognize. This claim of credibility is comprehensive in that it extends not only to character, but to action. The narrator aims to substantiate this claim through constant allusion to what he has discovered through his continuing personal relations with Joseph, Fanny, Abraham Adams, and Mr. Wilson, eyewitness report, and occasional documentation. All these underscore the narrator's concern to establish the veracity, not only of characters, but of the entire narrative *as history.* It follows that, as an honest historian, the narrator acknowledges the limits of his knowledge. He denies omniscience and offers what retrospective reconstruction renders possible. All this is real and easily underestimated in *Joseph Andrews.*

At the same time, the narrator makes manifest that he does not lack a point of view. He does nothing to hide the fact that his particular retrospective arrangement has, in his judgment, not only local but general significance. He compels the reader to draw a moral. To this end, the reader of *Joseph Andrews* finds herself exhorted to cultivate her "sagacity" in response to the challenges posed by this telling:

> It is an observation sometimes made, that to indicate our Idea of a simple Fellow, we say, *He is easily to be seen through:* Nor do I believe it a more improper Denotation of a simple Book. Instead of applying this to any particular Performance, we chuse rather to remark the contrary in this History, where the Scene opens itself by small degrees, and he is a sagacious Reader who can see two Chapters before him.
>
> For this reason, we have not hitherto hinted a Matter which now seems necessary to be explained . . . [21]

It is typical of the narrator to couple assertion about the writing of "this History" with proffered suggestion about how it is best read. When the reader squirms out ⸢f the rhetorical pinhold, however, what is most striking is that, in one respect, *Joseph Andrews* is in fact quite easily seen through: it is a love story and its consummation is the marriage of those worthies who deserve each other, Joseph and Fanny. This stands as a judgment that works as a fact in the narrative: Joseph and Fanny wish to be married, are entirely worthy of, indeed deserve, each other. This is the point from which the reader must take her bearings to make sense of *Joseph Andrews.*

Not so easily seen through, however—and the true subject of the novel— is the way in which the twists and turns of the world do and do not conduce to this union. Here the scene unfolds slowly, and many impediments block the human capacity to judge and to discern resolution before it occurs. This narrator's poetics, then, are not those of Aristotle's celebrated emphasis upon the presentation of what is possible. Rather, *Joseph Andrews* aims to place the reader in the midst of the circumstantial fray. Here character and action (like life, as Aristotle recognized) will *not* be fully or directly congruent, and full judgments about the implications of character will not be immediately accessible. This is what will unfold, and the sagacious reader is the one whose concentration on this process ultimately yields some discernment beyond the present. The reader who follows the narrator in discerning cause and effect and in comprehending pattern may, the narrator intimates, make some progress on the broader scale of event in the sort of discernment invoked by the description of seeing through another person. Implicit is the suggestion that one's reading might be sagacious. But what does sagacity mean here? The above passage suggests that it is the ability to discern beyond the present. The reader who attends to the patterns of events will find, the narrator intimates, the discernment that the narrative—and, by implication, the reader's own life—tends to frustrate.

It is, then, a distinctive brand of mimesis that *Joseph Andrews* offers. It aims immediately to render the vicissitudes of life that challenge and frustrate comprehension, and in doing so to test the reader's sagacity and judgment just as life itself does. The narrator's direct address formulates this as nothing less than a challenge, and such discernment is coin of the realm in this novel. Everyone does it, starting with the narrator and extending to not only the reader but the entire cast of characters in the novel.[22] Fielding's narrator constantly forces the aware reader to weigh the evidence and judge, and the substance of that narrative is the way in which its characters engage, with varying degrees of success, in that process.[23] Lady Booby, torn between her attraction to Joseph Andrews's creature charms and her deep humiliation at his principled obliviousness to hers, by turns orders Slipslop to send Joseph to her and to turn him out of the house. After four reversals by her ladyship, the narrator interposes: "This wavering in her Mistress's Temper probably put something into the Waiting-Gentlewoman's Head, not necessary to mention to the Sagacious Reader." Lady Booby's previous behavior renders transparent to the reader her conflicting emotions, and the narrator records a similar recognition by Slipslop. This doubling underlines Lady Booby's mercurial disposition and the influence passion has over her (better) judgment. In recording Slipslop's own belated recognition, it also serves to remind the reader of what she should already know.

This is the central activity of *Joseph Andrews:* by implication it is the basis of the narrator's rendition, and the narrator in turn writes to put the reader through the paces of such discernment. Slipslop on occasion exercises a sagacity that is absolutely critical to events. Her recognition of Lady Booby's infatuation with Joseph differs from the reader's to the degree that she herself has pretensions to Joseph's attention and at several times displays her own unique combination of deep infatuation and remorseless outrage toward him. Slipslop's sagacity coincides with the reader's when she recognizes the depth of Lady Booby's infatuation with Joseph even as it diverges from the reader's in its degree of disinterestedness. The reader seeks what will make possible the union of Joseph with Fanny, while Slipslop seeks the means for advancement in her ladyship's household. However different their relationship to the narrative, both the reader and Slipslop must each employ the same method.[24]

No character in *Joseph Andrews* exercises the reader's powers of judgment more strenuously than Abraham Adams. And it is no coincidence that no character illustrates more fully the themes the narrative compels the reader to ponder. The good parson's capacity to delight, to amaze, and to confound proves so spectacular that these effects extend beyond the reader to the narrator himself. Nowhere else in Fielding's corpus does a character so fully embody both the grand promise and the deep pitfall of simple good nature and determined religious belief.[25] Adams responds to anyone in need with an unmatched and absolutely winning alacrity, yet an alacrity matched only by a lack of discretion that unfailingly aggravates, rather than relieves, the difficulty at hand. Adams liberally—much more so than Fielding's narrator—invokes providence as a bulwark for his good-natured bungling, and it is no accident of the narrative that such confident invocations frequently accompany his acts of charitable transgression. Adams presents the highest possible irony for the theme of *Joseph Andrews:* the character who most confidently affirms a divinely providential order also most consistently acts to imperil the most persuasive witness to such an order—the union of Joseph and Fanny. However unwitting, the consequences of his actions are more genuinely consequential than any of Adams's pronouncements about providence.[26]

Adams's failure, despite his fervent avowals and wholly honorable intentions, to aid and abet the desirable direction of events goes hand in hand with an unmatched credulity about human character. Continually taken in by the most transparent hypocrisy, what Adams smokes best is his pipe. The character with by far the greatest human appeal in *Joseph Andrews,* and the one who most directly speaks and acts to the questions raised by the narrative, is also the least sagacious. Abraham Adams embodies the pitfalls of the confident, absolute invocation of a providential order. He becomes in *Joseph Andrews* the crux of Fielding's own diffidence about claims for providence in the world.

Two episodes illustrate these paradoxes. Each consists of an exchange between Adams and Joseph Andrews about judgment and the real ways of the world—further exercises in sagacious understanding. In Book II, ch. xvi, Adams awaits with Joseph and Fanny for the proffered assistance of a purportedly wealthy man who befriended them late one evening of their journey. They are penniless and he volunteered munificent assistance. This nameless benefactor is in fact a fraud, as the unhappy trio discover when messages sent to his home return with the report that he has suddenly departed and is unavailable to honor his offers. Adams, unlike Joseph and Fanny, fails to discern the implication of this report and imagines illness or sudden calamity as the cause. Joseph's smile betrays his superior understanding, and he attributes it to his experience of denying Mr. Booby when in his service as a footman. Shocked, Adams laments the wickedness of the Christian world, and its uncomfortably close approximation to the wickedness of its heathen predecessor. Adams then turns to speculation: why would this man do such a deed when its discovery is inevitable? On this point Joseph defers to the Parson:

> "It is not for me," answered *Joseph*, "to give Reasons for what Men do, to a Gentleman of your Learning." "You say right," quoth *Adams*, "Knowledge of Men is only to be learnt from Books, *Plato* and *Seneca* for that; and those are Authors, I am afraid Child, you never read." "Not I, Sir, truly," answered *Joseph*, "all I know is, it is a Maxim among the Gentlemen of our Cloth, that those Masters who promise the most perform the least; and I have often heard them say, they have found the largest Vailes in those Families, where they were not promised any. But, Sir, instead of considering any farther these Matters, it would be our wisest way to contrive some Method of getting out of this House: for the generous Gentleman, instead of doing us any Service, hath left us the whole Reckoning to pay." *Adams* was going to answer, when their Host came in . . . [27]

In this instance, as in many others, the maxim of the footman proves more sagacious than that of the learned clergyman. There is no doubt about which gentleman of the cloth is more suited to divine character. Joseph suspects before Adams wonders, recognizes before Adams suspects, and finally must lead his disbelieving mentor to the truth. Training in the classics takes a back seat to worldly experience in this history. Most galling is that Adams, once enlightened to the truth, proceeds to draw precisely the wrong conclusion about what it all means. Utterly unchastened by his gullibility, Adams pounces on Joseph's deference to his learning to affirm the opposite of what the scene manifests, suggesting that Joseph's knowledge of human nature is deficient because he lacks Greek and Latin. Not only do the classics afford Adams no protection against deceit; his quick proclamation of superior understanding on their basis only compounds his initial error. There are of course occasions when such blithe ignorance endears Adams to us, for its source is the same heedless confidence that leads him, at the cry of Fanny, to fling his beloved Aeschylus into the fire and speed immediately to her rescue. However genuinely endearing, such literal mindlessness nonetheless renders Adams at once the most lettered and the most genuinely ignorant character in *Joseph Andrews*.[28]

Adams himself unwittingly names the subject of his ignorance: wickedness, in the above scene without motive and wantonly cruel. Here sagacity consists in recognizing evil as a genuine force in the world. Adams cannot imagine that such malice could exist in a Christian breast. Joseph can and does, and while he does not presume to explain it, he stands superior to Adams in the crucial capacity of recognition. Recognition may not be explanation, but it trumps ignorance. (It is Joseph who aims to conclude the conversation and turn the trio's attention to their situation.) Adams is most seriously naive, and however benevolent, this flaw renders completely ineffectual his immense energy and intention for the good. He fails to recognize that there are genuine threats to the workings of providence in the world.

Perhaps no scene in *Joseph Andrews* more dramatically illustrates Adams's imaginative failure than the one found in Book IV, ch. viii. In part as eyewitness and in part through report from Fanny, Adams has learned of her abduction, incarceration, and attempted rape by a young gentleman and his retinue. Following her liberation, Joseph resolves to marry Fanny immediately to ensure her safety. Fanny concurs, as does the narrator and the reader. All that stands in the way of the universally desired ceremony is Parson Adams, who insists that Joseph and Fanny follow ecclesial regulation and publish their wedding banns for three weeks before the nuptials may occur. Adams's capacity to act precisely against what is best is of course given particular poignance because the banns exist to inform society of the impending event, and to allow objections to be aired and resolved in advance. His ecclesial interposition, then, only enhances the prospects of Fanny's captors, whom the marriage (and Adams himself, of course) would thwart. Given that their marriage is the transparent telos of the novel, Adams literally stands in the way of what would be the symbolic confirmation of the providence that he invokes with such confidence and regularity.

On this occasion Joseph proves less deferential to the parson, and in response to his entreaties Adams counsels patience and offers a sermon on the text of Matthew 5:28 ("But I say unto you, That whosoever looketh on a woman to lust after her hath committed adultery with her already in his heart"). Adams's theme is twofold: patience is the appropriate antidote to lust, which he imagines, permitting ecclesial regularity to replace his knowledge of the situation, to be the actual reason Joseph wants to dispense with the banns; and fear of malfeasance argues a distrust in "that Power in which we should alone put our Trust," namely "the Will of Providence." Having invoked the first theme on the dubious foundation of his experience of the world, Adams turns with earnest to the second when the tables are roundly turned on him:

At which words one came hastily in and acquainted Mr. *Adams* that his youngest Son was drowned. He stood silent a moment, and soon began to stamp about the Room and deplore his Loss with the bitterest Agony. *Joseph,* who was overwhelmed with Concern likewise, recovered himself sufficiently to endeavour to comfort the Parson; in which Attempt he used many Arguments that he had at several times remember'd out of his own Discourses both in private and publick, (for he was a great Enemy to the Passions, and preached nothing more than the Conquest of them by Reason and Grace) but he was not at leisure now to hearken to his Advice. "Child, Child," said he, "do not go about Impossibilities. Had it been any other of my Children I could have born it with patience; but my little Prattler, the Darling and comfort of my old Age—the little Wretch to be snatched out of Life just at his Entrance into it; the sweetest, best-temper'd Boy, who never did a thing to offend me. It was but this Morning I gave him his first Lesson in *Quae Genus.* This was the very Book he learnt, poor Child! it is of no further use to thee now. He would have made the best Scholar, and have been an ornament to the church—such Parts and such Goodness never met in one so young." "And the handsomest Lad too," says Mrs. *Adams,* recovering from a Swoon in *Fanny's* Arms.—"My poor *Jacky,* shall I never see thee more?" cries the Parson.—"Yes, surely," says *Joseph,* "and in a better Place, you will meet again never to part more." I believe the Parson did not hear these Words, for he paid little regard to them, but went on lamenting whilst the Tears trickled down into his bosom. At last he cry'd out, "Where is my little Darling?" and was sallying out, when to his great Surprize and Joy, in which I hope the reader will sympathize, he met his Son in a wet Condition indeed, but alive, and running towards him. . . . The Parson's Joy was now as extravagant as his Grief had been before; he kissed and embraced his Son a thousand times, and danced about the Room like one frantick . . . When these Tumults were over the Parson taking *Joseph* aside, proceeded thus—"No, *Joseph,* do not give too much way to thy Passions, if thou dost expect Happiness."—The patience of *Joseph,* nor perhaps of *Job,* could bear no longer . . . [29]

Here Adams is made to veer dangerously close to what may be the greatest sin of character in Fielding—hypocrisy. The narrative tests its Abraham in the most personal terms, providing if not an exact parallel then certainly a genuinely analogous situation to that of Genesis 22. Adams responds appropriately, as a father rather than a clergyman, and in a reversal of roles it is now Adams who ignores, or decisively dismisses, those consolations he himself was offering moments earlier. His responses to both the report of the drowning and Joseph's entreaties confirm his essential goodness, but also highlight the artificiality of his earlier insistence on the publishing of banns. Nor has that problem disappeared at this point in the narrative: the threats to Fanny loom ominously on the horizon of this scene, and Adams's behavior renders his insistence at best fastidious, and perhaps insidious. Adams abruptly dismisses the moral he had only moments earlier so confidently propounded for Joseph's benefit; he expects Joseph to submit to God's will, however horrible the prospect, as providential, yet is himself incapable of such submission. In his state of lamentation the consolations he so assiduously endeavors to teach Joseph are, when offered to him by an apt pupil, either entirely ignored or immediately and decisively dismissed.[30]

This reading of the passage would be harsh toward Adams were it not for its two-part resolution: the immediate discovery that his son was not drowned, and Adams's abrupt, unmodified return to his theme of total submission to the divine will in all circumstances. The only unacceptable reaction on Adams's part to the news of his son's death would have been a reaction that followed his counsel to Joseph: stoical resignation to such tragedy as an act of the divine will. Adams would then have struck the pose of Voltaire's Pangloss. This, however, would not have been at all like Adams. In this he proves decidedly not the clergyman: he professes himself "not at leisure to hearken to [Joseph's] advice," words which testify to just the sort of experiential duress against which he has previously marshaled similar counsel, and he is deaf to Joseph's reminder that Adams and his son will be reunited in a far better place. We see Adams at his best, and doing so requires that he discard the bulwarks of his faith—providential will and the consolation of the final judgment![31]

The final stroke in the passage is to show that even so calamitous a series of events as the death and resurrection of his beloved son cannot instruct the uninstructable Adams, for after his passions settle he recommends to Joseph with renewed vigor the dispassionate life as the true source of wisdom in even the most debilitating circumstance. Utterly lost to Adams in his topsy turvy psychodrama is Joseph's trenchant apprehension for Fanny's safety, based equally on an awareness of her experience and a sage view of the nature of her captors. Perhaps the only passion in *Joseph Andrews* equal to Joseph's love for Fanny is Adams's love for his young son; Adams's failure to recognize in Joseph what he manifestly knows in his own life underlines the nature of his failing. Circumscribed by classical texts and orthodox exegesis—all scripture and tradition, but no experience—Adams's world is entirely at odds with the world the narrator presents in *Joseph Andrews,* specifically, and decisively, on the relationship of providence and evil.[32]

This is aptly illustrated by the complementary facts that Adams's trust in the divine dispensation is unassailable, and that he completely and immediately accepts as gospel whatever people tell him about themselves. Events never persuade him to qualify either his trust or his acceptance, while the narrative usually has precisely this effect on the reader. The inverse of effect is exact: the more unflinching Adams's credulousness, the more the reader's incredulity increases. Over the course of the novel this distances the one from the other—and not simply for comic purposes.[33]

It is also important that the incident is itself the result of caprice: the reporter of the drowning witnesses the son's fall into the water and, rather than dive to his assistance or call for help, races to report his death. At best premature and at worst self-fulfilling prophecy, it is also the opposite of Adams's own instinctive reactions to similar circumstances throughout *Joseph Andrews*. Such details, however, are lost to him (but not, thanks to the narrator, to the reader). Adams never conjectures about the disturbing source of his deep, albeit brief, agony. It measures his extraordinary confidence in providence, and his sense of duty in its propagation, that his return to his sermonizing mode is unimpeded by any speculation whatsoever concerning the source of the misleading report that caused him such anguish. It is a nice calibration of the cost of his good nature. Instead he returns with uncompromised confidence to his earlier lesson, sealing it and punctuating the entire scene with the remark that happiness can only be ours if we avoid passionate responses to the circumstances of our lives.

The reader is meant to conclude otherwise. In the context of Fanny's danger and Joseph's justified concern, Adams's sermon can only seem significantly removed from the immediate reality. His assured and all-encompassing invocations of providential design, when they counsel against available direct action to combat impending evil, contradict his own amply documented instincts. His immediate agony at the ensuing news of his son's death shows what we would have wanted to see previously: that his sensitivity is greater than his sense, that his human compassion can overcome his regard for ecclesial and theological dogma. The reader fully shares his agony, which, if in retrospect brief, is detailed and completely realized in the narrative. It is all the more shocking, then, to witness in its aftermath Adams's return to the "sense" of his sermon, when it is precisely the sensitivity he has just manifested that Joseph really needs.[34]

The juxtaposition here of sermon with brute reality calls into question the tenability of providence by presenting the fact of evil and its incursion into even the most honorable and trusting life.[35] There can be no doubt that Adams completely believes the counsel he offers Joseph about providence, and any sense that he might harbor doubts is eclipsed by his unimpeded return to his theme. *Joseph Andrews* thoroughly debunks the ensuing iteration by the way in which the narrator puts Adams through his paces to illustrate the great contradiction between his trusting invocations of providence and his rejection of providence's traditional consolations when personally faced with evil.

Adams himself embodies the fundamental conflict in *Joseph Andrews* between the manifestly desirable union of Joseph and Fanny, and the random but very effective forces that conspire against it. The sentiment that their marriage is for the good is weighed in this narrative against the fact that such a marriage, however desirable and praiseworthy, is far from easily accomplished. This conflict parallels Adams's reaction in the above scene: his own sentiment that providence conquers all, and his momentary and passing acknowledgment, when faced directly by evil, that such confidence appears unwarranted at times by the facts of life. He is utterly ignorant of the world's capacity for evil; it must literally stare him in the face before he recognizes it. When, under duress, he does, his reaction is disconsonant with his beliefs. No one more strongly supports in principle the marriage of Joseph and Fanny than does Parson Adams, and no one at the same time does more to impede it.[36]

The narrator in *Joseph Andrews* limns the theme of his narrative most expressively not through characterization, but through the juxtaposition of character and event. Yet while the conclusion may be ours to draw, the narrator hardly disappears: note his nod to Joseph's impatience at the passage's conclusion through his comparison of Joseph with Job on the matter of extraordinary trials. While not so overt in his judgments as his counterpart in *Tom Jones,* the narrator of *Joseph Andrews* succeeds in suggesting concretely the substance in which sagacity consists. Even as the narrator satirizes Parson Adams to the effect of debunking his learning as a source of true sagacity, he also offers his own book lessons in sagacity. Adams's worldly failures in understanding result from an unwarranted overconfidence in the ability of books to teach us about the world; the reader of *Joseph Andrews* must presume that its narrator does not suffer from the same vice, and that this book will somehow prove of greater utility in negotiating the world's ways than Plato, Seneca, or the Bible do for Adams. Adams is said to be without peer as a classicist, but however prodigious, it is ineffectual in guiding him (and others) through the world in which he lives. We should not read the present history as Adams has read his classics, without knowledge of the world and without a resulting sense of what is and is not relevant to us. Otherwise, the parallel suggests, the good things we desire will happen (if they do) only in spite of us, much as Adams presides with delight over the nuptials of Joseph and Fanny despite himself and his unwitting actions to the contrary.[37] While the resolution of *Joseph Andrews* vindicates Adams's great faith in providence, the cumulative effect of the full narrative forces the reader to recognize the fragility of such faith and the way it blinds Adams to the realities of evil— realities with which any honest sense of providence must contend.[38]

The perspective with which the reader closes *Joseph Andrews,* then, is removed from the unqualified faith in providence that Adams evinces throughout the novel. This results from the effect of a narrator whose sensibility is equally removed, and whose affection for Adams and delight in the final union of Joseph and Fanny reflects, not an unqualified endorsement of eternal providence, but the sense that the happy resolutions of these characters' lives are not fully explained even as they are fully rejoiced.[39]

The History of Tom Jones, A Foundling

While the narrator of *Tom Jones* possesses striking family resemblances to his counterpart in *Joseph Andrews*—in tone, in didactic intention, and, most significantly, in narrative purpose—he more systematically calls the reader's attention to his craft.[40] The move from abstraction to experience is a structural principle of *Tom Jones:* each of its eighteen books begins with an introductory chapter that functions as a kind of sermon, sometimes straight and occasionally facetious, on the reading and writing of history. A more digressive narrative than *Joseph Andrews, Tom Jones* not incidentally treats the themes of providence and evil more explicitly in its narrative commentary. Crucial to understanding the connection between Fielding's narrative art, the deism controversy, and the debate about poetic justice, the introductory chapters stand as nothing less than an extended contextualization of the story. They constitute a progressive meditation on the theme of providential design and the incursions of evil, and the appropriate rendition of this question in this "new" literary form of the novel. It follows that "the action" of *Tom Jones* should not be discussed apart from these chapters, which self-consciously parallel the unfolding events of the novel.[41]

While the bulk of this section will offer an extended discussion of these chapters, it is worthwhile at the outset to underline that Fielding's commentary is not restricted to them, and that the themes of providential design and the incursion of evil pervade not just the introductory chapters but the entire novel. The specific connection of *Tom Jones* to the deism controversy first becomes explicit, not in an introductory chapter, but in the novel's early scenes from its hero's youth. These are themselves the subject of commentary by the tutors Squire Allworthy has retained at Paradise Hall for the education of Masters Jones and Blifil: the Reverend Thwackum, an Anglican divine, and the philosopher Square, whose lofty thoughts have on occasion resulted in charges of deism. In Thwackum and Square, *Tom Jones* dramatizes in miniature the deism controversy. Divine and deist claim to argue from revelation and reason, respectively.[42]

The narrator reports that Squire Allworthy retained the tutors in tandem in the hope that they would balance each other out to the cumulative benefit of their young charges. In fact, the tutors prove so fundamentally at odds[43] that their appearances in *Tom Jones* are spent in personal debate rather than active pedagogy. Square's philosophizing regularly evokes from Thwackum heated proclamations that mock the reductionist propensities of the outraged eighteenth-century theologian facing arguments for natural or revealed belief: " . . . nor is Religion manifold, because there are various Sects and Heresies in the World. When I mention Religion, I mean the Christian Religion; and not only the Protestant Religion, but the Church of

England. And, when I mention Honour, I mean that Mode of divine Grace which is not only consistent with, but dependent upon, this Religion; and is consistent with, and dependent upon, no other . . . '"[44] In controversial fashion, Thwackum charges Square with atheism and hints darkly in response to Square's protesting rejoinders that he must then in fact be the same thing—a deist. He belittles Square's affinities with Plato and Aristotle and the philosopher's proclamations of *"the natural Beauty of Virtue."*[45]

In fact, however, these controversialists rarely debate so abstractly. Their usual context is some recent act of young Tom Jones, whose high spirits make him a far more active figure than his sober counterpart Master Blifil, rendering Tom the frequent object and stimulus of controversy between Thwackum and Square. These men, who would speak from the Book of Scripture and the book of nature respectively, are thus thrust into the frame of the book of experience, much as Parson Adams in *Joseph Andrews.* What emerges is that, for all their proclaimed differences, Thwackum and Square share a motive utterly beneath Parson Adams. Each seeks through his pronouncements to curry Allworthy's favor by championing the boy whom he imagines to be Allworthy's favorite, and so to achieve for himself a place of favor in the one document each actually reveres: Allworthy's last will and testament.[46]

The narrator provides us with this knowledge, and in a subsequent, extended commentary upon it remarks the perplexed relationship between religious belief and its advocates:

> A treacherous Friend is the most dangerous enemy; and I will say boldly, that both Religion and Virtue have received more real Discredit from Hypocrites, than the wittiest Profligates or Infidels could ever cast upon them: Nay, farther, as these two, in their Purity, are rightly called the Bands of civil Society, and are indeed the greatest of Blessings; so when poisoned and corrupted with Fraud, Pretence and Affectation, they have become the worst of civil Curses, and have enabled Men to perpetrate the most cruel Mischiefs to their own Species.[47]

This is part of one of the earliest and most striking examples of the narrator's propensity to comment at length on the action in *Tom Jones.* It is also one of the first of numerous occasions when the narrator attempts to anticipate the reader's misunderstanding and correct it, while insinuating his own beliefs. As such, it announces a major theme (and not incidentally links action and commentary). Square and Thwackum exemplify what we will witness again and again in *Tom Jones:* those who claim to act in the name of religion or virtue can be, and often prove to be, agents of evil. The narrator aims to promote both religion and virtue, but distrusts their invocations in the abstract and, most especially, those who invoke them. It is relatively easy to act maliciously in the name of religion or virtue, not least because such discussions are so often divorced from the very realm of experience which they pretend to improve. So it is with Thwackum and Square.

While the roles of Thwackum and Square recede as the novel progresses, the themes they are made to announce are decisively the themes of the novel, and it is Fielding's narrator who carries them forward. His voice pervades the novel, and establishes these continuities of tone and theme. Perhaps no passage better illustrates this voice than a passage from the conclusion of Book XII, ch. viii. The facts as the reader has them from the narrator are, of course, crucial. Tom and Partridge have at this point resumed their travels following the fiasco at Upton, Tom now himself in determined and anguished pursuit of Sophia Western rather than she of him. Tom had arrived at Upton with Mrs. Waters, whom he had rescued from abduction, and after securing lodging and food for her there, has been seduced by her (albeit not unwillingly). At this point Sophia herself arrives at Upton with Honour, and discovers through Honour that Jones is there. She also learns to her dismay that he is with Mrs. Waters and that a servant girl—along with everyone else at the inn—"knows" that Sophia is in search of Jones, that he has refused her hand in marriage, and that he is fleeing to the army to take refuge from her advances. Her momentary anticipation at the prospect of meeting her true love now thoroughly dashed, Sophia departs Upton immediately—but not without first leaving her (signed) muff on Jones's empty bed for his anguished delectation. The message has its desired effect, and Jones returns to the road with new purpose: he will follow Sophia's trail wherever it may go to overtake her so that he may restore her muff and his reputation.

The narrator draws together all this information and its implications— real and imagined—in Book XII, ch. viii. Resting briefly from the arduous pace of his journey, Tom encounters a boy who led Sophia and Honour on part of their journey. Eager for any news of his beloved, Tom leads the boy to a separate room at the inn for a discreet interview. At this point the narrator interjects, ostensibly in anticipation of the sagacious reader's outrage that Tom's exemplary delicacy with Sophia's name is unknown to her:

Hard therefore was it, and perhaps in the Opinion of many sagacious Readers, very absurd and monstrous, that he should principally owe his Present Misfortune to the supposed Want of that Delicacy with which he so abounded; for in reality *Sophia* was much more offended at the Freedoms which she thought, and not without good Reason, he had taken with her Name and Character, than at any Freedoms, in which, under his present circumstances, he had indulged himself with the Person of another Woman; and to say Truth, I believe *Honour* could never have prevailed on her to leave

Upton without seeing her *Jones,* had it not been for those two strong instances of a Levity in his Behaviour, so void of Respect, and indeed so highly inconsistent with any Degree of Love and Tenderness in great and delicate Minds.

But so Matters fell out, and so I must relate them; and if any Reader is shocked at their appearing unnatural, I cannot help it. I must remind such Persons, that I am not writing a System, but a History, and I am not obliged to reconcile every Matter to the received Notions concerning Truth and Nature. But if this was never so easy to do, perhaps it might be more prudent in me to avoid it. For instance, as the Fact at present before us now stands, without any Comment of mine upon it, tho' it may at first Sight offend some Readers, yet upon more mature Consideration, it must please all; for wise and good Men may consider what happened to *Jones* at *Upton* as a just Punishment for his wickedness, with Regard to Women, of which it was indeed the immediate Consequence; and silly and bad persons may comfort themselves in their Vices, by flattering their own Hearts that the Characters of Men are rather owing to Accident than to Virtue. Now perhaps the Reflections which we should be here inclined to draw, would alike contradict both these Conclusions, and would shew that these Incidents contribute only to confirm the great, useful and uncommon Doctrine, which it is the purpose of this whole work to inculcate, and which we must not fill up our Pages by frequently repeating, as an ordinary Parson fills his Sermon by repeating his Text at the end of every Paragraph.

We are contented that it must appear, however unhappily *Sophia* had erred in her Opinion of *Jones,* she had sufficient Reason for her Opinion; since, I believe, every other young Lady would, in her Situation, have erred in the same Manner. Nay, had she followed her Lover at this very Time, and had entered this very Alehouse the Moment he was departed from it, she would have found the Landlord as well acquainted with her Name and Person as the Wench at *Upton* had appeared to be. For while *Jones* was examining his boy in Whispers in an inner Room, *Partridge,* who had no such Delicacy in his Disposition, was in the Kitchin very openly catechising the other Guide who had attended Mrs. *Fitzpatrick;* by which Means the Landlord, whose Ears were open enough on all such Occasions, became perfectly well acquainted with the Tumble of *Sophia* from her Horse, &c. with the Mistake concerning *Jenny Cameron,* with the many Consequences of the Punch, and, in short, with almost everything that had happened at the Inn, whence we dispatched our Ladies in a Coach and Six, when we last took our Leaves of them.[48]

Almost the length of a shorter introductory chapter, the narrator's "digression from the action" underlines the sort of reading the narrator exacts from the reader. It is not coincidental that it is also itself a meditation on such reading. The entire passage hinges on the narrator's revelation that Sophia left Upton more out of disgust at what she presumed with good reason to be the case (his indelicacy with her name and reputation) than out of disapproval of what she knows to be the case (his dalliance with Mrs. Waters). No such distinction was drawn at the time, and the narrator presumes that most readers assume that Sophia ranks the importance of these dual indignities in the opposite order. Having suggested that this revelation, being the case with Sophia, is more true to the female nature than most readers would suspect, the narrator establishes his theme: Jones lost his opportunity to meet Sophia because she presumes his indelicacy with her name, but this presumption—like the reader's about Sophia's reasons for leaving Upton without seeing Jones—is in fact incorrect. It is rather the case both that Jones abounds with such delicacy, and that Sophia is entirely justified in her presumption that he does not.

Having established this understandable misunderstanding, the narrator proceeds to meditate on what conclusions the sagacious reader may draw from it. He dismisses disbelief as the refuge of systematicians who would mold history to some preconceived formula of truth or nature. Readers who object that it is unnatural must recognize that what happened is most certainly true, for it is historically the case—"so Matters fell out." Once he has vouched for the veracity of his account, and not coincidentally for the ways in which narrative verisimilitude defies systematic analysis, the narrator then sketches two kinds of interpretations of the facts of the case. The "wise and good" reader will regard Sophia's misunderstanding as just punishment of Jones for his philandery, while "silly and bad" readers may regard it as illustrative of the fact that good character is a function of accident rather than genuine virtue. These can be readily dismissed, not only for their inherent pretensions of superiority but because they systematize what has already been declared beyond systematic understanding.

At this point the narrator announces "the Reflections which we should be here inclined to draw" in opposition to these alternatives, but the subjunctive mood does not give way to the declarative: succeeding phrases employ "would" and refer to a "great, useful and uncommon Doctrine" which is characterized but not enunciated. This is all the more striking because it is avowedly the purpose of this history to "inculcate" it, and there are strong hints that it is religious: it is a "Doctrine," and like Scripture in a sermon might lend itself to constant repetition when meditating on matters such as these. It is surely this which the sagacious reader must aim to discover and cultivate in reading *Tom Jones*, and it is equally clear that it addresses not merely human nature, but the paradoxes of history in which partial knowledge and misunderstanding are the characteristic engines of activity. The fact that the narrator clears away certain misreadings clarifies this direction: the reader who exercises sagacity in *Tom Jones* ponders such mysteries that encompass, but are not exhausted by, human nature.

If the narrator is guilty of anticlimax at this point, his loquacity is still not entirely spent (and the sagacious reading has only begun). In lieu of an explicit statement of a doctrine of providence, the narrator offers at last an explanation for the understandable misunderstanding which is historical and natural. Sophia's reasonable offense results from Partridge's indelicacy rather than Jones's; and while Jones inquires discreetly, Partridge simultaneously undoes his discretion by relating their adventures with an eye to whatever advantage appears to suit the moment: always his, often Tom's, never Sophia's. The narrator's report of Partridge's propensity to bandy names and actions with neither discretion nor accuracy falls entirely within his character—indeed, was witnessed earlier at Upton when Partridge encountered Honour in the kitchen at the inn.

So if we lack an explicit statement of the great, useful and uncommon doctrine of *Tom Jones*, what do we possess at the conclusion of the passage? The passage provides a sense of the dynamic nature of the narrative itself, and an indication of the kinds of questions appropriate to its sagacious interpretation. This narrative is historical, which is to say first that it repels the systematic explanations of traditional theology and philosophy. It is also to say, more positively, that it is natural, it has verisimilitude. The explanation of how Sophia's name comes to be so widely and indelicately known when Jones exhibits such discretion and delicacy turns out to possess complete narrative integrity: it neither surprises nor appears remotely unlikely. Its larger question, dressed in comic garb and laced with coy indirection, is that of why bad things happen to good people. Here that question can be formulated very concretely: why is Tom and Sophia's union delayed by factors beyond their control, even if those are at least partly of their own doing?[49]

This question is addressed, indeed nurtured by the novel's eighteen introductory chapters in which the narrator gives free rein to his penchant for commentary and intrusive loquacity. The issues introduced in the debates of Square and Thwackum, and elaborated in the aftermath of Upton are addressed explicitly in the introductory chapters and are developed throughout the course of the novel to the point of elucidating "the great, useful, and uncommon Doctrine." Two chapters focus the commentary at the outset by establishing an explicit relationship, culminating in a contractual agreement the narrator establishes with the reader. On the basis of this, the narrator predicates concepts of the marvelous, the incredible, and the supernatural as they play their parts in the narrative.

Frank Kermode's helpful if passing remark that *Tom Jones* in fact has two beginnings provides a useful frame for any discussion of the introductory chapters.[50] The novel opens with "The Bill of Fare to the Feast," the initial introductory chapter, which announces the presentation of human nature as the essence of the narrative. The narrator introduces himself and comments on the nature of the action before he actually presents any action. The action "proper" appears with chapter two, with the description of Paradise

Hall and Squire Allworthy. The narrator's proposal—presented through the simile of narrator as honest Victualler operating a "common Ordinary" at which readers may dine on courses in human nature—places, as it were, his menu on the door of his establishment and provides the reader/diner with the opportunity to read on/enter or close the book/depart. In completing the simile the narrator refers to what has been "premised," and a bargain has been offered and (if the reader proceeds) accepted.

By the conclusion of Book V the reader has had ample opportunity to sample the narrator's various culinary feats of character and action, and the introductory chapter to Book VI refines the initial bargain into the more formal language of a contract. From this point more than simple acquiescence to the topic is required. The narrator discusses the human quality of love in a mock-philosophic dialogue with certain absent and unnamed philosophers. The premise, explicitly named, is that in each human breast exists "a kind and benevolent Disposition, which is gratified by contributing to the Happiness of others." Readers who balk at this assertion, or who have no experience of it, are presented with the following directive:

> Examine your Heart, my good Reader, and resolve whether you do believe these Matters with me. If you do, you may now proceed to their Exemplification in the following Pages: if you do not, you have, I assure you, already read more than you have understood; and it would be wiser to pursue your Business, or your Pleasures (such as they are) than to throw away any more of your Time in reading what you can neither taste nor comprehend.[51]

What was presented in Book I as a matter of easy preference is transformed by Book VI into a matter of shared faith. The reader who does not share the narrator's conviction concerning the human capacity for love cannot understand this narrative—in fact, has already missed its import. On the narrator's terms, at least, readerly sagacity in *Tom Jones* will depend upon this tenet about human nature. The narrator's forthright, unapologetic dismissal of readers who dispute or disagree nicely underlines the narrator's confident didacticism.[52]

The rhetoric of this claim urgently underscores that the reliable pronouncements in *Tom Jones* belong almost exclusively to its narrator. Note that he bases this covenant of critical faith on common experience *independent of the narrative*.[53] This appeal corroborates the verisimilitude of *Tom Jones*—what you read is what you get in life—and at the same time claims for the novel a general theme. Experience may resist system, but the reader must recognize that here nonetheless is the stuff of life. If he acknowledges that not all readers will share this recognition, the narrator nonetheless displays confidence that such readers exist and dismisses the rest with bravado.

His willingness to part company with some underlines that larger lesson he seeks to inculcate. Not incidentally, it also implies that his readership includes in its number some whose predilections ally them with those who would foil manifestly providential design. The narrator's rhetoric would banish them from the readership, even as his own narrative design will prove resolute in its refusal to banish evil from the world of Tom and Sophia.

Here the narrator writes straightforwardly, with none of the ironic misdirection or telling of partial truths found in the previous passage discussing "how events fell out" at Upton. Its declarative structure and straightforward arrangement typify the introductory chapters, in which the narrator speaks not only confidentially and cordially, but downright conspiratorially. A writer of Fielding's ironic capacities might on such occasions of candor elicit great wariness, but nowhere is such caution less warranted, and ostensive meaning more trustworthy, than in the introductory chapters to *Tom Jones*.

This covenant of critical faith carries into the narrative of the action, and brings with it the particular and crucial advantage that, thanks to the narrator's presentation of events, the reader is usually enabled in the end to see more than the characters can themselves.[54] The scene at Upton provides just one of many examples in *Tom Jones*. The privilege of this perspective, its enhancement of our vision, consists of a capacity to divine human motivations in a way that everyday life by its nature denies. The narrator can be sufficiently self-serving to note this explicitly. The most pertinent, famous, and to some pernicious example occurs when he announces the fact that Squire Allworthy—previously described as without peer in not only generosity but discretion—is ignorant of Thwackum's hatred for, and malicious behavior toward, young Tom: " . . . the Reader is greatly mistaken if he conceives that *Thwackum* appeared to Mr. *Allworthy* as he doth to him in this History; and he is as much deceived, if he imagines, that the most intimate Acquaintance which he himself could have had with that Divine, would have informed him of those things which we, from our Inspiration, are enabled to open and discover."[55]

Here as throughout *Tom Jones* the narrator cultivates that muse whose inspiration delivers insights into true human nature, while noting that such insights stand beyond the comprehension of even the most observant. Allworthy's failure goes not so much to his particular character as it does to the general limitations under which human awareness exists. Even the most powerful and accomplished goodness does not always recognize the evil under its eye. Whatever our frustration with the way Tom's table of life is set, our frustration cannot allow us to make judgments that imply a superiority to life's limitations. The necessity to surmise is a fact of human life in the present tense; retrospection teaches us not only the limits of perspective implied by that fact, but also the limits of judgment apart from retrospection. The meaning here of "judge not, lest ye be judged" is the meaning of the privilege of retrospection.

Here retrospection implies providential sweep, promising not merely knowledge but understanding of the narrative. A major part of what the lovingly sagacious reader learns, however, is the inherent limitations of any one human perspective. The privileged perspective serves to remind the reader of how much more difficult it is to negotiate the ways of the world when we lack it. The narrator's call for the reader to determine the verisimilitude of *Tom Jones* with reference to the reader's own life turns out to be two-edged: the rhetoric implies a coherence between the two worlds, but the history that is *Tom Jones* also underscores that this coherence can only be appreciated in retrospect.

This double quality of retrospection is the heart of *Tom Jones,* and its dual effects are complementary. Consider the two characters at the extremes of goodness and evil in the novel, Allworthy and Blifil. Allworthy demonstrates repeatedly the failure of good nature to effect, at times even to recognize, the desirable end. His oversight is not confined to the particular instance of not recognizing Thwackum's malice toward Tom. Most glaring is his failure to discern Blifil's devious machinations to discredit everyone whom Allworthy himself should know to be admirable. Sophia Western immediately recognizes Blifil's true character, as does Mrs. Miller when Allworthy and Blifil arrive together in London and take rooms in her house. Blifil certainly takes greater pains with Allworthy than with anyone else to conceal his deviousness, and his dubious courtship of Sophia allows her to see Blifil in a way that Allworthy never could. Given such considerations, it remains the case that Allworthy simply fails, until the evidence forces itself upon him, to recognize Blifil as an agent of evil who stands in the way of all that is good in Allworthy's world. Allworthy is more badly deceived about character than almost anyone else in the novel—certainly more so than one would expect of an avowedly great man.[56]

Just how much Fielding's narrator claims for his perspective and authority appears in this gap between his confident assertion of Allworthy's greatness and the significant limitations in Allworthy's sagacity that the ensuing narrative documents. The reader would be greatly mistaken to understand them as irreconcilable. Allworthy remains a great man for the nobility of his beliefs and for his efforts to do everything in his power to make those beliefs a reality in the assistance of others. The narrator provides abundant testimony to these traits. Even at the outer limits of human greatness, however, perspective has its limits, and insight into the motivations of others proves at best partial.[57] Personal merit, however great and munificent, affords no definitive protection against life in the present tense, where human vagaries and the twists of circumstance hold sway. Allworthy is not hopelessly or needlessly contradictory, but despite his endowments he remains human and thus subject to limitations of perspective.

If the manifestly best character in *Tom Jones* lacks prudence, his counterpart is its most effective marshal. No one in *Tom Jones* acts more prudently than Blifil, and the evil that intrudes upon Tom's rightful destiny always results from extremely prudent actions: Bridget Allworthy-Blifil's "hidden" parentage; the favoritism Square and Thwackum show toward Allworthy's "natural heir," Blifil, and their corresponding denigration of the "bastard" Jones; Western's assessment that his daughter must marry Blifil rather than Jones to ensure the alliance of his property with Allworthy's. Blifil, however, exhibits a singularity of purpose, and of action, in this regard. From his early youth he demonstrates this mastery in his consummate manipulation of Thwackum and Square. While his counterpart Tom Jones, all youthful candor and indiscretion, finds himself roughly tossed between Thwackum's theological discipline and Square's heartless stoicism, Blifil accomplishes the impossible: he manages to make *both* men his admirers, steering the favorite's course between Scylla and Charybdis with mock-Odyssean ease. With age Blifil's proclivities mature and his capacity for mendacity blossoms: he engineers Allworthy's dismissal of Tom from Paradise Hall, he proves an insincere suitor for Sophia Western (simultaneously the man perfectly situated to marry her yet the only one who is utterly unconscious of her true appeal), and, most crucially of course, he keeps from Allworthy the letter which discloses Tom's true lineage. No one in *Tom Jones* steers a more determinedly prudential course than Blifil; and the narrative clearly condemns it, and him.

Formulations of the message of *Tom Jones* that stress human virtue can miss this critical dimension of the narrator's distancing perspective, and fail to recognize that the reader is removed from the human limitations (including, not incidentally, virtue) which can inhibit understanding. Arguably the most powerful of these formulations has stressed the role of prudence in this message. Prudence, Martin Battestin has famously argued, is the human analogue to providence and so the virtue which allows us to steer the steady course of divine destiny. As Battestin himself recognizes, however, prudence can be used for good or ill, and in the hands of Fielding's narrator it is at least morally neutral, and possibly shows more affinity for the Blifils than the Allworthys of the world. This is best illustrated by the reconciliation scenes at the end of the novel between Allworthy and Tom Jones, when Allworthy recommends to Tom the cultivation of prudence as protection against the vagaries of the world. Battestin takes this to be Fielding's viewpoint. But the effect of the narrator's retrospective distancing allows for a more ambiguous reaction. The cardinal virtue is surely love—the benevolent disposition that precludes selfish motivation—and prudence's ambiguities contrast directly with the unambiguous sketch of the loving disposition presented in Book VI, ch. i. Thanks to Blifil's steady presence, the reader knows that prudence is not *Sophia* (even as Sophia herself, in counterpoint to Allworthy, embodies its positive dimensions). To be sure, Fielding's narrator commends prudence as a worthy goal of human behavior and as a recourse against the wiles of fortune. Yet this commendation is fleeting by comparison with the degree to which the total narrative perspective documents the moral neutrality of prudence, its capacity to be the tool of human motivation whether for good or ill.[58]

Tom Jones calls into question and finally negates the very compelling proposition that human qualities are the means to human happiness. Yet happiness is the manifest human good in *Tom Jones*. What, then, is the source of human happiness in a novel whose message and entire sentiment are suffused with its quest? The answer is found in the later introductory chapters of the novel.

In these the narrator discusses more broadly historical questions raised by a sagacious reading of the action. Book VIII ("much the longest of all our introductory chapters," the narrator notes) discusses "the Marvellous." Just two books earlier the narrator established with the reader a contract of privileged, retrospective understanding through his claims for love as an inherent human quality. Here the commentary is prospective: to understand what you are about to read, you must understand what role marvelous events may play in history. Events will oblige the narrator "to relate some Matters of a more strange and surprizing Kind than any which have hitherto occurred . . . ,"[59] but what will follow is emphatically not of a piece with the sixteenth- and seventeenth-century romance tradition. Christian "machines" and resulting divine machinations, and the arguments, especially in France, about the appropriateness of such godly interventions in narrative form are not what he expects the reader to have in mind.[60]

While distancing his new species of writing from these traditions, the narrator does not abandon religious language: he employs the terms possibility and probability, and the ways in which these will exercise the reader's "Historic or Poetic Faith" in reading *Tom Jones*. Readerly faith may range widely, and the narrator proves reluctant to insist on the same degree of fealty that accompanied his earlier discussion of love. Yet while he recognizes inherent variation among his audience, the narrator specifically protests any reading in which possibility and probability may consist only in what has been seen.

The narrator then lists the reasonable expectations of the reader who is asked to exercise such faith. *Tom Jones* must remain historically credible by meeting three criteria: possibility, probability, and conservation of character. Possibility requires the most extensive treatment. To be possible, any historical description of human action must remain within the compass of human agency. Here the relevant counterpoint is not the romance tradition but Homer, whose "Heathen" prospects are unavailable to the Christian writer. For the Christian writer, this "Doctrine" of resorting only to human agency must be de facto: "for as he cannot introduce into his works any of that heavenly Host which make a Part of his Creed," the Christian writer must settle for human action. Throughout the narrator contrasts "Heathen" polytheists with "modern" monotheists, but the exact reason for the Christian writer's limitation goes unexplained. The narrator remarks that Homer's gods appear unseemly when engaged in trivial errands, but he provides no "modern" counterpart. For good measure the narrator then provides a negative catalog of romantic supernatural agency: ghosts, elves, and fairies receive summary dismissals from *Tom Jones*. The apparent conclusion is, however, inconclusive:

> Man therefore is the highest subject (unless on very extraordinary Occasions indeed) which presents itself to the Pen of our Historian, or of our Poet; and in relating his Actions, great Care is to be taken, that we do not exceed the Capacity of the Agent we describe.

Banishment of the Homeric pantheon and romantic machines on the ground of impossibility, and the assertion of human agency as the Christian writer's de facto recourse do not result in a firm dismissal of the possibility of divinely providential activity. The possibility of providential activity is coyly left open. Structure highlights the exception: the historical discussion of possibility prepares the reader for a summary rejection of Christian providential activity, and the opening words of the above passage appear to confirm the dismissal. These six words, however, receive immediate parenthetical qualification in a way that manages, abruptly and briefly but pervasively, to make explicit the potential that this narrative will include divine action. What follows retains the ambiguity of reference to both humanity and divinity: "Agents" can be human or divine, and both have their capacities. The narrator's criticisms of supernatural and divine agency in previous literature addressed the credibility of the kind of agent or the timing of its appearance; such criticisms do nothing to eliminate the prospect of providential activity by the Christian deity.

In addition to being possible, the narrative must also be probable—any description of human action must consist of what human agents may be supposed to have done. Here the narrator takes issue with Aristotle's dictum that poets must reconcile their accounts not merely to what happened, but to what readers will accept as having happened. It is rather fully sufficient for the historian to render what occurred, save in the most extreme cases. This maxim results in a distinction between the marvelous and the incredible: "To say the Truth, if the Historian will confine himself to what really happened, and utterly reject any circumstance, which, tho' never so well attested, he must be well assured is false, he will sometimes fall into the Marvellous, but never into the Incredible."[61] There is a sure test for credibility: the marvelous will incite wonder, and the incredible contempt. The former is history, while the latter is fiction or romance.

Finally, the narrative must exercise conservation of character, meaning that *Tom Jones* must successfully represent private examples of individual virtue and vice. Such representations necessarily preclude recourse to public notoriety or concurrent testimony, demanding instead strict fealty to both the possible and the probable. Private examples may never stray from the agent's capacity or from strict historical accuracy. Here the narrator restricts his discussion to human agency, and underlines the role of human nature in the rendering. Characters may not act in ways that contradict their natures, for this is the most genuinely incredible or miraculous of representations.

The payoff of this catalog is a reiteration of Book VI's covenant of faith with the reader: "If the Writer strictly observes the Rules above-mentioned, he hath discharged his Part; and is then intitled to some faith from his Reader, who is indeed guilty of critical Infidelity if he disbelieves him."[62] Marvelous here joins Love as a clause in the contract between narrator and reader. The sagacious reader of *Tom Jones* now must share not only a certain sentiment, but the thesis that the historical and the marvelous do not exclude each other if certain conditions hold. Yet the narrator provides no examples of what would constitute the marvelous in this narrative. Negative examples from the Greek and Romance traditions abound, but specifically providential agency remains implicit.

What is explicit, however, may be reformulated as follows: verisimilitude is not at odds with what cannot be accounted for by cause and effect. The violation of verisimilitude instigates readerly contempt, but cause and effect hardly exhausts the range of readerly belief. Historical credibility, then, goes beyond accountable causation. "How matters fell out," so long as they are possible and probable, must command our credulity. If we recollect the narrator's commentary on Upton discussed earlier (but which follows this discussion in *Tom Jones*), the discussion here is decidedly in the manner of those events that serve to illustrate "the great, useful, and uncommon Doctrine which it is the whole purpose of this Work to inculcate." On very extraordinary occasions, history may indeed take as it subject an "Agent" greater than the human. Realism and supernatural agency, however unspecified the latter may be in a positive sense, may be reconciled in the history that is *Tom Jones*.[63]

Having established a place for the supernatural, and by implication the providential, in this history, the narrator in the introduction to Book XV addresses the single greatest test of any doctrine of providence: the existence of evil. The chapter begins with the following observation:

> There are a set of Religious, or rather Moral writers, who teach that Virtue is the certain Road to Happiness, and Vice to Misery in this World. A very wholesome and comfortable Doctrine, and to which we have but one Objection, namely, That it is not true.[64]

Here the narrator directly invokes the attacks on Christian revelation lodged by Toland and Tindal in the deism controversy. Each argued against an interposing providential agency because it implied that the general providential order established in the creation was insufficient, an implication incommensurate with the perfection of the Christian deity. It follows that virtue consists in the life lived in concord with nature, while vice resides in the (strange, nearly perverse) failure to do so. Their confident articulation of this in counterpoint to special revelation led Butler and Law each to find in this view a failure to account for the existence of evil in the world. If nature has been comprehensively ordered since the creation, how can one account for the plethora of examples of natural and moral evil we find in the world?

The introductory chapter to Book XV addresses these considerations. Virtue can and often does go unrewarded in this life; indeed, those who walk the virtuous path as often as not wind up jailed for their efforts. By comparison with the earlier discussion of the marvelous, the discussion of evil is brief, unbuttressed by philosophical argumentation. Instead the reader finds the brute assertion of fact: such is the world that virtue does not ensure happiness. This point is beyond dispute and (unlike claims for the marvelous) requires no lengthy justification of verisimilitude. The narrator concludes by noting that the virtuous behavior of Tom Jones has served only to make him less attractive to Sophia Western. As his worthiness of Sophia increases, his likelihood of marrying her diminishes. The narrator claims complete verisimilitude for this paradox, and concludes by returning to the "rule" of the "Religious, or rather Moral Writers":

> This therefore would seem an Exception to the above rule, if indeed it was a Rule; but as we have in our Voyage through Life seen so many other Exceptions to it, we chuse to dispute the Doctrine on which it is founded, which we don't apprehend to be Christian, which we are convinced is not true, and which is indeed destructive of one of the noblest Arguments that Reason alone can furnish for the Belief of Immortality.[65]

While it achieves its most emphatic expression here, this sentiment pervades *Tom Jones*. History, Christianity, and Reason all argue against the idea that virtue is rewarded. Note its affinity with the arguments of Butler especially, and of Law to a lesser degree: here we again find both the claim that there are many exceptions to the goodness of the natural order, and the Christian affirmation that only at the final judgment can we expect a just disposition of the rights and wrongs we witness and experience in the world. The narrator's terms and his logic explicitly address those of the deism controversy, and underline in turn the relevance of *Tom Jones* to it.

Book XV, ch. i functions as a hinge for the action of the novel: what happens just before and after pointedly illustrates the narrator's empirical pronouncement. Book XIV describes Tom's solitary, ultimately successful effort to save the Miller family from disgrace. Tom convinces the recalcitrant Nightingale that he is obliged to marry Nancy Miller, who is pregnant with Nightingale's child, despite the fact that the match is "beneath" Nightingale and means that his father, who intends Nightingale for a marriage of advantage, will disown him. At the same time, Tom persuades Nightingale's father to amend his intentions and bestow his fortune upon what he does not understand: a marriage based on love rather than money. The episode underlines Tom's virtue, understood as both his wholehearted assistance to anyone in distress and his ability as an intercessor. When the narrator returns to the action in Book XV, we learn immediately of Lady Bellaston's plot with Lord Fellamar to accomplish Sophia's marriage to the lord by arranging an opportunity for the lord to rape Sophia. As Tom's worthiness becomes more manifest, his likelihood of marriage to the woman he loves, and who loves him, becomes less likely. Tom's virtuous behavior is anything but a certain road to his happiness. The circumstances of the moment frame this in their contrast in two impending marriages—one benevolent, the other anything but.

Tom is of course unaware of the plot against Sophia, just as she is unaware of his actions on behalf of the Millers and Nightingale. Their mutual lack of knowledge is the larger point underscored by the narrator. Tom cannot know of Sophia's precarious state; and we know that if he did, he would certainly lay down his life to protect her. Such an opportunity for devotion, however, is qualified of necessity by his lack of knowledge. Once again the reader's perspective in *Tom Jones* is privileged: we learn, far more concretely than we could from daily life, the uncertain connections of virtue with happiness and vice with misery. The limitations of Tom and Sophia are inescapable human limitations, and these render them vulnerable to evil as a qualifying agent. Happiness is not finally a matter of direct travel, as the crow flies: it is a matter instead of circumstance and good fortune at least partly beyond our making. The "great, useful, and uncommon Doctrine," if it is inculcated everywhere, certainly is to be found in this moment.

What, then, is the source of their good fortune? As the narrative moves toward its conclusion, its narrator does not omit opportunities to comment on this question, most overtly in the introductory chapter to Book XVII. Here the narrator discusses the resolutions of comic and tragic narratives: comedy makes the principals as happy as possible, while tragedy aims for the full effect of misery. All that remains to make *Tom Jones* a tragedy at this point is "but a Murder or two, and a few moral Sentences." The comic task, however, proves more formidable:

> But to bring our Favourites out of their present Anguish and Distress, and to land them at last on the Shore of Happiness, seems a much harder Task; a Task indeed so hard that we do not undertake to execute it. In Regard to *Sophia* it is more than probable, that we shall somewhere or other provide a good Husband for her in the End, either *Blifil,* or my Lord, or somebody else; but as to poor *Jones,* such are the Calamities in which he is at present involved, owing to his Imprudence, by which if a Man doth not become a Felon to the World, he is at least a *Felo de se;* so destitute is he now of Friends, and so persecuted by Enemies, that we almost despair of bringing him to any good; and if our Reader delights in seeing executions, I think he ought not to lose any Time in taking a first Row at *Tyburn.*
>
> This I faithfully promise, that notwithstanding any Affection which we may be supposed to have for this Rogue, whom we have unfortunately made our Heroe, we will lend him none of that supernatural Assistance with which we are entrusted, upon Condition that we use it only on very important Occasions. If he doth not therefore find some natural Means of fairly extricating himself from all his Distresses, we will do no violence to the Truth and Dignity of History for his sake; for we had rather relate that he was hanged at *Tyburn* (which may very probably be the case) than forfeit our Integrity, or shock the Faith of our Reader.

One might argue that this passage is merely playful: the narrator belies the very expectation he has so assiduously cultivated throughout *Tom Jones* in his intimation that Tom and Sophia will not marry. This cannot be the case, and the currency of the narrative commentary is, on this reading, seriously diminished. That the previous introductory chapter suggested that these chapters have the status of prologues to plays—interchangeable, eminently forgettable, and irrelevant to what follows—would appear to underscore such a reading, and its basic thesis that the chapters cannot be read seriously. The most sensible interpretation of this passage, abetted by the narrator's own pronouncement, is to take it as little more than a winking acknowledgment of the deliverance to come.

Such an approach disarms the passage of serious intent. The presence of playfulness is no inherent compromise of seriousness of intent, least of all in an eighteenth-century writer of Fielding's rhetorical skills. Playful the passage is, and its playfulness extends to the transition from the first to the second paragraph quoted above. The first argues against precisely the happy (here equals comic) resolution every reader expects, and claims facetiously that a tragic denouement is in order: Sophia can marry Blifil, and Jones can be hanged. It is no accident that this formulation inverts precisely the reader's cultivated sense of justice. The second turns to the question of how a comic denouement can be achieved. Here the playfulness refers directly back to the narrator's discussion of the marvelous in Book VIII. There is here not only a repetition of the earlier terms—"integrity," "Faith," "Truth," "History"—but the same two-step declaration of intent about supernatural interposition, combining declaration with the qualification, found there: " . . . we will lend him none of that supernatural Assistance with which we are entrusted, upon condition that we use it only on very important Occasions."

The reader commences the denouement of *Tom Jones* with a final general invocation of providence in relation to the resolution of Jones's difficulties. As in the other cases we have discussed, the narrator formulates it ambiguously: there will be no providence unless on very special occasions indeed. What are these occasions, and what can be said about them?

Only humanly caused effects render the conclusion of *Tom Jones*. There is, in the sense of special providence, no such agency in its history. No specific act in its resolution can be attributed to direct divine action. The narrator underlines this in the narrative through frequent and explicit commentary that traces the origin of a particular action to earlier actions in the narrative, or to earlier implications of the action that the reader may not have noticed. When Partridge confirms with Tom that Mrs. Waters, who has visited him in jail, is the women he was with at Upton, and then informs Jones that she is in fact his mother, the narrator offers a textual cross reference: "If the Reader will please to refresh his Memory, by turning to the Scene at *Upton* in the Ninth Book, he will be apt to admire the many strange Accidents which unfortunately prevented any Interview between *Partridge* and Mrs. *Waters,* when she spent a whole Day there with Mr. *Jones.* Instances of this Kind we may frequently observe in Life, where the greatest Events are produced by a nice Train of little Circumstances; and more than one Example of this may be discovered by the accurate Eye, in this our History."[66] The reader's disbelief at the revelation that Tom has committed incest is immediately addressed by the narrator, who shows that the one "out" which suggests itself—that Partridge would surely have seen Mrs. Waters at Upton, and prevented Tom's folly or at least advised him of it much sooner—is shown to be impossible. The facts reinforce the preceding invocation of tragic denouement, both in their empirical detail and in their unmistakable allusion to *Oedipus Rex.*[67]

This allusion to Sophocles may seem farfetched if we consider only the stylistic differences between the two works, but the two works, so different in genre and tone, in fact possess important structural affinities. Sophocles utilizes his chorus much as Fielding utilizes his narrator—to divulge the workings of fate, and to emphasize the degree to which the characters are helpless to change or even materially to challenge a chain of events that will prove decisive for them. The parallel underscores the ways in which Fielding takes very seriously indeed the prospect that events could fall out to the negative, and that Tom could be hanged (a prospect he will explore even more explicitly in *Amelia*). The force of the happy ending depends upon the reader's recognition of this possibility. Tom's providential end, so different in its relative degree of happiness from Oedipus's unhappy demise, rests nonetheless on a similar structure of emplotment, and a corresponding recognition of the perilous relation between individual intent and happiness. This affinity in sensibility is abetted by the parallel between the Sophoclean chorus and Fielding's narrator, each utilized to divulge the workings of fate to its audience. It is also interesting to note that in each work the artist encourages his audience to scrutinize the details, and to query the possibility that something else might have happened. The sense of the ending is, in each case, one of inevitability followed by a scrutiny of the action that only serves ultimately to reinforce that sense.

In this way *Tom Jones* moves to its denouement: human events transpire that appear to stretch credulity, and the narrator immediately reminds the wondering reader that in fact they follow from earlier events and are possible, probable, and within conservation of character. For all his explanation, the narrator also seems to debate with himself about the implications of these events. Two such comments from Book XVIII, quite proximately placed, illustrate this ambivalence. The first introduces Allworthy's accidental but of course fortuitous discovery that Black George has the 500 £ that Allworthy bestowed upon Jones when he banished Tom from Paradise Hall: "Here an Accident happened of a very extraordinary Kind; one indeed of those strange Chances, whence very good and grave Men have concluded that Providence often interposes in the Discovery of the most secret Villainy, in order to caution Men from quitting the Paths of Honesty, however warily they tread in those of Vice."[68] A better gloss for Fielding's pamphlet on "Interpositions of Providence in the Detection and Punishment of Murderers" could not exist. Compare it with the following observation which accompanies the report that Allworthy's mind has undergone a "visible Alteration" in its attitude toward Jones: "Revolutions of this Kind, it is true, do frequently occur in Histories and dramatick Writers, for no other Reason than because the History of Play draws to a Conclusion, and are justified by Authority of Authors; yet though we insist upon as much Authority as any Author whatever, we shall use this Power very sparingly and never but when we are driven to it by Necessity, which we do not at present foresee will happen in this Work."[69] His retrospection begs the question, and the narrator acknowledges, but does not assert, the classical Christian reply.

The characters in *Tom Jones* exhibit no such reticence. Most prominently Allworthy, but also Jones, Mrs. Miller, Partridge, Mrs. Waters, and even the philosopher Square attest fervently to the wonders of providence. By contrast the narrator is notably more restrained, even ambiguous: perhaps providence plays a role, perhaps it does not. So matters fell out, and he is not obliged to reconcile his history to the expectations of systems.

This juxtaposition captures the fundamental dynamic of the novel's teachings about providence: retrospective viewpoint as practiced by the narrator results in cautious, ambivalent attribution, while those in the midst of the fray readily, even eagerly invoke the triumph of the divine design against their apprehensions of ominous, foreboding tragedy. The inversion is striking and unremarked, dismissed implicitly in the all-encompassing attribution of playfulness to the narrator's voice, or in the equation of him with God. As this analysis should make clear, however, neither mere playfulness nor divinity fit. *Tom Jones* actually presents the sagacious reader with two perspectives on providence: that of the actors in the moment, and that of the narrator in retrospect. They are not perfectly symmetrical. Those whose circumstances are immediate can do no other than attribute their happy conclusion to the designs of providence. The one who considers events retrospectively wavers.

The narrator's ambivalence is not replicated, however, on the directly related matter of evil. It is hardly incidental that this topic also exercises the narrator's ruminative powers in the closing book. He documents with equal vigor the tendencies toward the tragic as well as the comic in the resolution of this narrative. In fact he documents the inherent tensions between divine design and the incursions of evil, and exhibits no sense that the devil's presence in this world proves as elusive of attribution as the deity's: "And, indeed, I look upon the vulgar Observation, *That* the devil often deserts his Friends, and leaves them in the Lurch, to be a great Abuse on that Gentleman's Character. . . . he generally stands by those who are thoroughly his Servants, and helps them off in all Extremities till their Bargain expires."[70] This remark prefaces an explicit characterization of the devil as counsel to Blifil, and a contrast of Blifil's evil nature with Mrs. Miller's guileless good heart. The capacity to tell lies under the guise of truth refers to the lawyer Dowling, and we read a number of elliptical references to a better world where, it is implied, justice will prevail unambiguously.[71]

No specific instance of providence can be discovered by even the most sagacious reader of *Tom Jones*. The narrator by turns invokes and then rejects the possibility. Characters proclaim what they take to be epiphanic moments of providential interposition, but their attributions actually are general rather than specific. The reader is left with the story, and these views of it, upon which to exercise her sagacity. Taken individually, the circumstances that conduce finally to the union of Tom and Sophia seem clearly beyond the ken of providential attribution. Taken cumulatively, the combinations of events prove beyond the power of human history to render a full account. How the individual matter of the moment falls out turns out to be amenable to human attribution; how matters fell out, however explicable individually, turns out to be beyond the power of human history alone to explain. The notion of a divine design to the world, one unmistakably bolstered in the face of evil by reference to the future state, comprises the narrating of providence in *Tom Jones*.

It is precisely this cluster of questions that truly exercise the reader's sagacity. The great provision of human nature is in fact relevant to the degree that it illuminates how we might think about these questions of providential design and the incursions of evil. The narrator makes such rumination, from just the distancing perspective we have described, a focus of the concluding chapters of the novel. An enlightened Allworthy, flushed with Tom's now happy prospects at the conclusion of the novel, eagerly expounds upon just this theme:

> The World, I do agree, are apt to be too unmerciful on these Occasions, yet Time and Perseverance will get the better of their Disinclination, as I may call it, to Pity, for though they are not, like Heaven, ready to receive a penitent Sinner, yet a continued Repentance will at length obtain Mercy even with the world. This you may be assured of, Mrs. *Waters,* that whenever I find you are sincere in such good Intentions, you shall want no Assistance in my Power to make them effectual.[72]

Fielding's narrator then remarks that Allworthy's "goodness . . . savoured more of the divine than human Nature." His gloss nicely encapsulates the sense of the ending in *Tom Jones*. The sagacious reader takes this with a healthy grain of salt, because she knows that Allworthy's limitations are better documented than those of any other character in *Tom Jones*. The man with the greatest potential to make what is "providential" happen in fact proves integral to its near thwarting. In terms of character and a fully effectual happiness, what savors of the divine turns us to thoughts of a future and better state—eschatology and the Day of Judgment, images of an ideal next to which the resolution of *Tom Jones* affords but a dim reflection. The conclusion of the novel documents evil as much as providence; so Allworthy himself remarks also the "wonderful Means" by which "the blackest Villainy" is sometimes discovered. Blifil, explicitly associated with the devil and the main impediment to the happiness of Tom and Sophia, is not destroyed: he repairs elsewhere and contemplates a career in parliament. Deceit is not removed, and the concluding reports about the happy situations of all the characters—including the introduction of Parson Adams as tutor to Tom and Sophia's young children—suggest an idyllic preserve, a place both happy and (as the assurance of that happiness) insular. Fielding finally endorses All-worthy's fondly articulated hope, but the endorsement carries a qualification. The weight of that qualification as a factor in Fielding's making of novels is best testified by its role in his last novel, *Amelia.* The urgent sense that there must be a better world to come, and that this provides the ultimate warrant for belief in providence, proves to be the cardinal development of his fictional creativity.

Comparative Conclusion

While their relationship is clearly evolutionary, *Joseph Andrews* and *Tom Jones* present important family resemblances. *Joseph Andrews* presents the theme of divine design and the incursions of evil primarily through characterization and juxtaposition of incident, while *Tom Jones* adds extensive and comparatively explicit narrative commentary. Each speaks directly to the deism controversy's central issue of the place of providence in the world, and of what concern evil should be to the confident proclamation of a design that must reward the virtuous and punish the wicked.

Both novels yoke historical veracity (Ian Watt's "formal realism") with an affirmation of a supernatural agency in the form of providence (Hans Frei's "precritical" sense of biblical narrative). In *Joseph Andrews* and *Tom Jones,* the compatibility of realism and providence is the point: narratives that strive for verisimilitude must include both the marvelous, expressed specifically in the Christian doctrine of providence, and the fact of evil. Especially in *Tom Jones,* the interspersion of commentary with action unites those seemingly "incongruous bedfellows," historical verisimilitude and the marvelous. The result: the overarching theme of these novels is unmistakably what can be claimed for providence in the world. That the theme is abiding does not, however, mean that its treatment straightforwardly affirms a divine design. The narrator's commentary, and the resulting juxtaposition of his retrospection with the perspective of characters living the moment, suggests comprehensive affinities with the ethos of the deism controversy: an acute sense of the reality of human evil, and an abiding insistence that however much it qualifies belief in special providential interposition, evil cannot compromise belief in an overarching providential design with final recourse to the Day of Judgment.

In both *Joseph Andrews* and *Tom Jones,* narrative commentary places narrator and reader at a remove from the action in order to survey its interests and implications. This distancing is historical and therefore retrospective; through it, the narrator claims that the real significance of the action rests in its overall shape. That shape raises questions, and provides answers, about the disposition of events in human life. It should not surprise us that such discussion of the disposition of events raised for Fielding questions about providential design on the one hand, and the role of evil in at least threatening and sometimes even qualifying that design. In each novel, Fielding sharpens the discussion by placing it in the context of a manifestly desirable, indeed providential, marital union that is then threatened to the verge of tragic incompletion by the forces of evil in the world.

Explicitly in *Tom Jones,* this retrospective positioning of reader and narrative leads the narrator to a series of claims for a covenant of faith between himself and the reader. As the narrative extends, so do the terms of the covenant. These terms underline the need for common points of recognition in a narrative that discusses providence and evil. They also reflect the novel's didactic purpose. Here again, the terms of these contracts—the distinctively human nature of love, the correct place of the marvelous in modern history, and the fact of evil as manifest through the irregular relation of virtue with happiness and vice with misery—underline the central themes of the narrative.

Divine design and the incursions of evil, then, are the themes of these novels of Fielding as they were of the eighteenth-century controversialists who were Fielding's contemporaries. In the context of these debates, Fielding's narrator establishes a general position which speaks directly to their terms: there is a divine design, but our capacity to recognize the divine design is at best ambiguous, and goodness is no guarantee of happiness in a world fraught with evil. Providence can only be understood retrospectively, through acts of historical reconstruction, and such understanding suggests a general providential plan which excludes special providence through attributions of specific human agency which the narratives record, and which the narrator highlights retrospectively. There is no deus ex machina in Fielding: rather, events "fall out" in a way which may affirm providential activity, and certainly documents the pervasive threat of evil to any apprehension of a general providential design.

Such human virtues as prudence prove equally accessible to good and evil people alike in these novels, and such is the world that at times prudence and virtue are at odds. Joseph and Fanny, Tom and Sophia do ultimately marry and validate the design, but only after considerable strife. The sagacious reader's vicarious joy is qualified by the recognition, underscored to the last lines of the novel, that the path to these happy, manifestly desirable unions was fraught with difficulty. Those difficulties resulted often from the conflict of prudence and virtue. It would have been prudent for Joseph and Fanny to marry without banns, but ecclesiastical virtue as invoked by Parson Adams conflicted with that course. Tom's actions on behalf of the Miller family are virtuous, but they detract from his more prudent concern, which is to find Sophia and restore his reputation in her eyes.

These narratives share with the deism controversy and the debate on poetic justice the capacity to elicit interpretations from one of two opposed perspectives. One approach stresses the novels as moral *exempla* writ large, in which goodness is tested, found wanting, and finally allies itself with virtue under the aegis of a benevolent providence. The other approach treats the novels as historical narratives which deny the role of providence in the name of realism. Neither approach captures the truth in the cases of *Joseph Andrews* and *Tom Jones,* and either approach alone distorts what actually occurs in the narrative.

It is, then, a delicate balance that Fielding's narrator seeks to serve. To illustrate the limits of human understanding, while also affirming the existence of a providence that remains beyond our complete, assured cooperation: this, and nothing less, is his aim. The narrator's retrospective viewpoint provides the vehicle for propagating this claim and imitates, in its inimitable way, the necessarily retrospective recognition of divine design. In point of view, then, Fielding's narrator attempts exactly a providential narrative. The fact that he insists on its historical nature is of course not accidental, and highlights his insistence on yoking verisimilitude with the marvelous, and the historical fact of human evil with divine design.

History in these novels teaches us the vagaries of circumstance and the extraordinary limitations of such apparently useful human virtues as prudence. Prudence, supposed to be the human weapon against circumstance and seen by some as the natural analogue to supernatural providence, appears in *Tom Jones* either as the engine of evil intention (Blifil), or as the human quality sacrificed for the sake of virtuous action (Tom Jones). *Tom Jones* leaves little doubt about whether Blifil's exclusively prudential approach to life is preferable to Tom's heedless good nature, but its endorsement of Tom is qualified by the knowledge adduced throughout the history that such goodness is not invulnerable. Here again the narrator's covenant with the reader comes into play, and suggests that none of the characters who populate the narrative merit imitation. They are examples, not to be imitated but observed for what they tell us about the forces at work in the world. It is this interplay of divine providence and human evil that the historical narratives of *Joseph Andrews* and *Tom Jones* seek to portray.[73]

That so delicate a balance of narrative artistry would be the source of controversy in Fielding's last, "problem" novel, *Amelia* is perhaps unsurprising. Heralded, or rather condemned for its darker tone and pessimism, what the present chapter demonstrates is that the seeds of that difference in tone can be found in its predecessors. To *Amelia* we now turn for illumination of the role of evil in Fielding's fiction via yet another attempt at the delicate balancing act of verisimilitude between providential design and the machinations of evil.

Chapter 4 ~

Providence Displaced:
The Recourse to the Final
Judgment in *Amelia*

A s noted in chapter one, *Amelia* (1751) has a bewitched history in the Fielding canon. Long the object of condescension and even ridicule, it has in recent years enjoyed a minor renaissance among scholars. From the unhappy, anticlimactic afterthought to his career, *Amelia* has become the darling of those who regard it as a noble experiment in social realism, or as an exercise in new structures of characterization that at least implicitly acknowledges the merits of Richardson's approach to the novel.[1] *Amelia* thus pays recognition to *Clarissa* and offers a direct inversion of the relation of *Joseph Andrews* to *Pamela*. Fielding takes a new interest in psychology, and develops a complementary concern for the individual moral dilemma. To achieve this end he relinquishes some of the narrative control of the earlier novels—no small sacrifice, given that it was the chief distinguishing mark of his fiction when compared with Richardson's. A radically altered reading experience results: the misled reader in *Amelia* discovers the source of error not in the narrator's disingenuity but in a character's misapprehension. Readerly sagacity and discernment focus in *Amelia* not on its chains of cause and effect, but on the internal lives of its characters. Its special status, then, is that it is Fielding's "richest psychological study."[2]

In this chapter I make the case that *Tom Jones* and *Amelia* emerge from the same artistic mint in which Fielding fashioned a series of meditations in narrative form on the contentions between an overarching providential design and the fact of human evil. In this respect *Amelia* is fully coin of the realm, and its genuine differences from its predecessors are best understood in this frame. My argument, then, is not that *Amelia* does not differ from

Tom Jones, but that its real differences emerge from Fielding's common, overarching concern. I share the judgment of such earlier Fielding interpreters as Alter, Hunter, and Rawson that *Amelia* is lesser literary coin than *Tom Jones,* but I concur with successor approaches that *Amelia* is crucial to the corpus—but because it is a continuation of, rather than a departure from, his great theme. The proffered new variation holds intrinsic interest and affords important insights into its predecessors.

If lifted out of its place in the chronology of the Fielding canon, what might happen to *Amelia?* To put the point concretely (while retaining chronology), can we imagine a critically successful successor to *Tom Jones* written in the same vein? Earlier criticism answers resoundingly in the negative. What this answer means is that *Amelia* has been treated as an afterthought because it would have been impossible to take further the achievement of *Tom Jones.* It follows that, given Fielding's artistic accomplishment in *Tom Jones,* the question of what to do next required an answer that involved real difference. Repetition inevitably would mean diminishment. *Amelia* reflects Fielding's recognition of this problem and represents his attempt to address it.

Read in the context of the deism controversy and the debate on poetic justice, *Amelia* can be understood to represent a genuine theological, and so for Fielding artistic development from *Tom Jones.* Providence is not banished, but displaced from this world to the next. Evil enjoys, as a result, a fuller rein in *Amelia,* and Fielding's decision to mute the abundant narrative commentary of *Tom Jones* both complements the changing role of providence and alters notably the way the narrative works. I discuss these changes in what follows, but it merits emphasis at the outset that Fielding's decision to displace providential force in *Amelia* from this world to the next does not lack ample precedent in the religious climate of his age. Butler's recourse in his *Analogy* (1736) to the final judgment as the location of providential justice exactly parallels the position Fielding presents in *Amelia.* The issue that divides Dennis and Addison in the debate on poetic justice is whether the final judgment, which each takes to be the fulfillment of the deity's providential plan, ought to be represented in the drama. Recourse to the realization of providence in the final judgment, at the expense of its manifest activity in this world, is hardly unique to Fielding.[3]

The appropriate language in which to discuss *Amelia* is therefore the language of displacement. Displacement exists in two, complementary dimensions of the novel. There is the displacement of Fielding's intrusive narrator, whose role Fielding seriously diminishes in *Amelia.* The necessary complement follows: the displacement of providence from this world to the next. Providence remains in *Amelia;* the locus of providence is not seen, however, in the overarching pattern to the world's events (which we only dimly perceive, but from which we may draw assurance and direction), but as the final judgment in which the world's wrongs will be righted. Fielding fully reprises the theme of the battle of providence with evil that shapes the earlier novels. At the same time, *Amelia* shifts providential authority from this world to the next: from implied providential interposition to the final judgment.

The disjunction between Fielding's earlier novels and *Amelia* consists, then, not in the abandonment of providential affirmation, but in its relocation. The signal result of this shift is not so much a wider play for the forces of evil, but a dramatically stronger sense of evil's random nature, and the explicit threat that evil will prove unremitting and thus indomitable. The earlier novels are hardly bereft of evil machinations, but the forces for providential design are equally present and the narrator's commentary highlights the fact that there is a battle (and not incidentally that there will be a winner). Fielding chooses to forfeit this in *Amelia*, making the forces for providence less potent and forcing those who affirm a divine design to take recourse in the affirmation that at the final judgment, if not now, good will overcome evil. This unmistakable shift of providential affirmation from the present to the future tense results in less exhilarating, more sober narrative art. But it does not entail the abandonment of Fielding's great narrative theme.

Formal parallels underscore the continuity and spell out the terms of displacement. Parson Adams and Squire Allworthy have their counterpart in Doctor Harrison, the wise counselor who stands above but really lives within the fray. Harrison proves, however, to lack both Adams's alacrity and Allworthy's unremitting high seriousness, traits which, however troublesome in the worlds of *Joseph Andrews* and *Tom Jones,* would be most welcome in the world of *Amelia.* Like his counterpart Square in *Tom Jones,* the deist Robinson converts to Christianity on his deathbed (we learn subsequently that, unlike Square, he will live; this is the rare moment in which *Amelia* is comparatively more optimistic than its predecessors). Robinson's conversion, like Square's, inspires a confession about the truth of the past which proves instrumental to the happy resolution of affairs. Like Tom Jones, Booth is guilty of infidelity, but here the infidelity is of unmistakably serious consequence, with the result that he mends his ways not by a genteel endorsement of Allworthy's general invocation of providence, but by abandoning stoicism for Christianity. Booth's interview with Harrison sounds a theme similar to Allworthy's pronouncement at the conclusion of *Tom Jones,* but Harrison is both more explicit in his affirmation of providence, and in that affirmation more at odds with the world of the novel. Country life remains superior to that of the city, but an important aspect of the resolution is the sense of the country not as magnificent and complementary alternative, but as retreat, nearly fortress or bulwark, against the ways of the world. These particulars are matched by the fact that, in the end, the "very worthy Couple" at its center achieve their much-deserved state of happiness and relative security with the strong sense that without this recourse, they could not have survived.

A basic formal reversal matters a great deal, and it is announced in *Amelia*'s opening sentence: "The various Accidents which befel a very worthy Couple, after their uniting in the State of Matrimony, will be the Subject of the following History."[4] This bald declaration with its unambiguous reference to the forthcoming action contrasts utterly with both the excursus on biographical writing that launches *Joseph Andrews,* and the Bill of Fare that opens *Tom Jones.* Bad things happening to good people will be the subject, absent the clear framing intimation of a happy resolution. The shift in tone is unmistakable.

The most critical shift the sentence announces, however, is that when *Amelia* begins the good people are already married. The implications of this shift cannot be overstated. The earlier novels embody a magnificent aggressive streak toward the marital union, and the sheer energy of its impending consummation overwhelms all impending difficulties (and most readerly objections). There marriage is the great end to which everything tends, and whatever the troubling offstage rumblings, the sense that happiness has triumphed holds sway. *Amelia* effectively sacrifices the queen with its opening move: that end already has been accomplished, thus transforming the subject into domestic harmony in its widest sense, including not only love and understanding, but the complications of financial security that comprised an afterthought, however carefully inserted, in the earlier novels. *Amelia* adopts, as a result, a defensive posture of preservation against tides of ill will, rather than aggressive pursuit of a manifest good.[5] The details of the endgame are not particularly pretty or appealing.

The plot develops through various stratagems of dishonesty and deceit,[6] and the tensions and conflicts that these machinations create exacerbate our sense that the ground of the world has shifted. Rather than an extended and even convoluted courtship, *Amelia* offers a detailed examination, in uncomfortable detail, of the truths and falsehoods of domestic life. Like the poker player at the end of a series of raises, Fielding's last novel calls the bluff of the earlier novels by casting a searching look at the marital union that served as their unambiguous good. Here marriage is no longer a fortress against the vagaries of fortune, or the secure institutional insurance of fidelity against the temptations of the world. As a result, *Amelia* exhibits a defensiveness toward the world that replaces the earlier novels' liberality and confident impulse to consummation. The surrounding world in *Amelia* so constantly and unremittingly threatens domestic tranquillity that the Booth family's relocation at the end to Amelia's family estate is a complete retreat. Booth returns to the city only to pay his debts, and the visit is as abbreviated as possible.

Tom Jones's forgiveness of Blifil (an act, be it noted, that the noble Allworthy pronounces beyond the ken) in the world of *Tom Jones* would seem not merely foolhardy, but utterly imprudent in *Amelia.*

These reversals are crucial, but comparative discussion of *Amelia* with its predecessors must consider the shift in narrative point of view. The disjunctions are tonal as well as formal: "This is no longer the method of the patient, bemused, benevolent teacher, nor of the less jovial, many-faced satirist; it is more like that of a humorless policeman."[7] Far less formally intrusive than his counterparts, he provides almost none of the metacritical digressions that mark *Joseph Andrews* and, especially, *Tom Jones.* Only silence stands in *Amelia* for the ongoing commentary provided by the intercalary chapters of *Tom Jones.* The rhetorical flourish and command available on virtually every page of *Tom Jones* is nowhere to be found in *Amelia.* Gone, too, are the opening theoretical pronouncements: no counterpart to the discussion of the high art of biography, or of the public ordinary, begins *Amelia.* If not thrown into the action, we have been strikingly less prepared for it. The narrative provides no metacritical apparatus and its tone is largely declarative. In a nice irony, these differences tend to render the narrator of *Amelia,* for those who come to it from the earlier novels, far more disappointingly obtrusive. He appears by turns tentative or overbearing, finally diffident, unsteady, and definitely not in full control. This absence of extensive narrative commentary affords the most significant challenge to any argument for the continuity of *Amelia* with *Joseph Andrews* and *Tom Jones.*

The only proximate parallel in *Amelia* to the commentary of the earlier novels is the narrator's tendency to conclude some chapters with brief reflections, rarely longer than one paragraph, on the just concluded episode. The longest of these—and so by far the least typical—is the first. Miss Mathews has just prevailed upon Booth, by recourse to innuendo and mock accusation, to hear the story of her life since their last meeting. Her diatribe leads the narrator to interpose. The reader schooled in sagacity by *Tom Jones* anticipates delight and instruction, only to experience anticlimax. The narrator begins by likening Miss Mathews's outburst to those of a list of eighteen historical heroines renowned for their aggressiveness. There follows a spurious paragraph discussing the irrelevance of climate to such behavior, and a paragraph noting classical antecedents of contrariness. Then this conclusion:

I happened in my Youth to sit behind two Ladies in a Side-Box at a Play, where, in the Balcony on the opposite Side was placed the inimitable B—y C———s, in Company with a young Fellow of no very formal, or indeed sober Appearance. One of the Ladies, I remember, said to the other—"Did you ever see any thing look so modest and so innocent as that Girl over the way? What Pity it is such a Creature should be in the Way of Ruin, as I am afraid she is, by her being alone with that young Fellow!" Now this Lady was no bad Physiognomist; for it was impossible to conceive a greater appearance of Modesty, Innocence and Simplicity, than what Nature had displayed in the Countenance of that Girl; and yet, all Appearances notwithstanding, I myself (remember, Critic, it was in my Youth) had a few Mornings before seen that very identical Picture of all those ingaging Qualities in Bed with a Rake at a Bagnio, smoaking Tobacco, drinking Punch, talking Obscenity, and swearing and cursing with all the Impudence and Impiety of the lowest and most abandoned Trull of a Soldier.[8]

The concluding paragraph abandons the impersonal realms of classical allusion and scientific description for that of personal experience. This announces a more serious point and implies a weight of credibility by contrast with the preceding commentary. The moral is unmistakable and unnuanced: a particular woman appears quite differently from what she actually is, and the set of expectations we customarily associate with appearance are not axiomatic. The discord between appearance and reality shifts here from misunderstandings of the chains of circumstance to the misleading details of physiognomy. And the source of misunderstanding also shifts, from insagacious penetration of the real meaning of events to a naivete about physicality that might fool anyone.

The appeal to personal experience is hardly unusual. The tone, however, is more heavy-handed, at one and the same time less assured (even at his most digressive, the narrator in *Tom Jones* is at least amusing and never spurious!) and more resounding in pronouncement. It is at odds with itself in its blunt dismissals of the previous explanations. There is a standoffish quality of assertion that contrasts directly with the earlier persona of the avuncular companion with his rhetorical arm always around the reader's shoulder. The narrator of *Tom Jones* would, at this point, have offered something like the polite, mildly condescending disquisition concerning love that opens Book VI of *Tom Jones*. We might be told to read no farther, for we have already read more than we have understood. The absence of such rhetorical flourish makes the claim to authority in *Amelia* more pressing, more urgent, and significantly less refined. It is only a slight exaggeration, if that, to suggest that this narrator keeps us at arm's length: he was fooled, too, and has learned by hard experience (that he would not wish upon his reader?). Even if badly fooled, the gentle reader needs to continue.

The shift in commentary is yet more remarkable because it serves a point that readers of most limited sagacity will not miss: Miss Mathews is enamored of Booth, and will do what she can to command his affection. Unambiguous evidence displaces the need for commentary. Flirtatious with Booth, condescending to Amelia, cajoling of the husband's devotion to his wife, her intention is anything but dubious and would seem itself not to require comment. The surrounding narrative renders the commentary null to proper judgment. For readers of *Tom Jones* this is a warmup exercise.

As the novel proceeds it becomes increasingly evident that such a passage will not occur again. When the narrator concludes a chapter with commentary, almost always it is no longer than a paragraph, it summarizes more than elucidates, and it lacks classical or contemporary allusion. It is as if the narrator halfheartedly attempts the earlier digressionary style and abandons it as unsuitable. Nor does this new, briefer mode of commentary differ solely in tone and form. It also differs in substance, consisting almost entirely of direct, if brief, commentary on the immediately preceding action. At the conclusion of Book IV, ch. iv, the narrator remarks how unusual it is to find benevolence in the world:

> Here, Reader, give me leave to stop a minute, to lament that so few are to be found in this benign Disposition; that while Wantonness, Vanity, Avarice and Ambition are every Day rioting and triumphing in the Follies and Weakness, the Ruin and Desolation of Mankind, scarce one Man in a thousand is capable of tasting the Happiness of others. Nay, give me leave to wonder that Pride, which is constantly struggling, and often imposing on itself to gain some little Pre-eminence, should so seldom hint to us the only certain as well as laudable way of setting ourselves above another Man, and that is by becoming his Benefactor.[9]

The opening entreaty reflects the fact that, in *Amelia,* digression has become interruption. At this point in the narrative—about one-third of the way through the novel—it is unusual. Its theme—the grief the narrator feels that acts of simple kindness are remarkable because so rare—signals that, like its predecessors, *Amelia* claims verisimilitude; here, however, verisimilitude documents a world in which evil is the norm. If we recall the digression on love in Book VI, ch. i of *Tom Jones,* with its confident claims for a fundamental human disposition to goodness, buttressed rhetorically by the literal dismissal of any readers unacquainted with, or indisposed to it, our sense of the contrast is complete. In *Amelia,* the narrator informs us, the preponderance of evidence will suggest the contrary. In the above passage, the celebrated benefactor is Colonel James, whose generosity we later discover to be based upon an infatuation with Amelia's creature charms. The fact that the colonel uses the widespread perception of his generosity to forward such designs underlines the narrator's general point about the world (and, not incidentally, gives the lie to the attribution of goodness). The narrator is fooled. If this is irony, it is dark indeed, and far removed in effect from its counterparts in the earlier novels, where general statements about human nature are positive and borne out by the unfolding plot (exceptions are so categorized). Here the reverse is the case.

The narrator also interposes at the conclusion of Book V, ch. iv, following an interview between Amelia and Mrs. James, the colonel's wife. Heedless of Amelia's manifest penury, Mrs. James converses as if a visit from Amelia were not only expected but natural. She treats Amelia as if they are equals in wealth, and therefore subject to the rules of courtesy that govern relations among such people. Having forced Amelia to speak plainly of her circumstances, Mrs. James then declares her high regard for her friend. Circumstances conclude the interview, and allow the entrance of the narrator:

> At this Instant the Arrival of a new Visitant put an end to the Discourse, and *Amelia* soon after took her Leave without the least Anger, but with some little unavoidable Contempt for a Lady, in whose Opinion, as we have hinted before, outward Form and Ceremony constituted the whole Essence of Friendship; who valued all her Acquaintance alike, as each Individual served equally to fill up a Place in her visiting Roll, and who in reality had not the least Concern for the good Qualities or Well-being of any of them.[10]

The colonel's wife provides an excellent specimen of the sort of person utterly lacking the qualities of benefaction which the narrator noted above to be so unusual. As the plot unfolds Mrs. James's general disinterest will in fact render her a force for malevolence when she discovers her disaffected husband's interest in Amelia. Mrs. James's "dear friend" then becomes a sacrificial pawn in her ongoing domestic chess match with her husband about where she shall reside: she arranges for the colonel an "interview" with Amelia, in return for residing where she pleases when she pleases, and with the appropriate accoutrements. These developments render the distinction of Amelia's "Contempt" (as opposed to "Anger") unsubtle and irrelevant.

This, however, is the point: in *Amelia,* these moments of commentary underscore, most acutely when considered in the context of the full plot, that they are utterly in the power of the action at hand.[11] The narrator possesses no general authority apart from the facts; indeed, the facts can and will contradict him, as in the case of Colonel James. Unlike *Tom Jones,* in which narrative commentary controls the action, in *Amelia* the action controls the commentary. And in this consists *Amelia's* own unremitting insistence on its verisimilitude. Forced into brevity, concision, and specificity by the facts, the commentary highlights formally and thematically—and at its own expense—the evil propensities of the world. It is as if the narrator's remark in *Tom Jones,* that he is only providing us the facts and cannot help it if readers find this offensive, were rendered literally true in *Amelia.*

Here facts alone dictate the course of the narrative, and they control the commentary with an iron hand. Consider the following interposition, comparatively lengthy for *Amelia,* which concludes Sergeant Atkinson's interview with Colonel James:

> Tho' some Readers may, perhaps, think the Serjeant not unworthy of the Freedom with which the Colonel treated him, yet that haughty Officer would have been very backward to have condescended to such Familiarity with one of his Rank, had he not proposed some Design from it. In Truth, he began to conceive Hopes of making the Serjeant instrumental to his Design on *Amelia;* in other Words, to convert him into a Pimp; an Office in which the Colonel had been served by *Atkinson's* Betters; and which, as he knew it was in his Power very well to reward him, he had no Apprehension that the Serjeant would decline: An Opinion which the Serjeant might have pardon'd, though he had never given the least Grounds for it, since the Colonel borrowed it from the Knowledge of his own Heart. This dictated to him, that he, from a bad Motive, was capable of desiring to debauch his Friend's Wife; and the same Heart inspired him to hope that another from another bad Motive, might be guilty from the same Breach of Friendship, in assisting him. Few Men, I believe, think better of others than themselves; nor do they easily allow the Existence of any Virtue of which they perceive no Traces in their own Minds: For which Reason I have observed, that it is extremely difficult to persuade a Rogue that you are an honest Man; nor would you ever succeed in the Attempt by the strongest Evidence, was it not for the comfortable Conclusion which the Rogue draws, that he who proves himself to be honest, proves himself to be a Fool at the same time.[12]

Here the narrator aims to ensure the reader's sagacity by stating explicitly the motivations of Colonel James. There is, however, some amplification: it is also important for the reader to understand that the colonel's behavior is not unusual, either for his rank or for general humanity. The imperturbability of the rogue is rendered all the more formidable by the incapacity of the honest person to make any true impression of character on him. As throughout *Amelia,* enlarging commentary only reinforces cold, hard fact. The fact that the formal commentary follows, rather then precedes, the action only confirms the narrator's resignation to the impregnability of evil.

Amelia thus reverses the relationship between narrator and history found in the earlier novels, and the narrator's commentary highlights the facts. What, in general terms, are these? A novel that focuses so closely on marriage raises the issue of fidelity, and characters in *Amelia* constantly deceive one another. The novel offers, in Booth and Amelia, a sustained depiction of the marital relationship, and it affords glances throughout at the marriages of Colonel and Mrs. James, and Sergeant and Mrs. Atkinson. None of these unions realizes in fact the promise of the unions proposed and finally consummated in the earlier novels. Booth, of course, sustains through most of *Amelia* a front of absolute integrity and devotion to his wife despite his gaoling infidelity with Miss Mathews. The truth about Colonel James's character becomes most clear when we see that his marriage with Mrs. James is a perpetual negotiation of travel and social calendars to minimize their time together. Amelia decides that she cannot inform Booth of Colonel James's adulterous intentions because she speculates that his rage would dash his hopes of preferment from the colonel, and in turn the family's chance for relief from poverty. Dr. Harrison serves first as her counsel and then as her partner in withholding this information from Booth. The point is not that these deceptions are all of a piece, or share a common degree of moral culpability. In fact they elicit complex responses. Rather each describes an instance of deception utterly at odds with the public appearances of truth and candor that these characters maintain. Each not coincidentally impugns the ideal of fidelity his or her marriage seems to proclaim.

At the same time it is also the case in *Amelia* that the victims of deception either accept it, or live under its delusions with at most feeble protest. When Booth finally confesses his infidelity, Amelia's revelation that she knew all along, and has long since forgiven him, is both entirely credible to her character and utterly unsatisfying to the reader who is aware of the ends to which Booth has gone to deceive his wife. The best to be made of it is Dr. Harrison's rather convenient judgment that this is manifestly not a union of equally worthy individuals. The James' mutual deception is an open secret between them, at best obliquely acknowledged in their private conversation. Amelia herself must be told, by the ever vigilant and experienced Mrs. Atkinson, the truth about Colonel James's attraction to her, which she at first discounts and only gradually recognizes. Amelia all but tells Booth the truth about Colonel James, but Booth is so enchanted with the prospects the colonel offers him for advancement, and so convinced of the colonel's stellar character, that he reacts with disbelief and justifies Amelia's deception. Again, these facts appropriately elicit varying degrees of sympathy or contempt from the reader. The point is that in *Amelia* gullibility often serves as the handmaid of guile; and if deception is the hallmark of human relations, the objects of deception frequently offer the complement of malleability or complaisance.

This focus on the facts of marriage rather than the promise of courtship, and the troubling theme of deception which emerges from it, has the important consequence that the characters who engage our sympathy in *Amelia* are placed in double jeopardy by the evil portrayed in the novel. Contrast the central couples in *Amelia* and *Tom Jones*. Booth's infidelity has far graver consequences than Tom Jones's philandering because he is married and, not coincidentally, because he openly proclaims his fidelity and genuinely loves his wife. In attitude, Booth mirrors Jones exactly: he knows whom he loves, and his infidelity galls him. For Booth, however, infidelity is potentially far more than galling because it flies in the face of a proclaimed sacred trust: hence, when faced with the contrast of their pledges and their peccadilloes, Booth goes through anguished deceit and shamefaced, forced revelation, while Jones pledges fealty and pleads that possession will secure his troth. Booth must be saved by Amelia's prior, independent knowledge and long-standing forgiveness; Jones, by Sophia's mild dubiety and public declaration that she marries to please her father. In turn, Amelia's marital status literally limits the range of her possible responses to Booth's infidelity, and she faces it without the freedom Sophia Western so expertly employs at Upton: she lacks Sophia's means, and she has children.

Sexual infidelity, which in *Tom Jones* has ultimately modest consequences and proves at least substantially eradicable, is thus far more complexly rendered in *Amelia*. That it occurs in the context of marriage limits the human resources to respond to it. The characters face a world in which the bad actions of good people will cost them, largely because their range of response is effectively halved. Booth can regret like Jones, and Amelia can express disappointment; but a husband cannot credibly take recourse in the inspiring image of his wife, and a wife cannot leave her children and test her beloved's devotion by making him chase her.

As readers, we face this world without the benefit of the narrative presence that eased our way with such insight and pleasure through the earlier novels. The shift in *Amelia* is not that the good characters suddenly become evil, or even that they are now thrust into the arena with the evil ones in ways unfamiliar in Fielding's fiction. The consequences of Booth's infidelity are understandably far more serious than Jones's, both because he is in fact married and because he claims to live up to the ideals of marital fidelity.

Since *Amelia* both presents this range of deception and limits its characters' capacities to respond, does the novel offer any promise of respite from its pessimistic scenario? How, if at all, is the providential design represented in *Amelia*?

The answer begins with the fact that while the authorial commentary virtually disappears in *Amelia,* the characters themselves assume parts of this role. Amelia and Dr. Harrison form a disjunctive question and answer team in the novel, the former articulating in her despair the classical issue of theodicy, the latter ruminating on the inscrutability of providence and the consolations of the final judgment. Amelia and Dr. Harrison do not speak directly to each other on these specific issues, but their single reflections provide throughout the second half of the novel a point/counterpoint dialogue on the evils of the world and human prospects to flourish despite it. While far removed from the seamless disquisitions of the earlier novels, Fielding's art here resides in the contrast not just of perspective, but of detail: Amelia's plaints are rooted in her difficult circumstances, while Harrison's pronouncements come to us from "on high," removed—despite, as we shall see, his protestations of concern—from the fray. In this juxtaposition Fielding plays out a new, sharper challenge to the question of providence, and it ultimately leads to the displacement of divine design from this world to the next.[13]

Despite herself, Amelia proves prone to despair whenever Booth's prospects become especially bleak and relief seems not even a remote eventuality. Her show of confidence in Booth's presence falters in his absence,[14] and her children, who when present unfailingly contextualize her despair, elicit her most acute questionings. On these occasions she explicitly raises the question of how we might make sense of the evil in this world. The first instance occurs in Book IV, ch. iii, following Booth's receipt of two letters: one, from Miss Mathews, announcing that she expects his presence at dinner that evening, and that his failure to arrive will force her to reveal Booth's infidelity; the second, from Dr. Harrison, excoriating Booth for maintaining an equipage when his circumstances are so slight. Booth's manifest dejection results from the first communication, but he shares only the second letter with Amelia and leads her to believe that Dr. Harrison's censure alone accounts for his low spirits. Shortly thereafter, Booth leaves and Amelia's vexation quickly emerges. Her son's inquiry about his father's despondence elicits her tears and despair, and these immediately focus on the uncertain fate of the children. The son draws the implication of his mother's lament—that a good man can come to ill in this world—with the ensuing exchange:

> . . . the Boy, who was extremely sensible at his Years, answered, "Nay, Mamma, how can that be? Have not you often told me, that if I was good, every body would love me?" "All good People will," answered she. "Why don't they love Papa then," replied the Child, "for I am sure he is very good." "So they do, my dear," said the Mother, "but there are more bad people in the World, and they will hate you for your Goodness." "Why then bad people," cries the Child, "are loved by more than the Good."—"No Matter for that, my Dear," said she, "the Love of one good Person is more worth having, than that of a thousand wicked ones; nay, if there was no such person in the World, still you must be a good Boy; for there is one in Heaven who will love you; and his Love is better for you than that of all Mankind.[15]

Amelia's despair at her family's impending ruin is most clearly expressed in this extended exchange, under duress, with her son. In it she beats a speedy and abrupt retreat from the orthodoxy she has taught her children. The fact that she does so only after Booth's departure underscores her desperation: the simplicity of the children's reactions and her son's questions and her direct response complement Booth's absence to tell the reader that this is what Amelia really feels. As a revelatory tactic, this is quite different from *Tom Jones* and its effect is to underscore much more specifically and, not coincidentally, urgently what is involved when bad things happen to a good person.

Amelia's responses to her son, rather than a narrative interposition, thus introduce explicitly the theme of providence and evil as it informs *Amelia*. Booth's goodness, she announces, is the source of his penury and their problems (and thus of her anguish). The son—who appears to have digested a particular reading of *Tom Jones*—detects in this pronouncement a qualification of the worldview Amelia has fostered: is not goodness rewarded? Amelia's first response is to qualify the principle: good people will love good actions. This scarcely satisfies her interlocutor (or his question), so Amelia goes on to explain that there are more bad than good people in the world, and bad people hate goodness. The son concludes that the opposite of what he has been taught is in fact the truth: if one wants love in this world, one is more likely to obtain it by being bad than by being good. This forces Amelia to take her final stand: you must be good even if there was only one person or no person in the world to love you for it, for God in heaven will love you for your goodness. The final judgment and the future state justify goodness as the ways of the world cannot. Amelia's use of the future tense in this affirmation is the final note of her despair.

This passage presents in microcosm the movement in Fielding's fiction from *Tom Jones* to *Amelia*. It raises and develops explicitly the issue of theodicy, and presses urgently the absence of providential order in the world. The passage not only fulfills the dramatic imperative of showing that Amelia feels her circumstances; it also dramatizes the substance of her desperation to acknowledge under the pressure of events that faith in providence can only be placed with assurance in the next world.

Hand in hand with the displacement of providence from this world to the next is the displacement of the narrator from the scene. The work of the passage is done through the descriptions of Amelia's distress and her dialogue with her son. The narrator interposes only in the conclusion, and at a considerable remove from what we have just seen. He begins by applauding Amelia's example and offering the spurious explanation that he included the passage for "the excellent Example which *Amelia* here gives all Mothers."[16] What becomes clear, however, is that he is concerned that the lesson Amelia proffers is so at odds with the facts of the world portrayed. Nonetheless, the narrator says, it is crucial: sneer at its simplicity at your peril, for from such apparently meager and naive matter as a mother's assiduous instruction resides the solution to the problem of evil as presented in *Amelia*. The implication—brief, but consistent—is that in the absence of such instruction the sources of goodness are two: the approbation of other good people in this world (in Fielding's fiction always a matter of a fortune); and the undergirding assurances of the future life, with the utter justice of the final judgment.[17]

As the novel progresses Amelia becomes increasingly less certain that there is any goodness in the world, and these laments go unassuaged by recourse to consoling assurances of a future state. When she learns that Booth has been jailed because of Dr. Harrison, she replies: "Dr. *Harrison!* . . . Well then, there is an End of all Goodness in the World. I will never have a good Opinion of any human Being more."[18] Later distressed when she meets her children while Booth is jailed, Amelia questions the act of having brought them into the world: "Why have I produced these little Creatures only to give them a Share of Poverty and Misery!"[19] The narrator reports that "The scene that followed, during some Minutes, is beyond my Power of Description: I must beg the Readers' Hearts to suggest it to themselves."[20] Finally, in Book XI, ch. ix, when she reads Colonel James's letter, alluding to Booth's engagement that evening with Miss Mathews and demanding that they duel for her, Amelia turns pale, trembles, taps a bottle of wine, and again laments the fate of her children. This time her lamentation elicits from her son, not queries about the disparity between what he has been taught and the ways of the world, but an affirmation that his father is only the victim of an accident, and that the family will be fine. Amelia then contradicts her son:

> "Mention him no more," cries *Amelia*—"your Papa is—indeed he is a wicked Man—he cares not for any of us—O Heavens, is this the Happiness I promised myself this Evening!"—At which Words she fell into an Agony, holding both her Children in her Arms.[21]

The scene mirrors its predecessor: the children's prospects trigger Amelia's despair and elicit bitter invectives about the evil of the world. Here, however, Amelia extends her theme, making the one good man who was then the subject of the lesson (because the victim of evil in the world) its primary object, the true source of their despair. Booth can no longer be trusted. Only the wine prevents the full consequences of a "relapse," and Amelia soothes her children and sends them off to bed. Looming in the background are the echoes of the earlier conversation and its uneasy affirmations, and it is impossible to imagine that in these still more desperate circumstances Amelia could be more sanguine.

Amelia's progressive despair expresses a fundamental reaction to the narrated events. She is a kind of psalmist of the narrative, and her laments work at the most personal level and bid to resonate as intimately as possible with the reader. Yet the reader who examines these moments as clues to Amelia's character will be disappointed: they point outward, offering a new kind of commentary on events, rather than inward to deep psychological insight. They do their primary work as signposts to the narrative, making Amelia the fulcrum of all the deceit and treachery in *Amelia*. Through her we witness most intimately at least three dimensions of evil: the sexual (Booth's philandering and Colonel James's designs); the financial (Booth's poverty and the several subplots in the novel, legal and personal, to keep him and his family in penury); and the social (the machinations of those like Mrs. Ellison, well-versed in the ways of the world, who see in Amelia's creature charms the solution to her family's poverty). Amelia's lamentations carry the signature of utter credibility, thanks partly to her innocence but primarily to her status as victim. Her vocalizations of despair are aimed to resonate with the deepest chords, not of her character, but of the reader's sensibility. When she despairs, she encapsulates comprehensively the problem the narrative seeks to address.

If Amelia presents in her moments of despair the narrative's thematic problem and question, Dr. Harrison offers reflections on the problem and its provisional answer. Man of the cloth like Parson Adams and benefactor (albeit of lesser means) like Squire Allworthy, Harrison can at first tempt the experienced reader of Fielding to anticipate a heady amalgam of his predecessors. This is not the case. Harrison is far more worldly than Parson Adams, and while in principle an undeniable advantage, at many moments in *Amelia* the reader would welcome a strong dose of Adams's penchant for quick, direct action. In place of the Parson's quicker trigger (and solid fists), Harrison musters sharp words; and while his eloquence formally matches Adams's pugilism in skill and dexterity, its effects are less direct and more indeterminate. With regard to his predecessor Allworthy, Harrison's virtue is not married to sizable personal fortune,[22] so he does not automatically command the world's attention and respect. His judgments and actions (unlike Allworthy's) make their impression solely on the basis of religious suasion, without the benefit of hard cash to induce fealty in the wavering.

Harrison is not shy of the soap box, and his speeches take the sorts of evils found in *Amelia* to be the rule rather than the exception. This pessimism proves warranted not only by the events of the narrative, but by the frequency with which Harrison's clerical standing carries little, if any, authority. His attempts to exert authority to protect Amelia or promote Booth fall on deaf ears or get brushed aside. When this happens, Harrison resorts to extenuated rhetorical gambits that appeal to common decency. Unlike Parson Adams, for whom the discovery of deceit is a momentary revelation from beyond the horizon of possibility, Harrison takes deceit to be the way of the world. Suspicion edges his judgment, and he is as likely to be severe with a friend's fault as with an enemy's maleficence. Unlike Amelia, Harrison assumes, even anticipates, the evil of the world.

Harrison's outlook is manifest from our first introduction to him, via Booth's narrative to Miss Mathews in the opening chapters of the novel. Harrison advises Booth that he must honor a commission to the army which will force him to leave Amelia and his young children, despite the fact that arrangements have been made, but not formalized, which would allow Booth to remain with his family. Harrison invokes Booth's duty to king and country, and the prudential consideration that remaining at home would ultimately blemish Booth's character regardless of the validity of his reasons. Harrison implies this last point in a matter antithetical to Falstaff's famous meditation upon honor:

> As the malicious Disposition of Mankind is too well known, and the cruel Pleasure which they take in destroying the Reputations of others; the Use we are to make of this Knowledge is to afford no Handle to Reproach: For bad as the World is, it seldom falls on any Man who hath not given some slight Cause for Censure, tho' this, perhaps, is often aggravated Ten thousand Fold; and when we blame the Malice of the Aggravation, we ought not to forget our own Imprudence in giving the Occasion. Remember, my Boy, your Honour is at stake; and you know how nice the Honour of a Soldier is in these Cases. This is a Treasure, which he must be your Enemy indeed who would attempt to rob you of. Therefore you ought to consider every one as your Enemy, who by desiring you to stay would rob you of your Honour.[23]

Most striking is not Harrison's invocation of prudence as the necessary virtue for success, but his catalog of ways the world would excoriate Booth if he does not honor the commission. Harrison quickly passes over the legal issue that raised the question in the first place and dwells at length instead on deleterious consequences. Booth can expect that many will leap at the chance to diminish his honor, even under false pretense. Whatever solid legal basis may exist for a decision to remain with his family, the world will not acknowledge it. Malicious creatures take pleasure in dismantling good reputations. Almost as an afterthought, Harrison intimates a rough justice in this: those who suffer the cruelties of the world usually have done something to deserve what they get. He does qualify this, noting that on such occasions the world magnifies the error ten-thousand fold, but he introduces a new kind of realist discretion here that overwhelms any notion of patriotic duty. His advice is not the complementary, two-pronged argument he initially promises, but the determination that patriotism is a formal consideration, and far outweighed by the pragmatic implications of the fact of life. It is a sobering message: we readers are not in Kansas anymore.

Harrison's rationale for honoring the commission provides a barometer for the action of the novel. Reading back from the subsequent action of the novel to his advice, its essential defensive posture becomes clear: prudence counsels the avoidance of any act that would make us vulnerable to insidious implication. With this, indeed as a consequence of it, *Amelia* severely questions the idea of providential assurance. By the conclusion of the novel readers are forced to question not just whether even Harrison's recommended defensive posture is possible, but the serene theological calculus which posits that, however random, evil acts tend in the end to punish the wicked and reward the virtuous. Harrison's pronouncements over the course of *Amelia* retreat from the confident invocation of a general providential ordering in events to a fervent, and fevered, affirmation of the assurances of the final judgment. In these the reader witnesses the displacement of providence from the world of the text to the next.

Again the opening notes of this theme are sounded in Booth's narrative to Miss Mathews. Doctor Harrison, he reports, wrote Amelia and Booth to inform them of the death of Amelia's mother. A substantial portion of the letter, however, addressed the terms of her will. She bestowed her entire fortune upon her other daughter, Amelia's sister. Harrison's lengthy letter reflects initially on the vagaries of reputation, and the fact that honest people can do nothing to preserve their reputations when they are not present to defend themselves:

> ... The Reports concern(i)ng you have been various; so is always the Case in Matters where Men are ignorant: for when no Man knows what the Truth is, every Man thinks himself at Liberty to report what he pleases. Those who wish you well, Son *Booth,* say simply that you are dead; others that you ran away from the Siege, and was cashiered. As for my Daughter, all agree that she is a Saint above; and there are not wanting those who hint that her Husband sent her thither. From this Beginning you will expect, I suppose, better News than I am going to tell you; but pray, my dear Children, why may not I, who have always laughed at my own Afflictions, laugh at yours, without the Censure of much Malevolence? I wish you could learn this Temper from me ... [24]

Had he sought to arouse foreboding and unease, Harrison could do no better. The quasi-jocose tone hardly matches the details he offers about Booth, his laughter at affliction (unnamed, and not his own) is, if not intrinsically inappropriate, certainly presumptuous. Harrison proceeds to explain the source of his good humor in the face of bad news, and to recommend his attitude to Booth and Amelia. That source is the assurance of a final judgment beyond the unjust world we occupy, in which all will be set right forever. Our failure to countenance misfortune directly reflects our forgetfulness of the future state. We allow the cares of the world to arrest our attention, and neglect the truth that we are assured a future of everlasting comfort. And we forget this not only in the most mundane, but in the most sacred moments—when we hear a sermon! Then, at last, the news of the letter:

> Your good Mother, you are to know, is dead at last, and hath left her whole Fortune to her elder Daughter.—This is all the ill News I have to tell you. Confess now, if you are awake, did you not expect it was much worse? Did you not apprehend that your charming Child was dead? Far from it, he is in perfect Health, and the Admiration of every Body; what is more, he will be taken Care of, with the Tenderness of a Parent, till your Return. What Pleasure must this give you! If indeed any thing can add to the Happiness of a Married Couple, who are extremely and deservedly fond of each other, and as you write me, in perfect Health. A superstitious Heathen would have dreaded the Malice of *Nemesis* in your Situation; but as I am a Christian I shall venture to add another Circumstance to your Felicity, by assuring you that you have besides your Wife a faithful and zealous Friend.[25]

Harrison's epistle to the bereft contains little of what we might expect: news of the nature of the death, information about the burial, some expression that the departed might rest in peace. The actual news is briefly, even tersely related. His address, to "My dear children," does announce obliquely the death, but this only underscores the fact that the letter's central concern is not the news, but the implications of it for Booth and Amelia. Its apparent genuine regard for its readers ought not to obscure the fact that this letter more than flirts with the unseemly: namely, talking about the practical implications of someone's death before mourning their departure. Harrison seems at odds with himself in the letter, but not in terms of whether it is appropriate. He appears uneasy instead about whether it has the philosophical effect he intends, and he offers a series of consolations apparently aimed to underscore that the mother's will is not such a big deal. Booth and Amelia enjoy a happy marriage; they have a fine son, and friends who take excellent care of him; and they have a friend in the doctor, who subsequent to the above passage reports that he has sent them a hundred pounds. He concludes that Booth and Amelia are truly richer than many who have so much more.

Behind this is Harrison's view that the assurances of the final judgment become the source of a perspective on the evils of the world that sustains humanity through the most grievous misfortune. As the Booth family's poverty makes their prospects ever more precarious, *Amelia* tests this view. There are the desperate circumstances they face: Booth imprisoned, Amelia and the children in rags without money for a simple meal or shelter, the vulnerability of Amelia under such circumstances to the whims of Colonel James. The narrative burnishes the ugly specter of such prospects. The sheer force of misfortune, drawn out and detailed in the narrative, damages the tenability of the doctor's suggestion that a cheerful countenance and a recollection of the future life can withstand the worst of times. Two facts of the narrative augment this effect. One is Amelia's despair, discussed above, which underlines her family's seemingly imminent demise. The doctor has no greater champion in the novel than Amelia herself, and no character is better suited to his formula for serenity.[26] Yet she still despairs, and the reader sympathizes.

The other fact of the narrative which questions this formula is the variability of the doctor himself, revealed especially in his "peculiar Manner" of conversation, but also in some of his actions. As his letter foreshadows, Harrison is a quirky conversation partner, often less than forthright in his dealings and at times seriously awry in his judgments. These habits make him a less than compelling exemplar of his own theological position. His jocosity is at best a poor synonym for the good humor he commends, and his erratic reactions to unhappy or difficult circumstances do not accord with the serene outlook that the assurance of the final judgment allegedly provides. Just as Allworthy's judgment in *Tom Jones* is asserted more than demonstrated, so Harrison's goodness of heart is reiterated at crucial points in the narrative as an antidote to his actual interactions with people.

Harrison loves disputation. It is central to his character and presents itself both outright and indirectly. Instances of its outright practice include the occasions when he endlessly provokes and teases Mrs. Atkinson for her classical learning, an aggravation which leads her to the not unwarranted conclusion that Harrison is a "conceited Pedant." He also disputes warmly and at length with a sneering young clergyman, the son of a friend, engaging willingly in a game of rhetorical badinage. Harrison's contrariness emerges even in the midst of his acts of goodness. At times he is particularly hard on Booth and, more remarkably, Amelia. A niceness of distinction often obtrudes in his conversations with the latter, which is difficult to reconcile with his own repeated statements of extremely high regard for her character. In a typical exchange, Amelia's declaration that she admires Harrison and loves him for his goodness leads him to say that he could dash the declaration in a minute. He attempts to do this by suggesting that Amelia is not handsome. Amelia is up to his rhetoric, and attributes his failure to do justice to bad eyesight; she then redirects their conversation to its real matter, the question of how she might deflect Colonel James's advances without risking Booth's knowledge and, in turn, either his incredulity to her or his rage against a benefactor. Harrison promises to sleep on it and counsels Amelia not to worry. Amelia replies:

"Well, Sir," said she, "I put my whole Trust in you."
"I am sorry to hear it," cries the Doctor. "Your Innocence may give you a very confident Trust in a much more powerful Assistance. However, I will

do all I can to serve you; and now if you please we will call back your Husband . . ."[27]

The context is an earlier conversation concerning Colonel James in which Harrison has responded to Amelia's report with meditations on the evils of the world, but relatively little in the way of practical advice. Amelia gives Harrison every sign that the matter is urgent: their audience is private and her news is not good. The doctor introduces a discordant note of levity with his teasing rejoinder about Amelia's declaration of love for him, and his abjuration that she misplaces her trust in him, when she could place it in the deity, clearly seems to devout Amelia at best a secondary consideration. Such instances of detouring from the matter of the moment glare especially because the doctor questions two points which are, or should be, beyond question: Amelia's regard for him, and her trust in providence. The narrator then reaffirms Harrison's essential good nature, basically acknowledging the problems readers may have with his part in his conversation with Amelia.

At other points in *Amelia,* Harrison is severe rather than merely jocose with Fielding's heroine. Invited by Booth and Amelia to arbitrate their disagreement about whether Amelia shall accompany her husband on a commission obtained for him by Colonel James, Harrison begins by noting how delicate such situations are, especially for one in his position. He then assumes a mock-Socratic pose, refusing to reveal his own position while appearing at alternating moments to side with each spouse against the other. Amelia and Booth are soon utterly befuddled by this dubious, and certainly indelicate, approach to pastoral care. Only then does Harrison say what he thinks:

> " . . . What, in the Name of Goodness, do either of you think that you have made a Union to endure for ever? How will either of you bear that separation which must some time or other, and perhaps very soon, be the Lot of one of you? Have you forgot that you are both mortal?—As for Christianity, I see you have resigned all pretensions to it: For I make no doubt, but that you have so set your Hearts on the Happiness you enjoy here together, that neither of you ever think a word of Hereafter."
>
> *Amelia* now burst into Tears, upon which *Booth* begged the Doctor to proceed no further. Indeed, he would not have wanted the Caution: For, however blunt he appeared in his Discourse, he had a Tenderness of Heart which is rarely found among Men; for which I know no other reason, than that true Goodness is rarely found among them: For I am firmly persuaded that the latter never possessed any Human Mind in any Degree, without being attended by as large a Portion of the former.[28]

Like the previous passage, here Harrison's conversational tropes vex his partners. His own proclaimed need of delicacy is then belied by its want in his subsequent behavior. When he does weigh in with his judgment, he sounds the theme of the immortal world to come as the guiding principle for resolving the puzzles of this world. Part of Amelia's motivation for attending her husband has to do with the threats posed by Colonel James; and while Amelia has not yet informed Harrison of this matter (this passage just precedes the scene where she divulges this secret), the doctor's castigations are sufficient in severity and sweep that they fail to acknowledge the possibility of such complications. The point is not that Harrison would permit Amelia to subject herself to Colonel James—his standing offer to house Amelia and her children is reiterated throughout the novel. It is rather that Harrison's behavior in such scenes is at odds with his both proclaimed awareness of the evil of the world, and his recognition of Amelia's fidelity and goodness.

A final example of Harrison's erratic behavior is his decision to swear out a warrant for Booth's arrest because Booth owes him money. The doctor's behavior is subsequently explained: he paid a call on the Booths when they were absent and saw the collection of trinkets and gewgaws that Colonel James had given the Booth children. He concluded, on the basis of this "ocular Demonstration," that Booth and Amelia were a pair of profligate fools who had spent his money on trifles while living hand-to-mouth. The narrator goes to some pains to accentuate the doctor's hasty rectification of his error, and his delight in discovering that he was wrong.

Harrison, then, can be mistaken in his judgments and erratic in his pronouncements. He is as often a source of destabilization as he is a rock-like refuge from the calamities of circumstance. His religious convictions, specifically those about the future state and the perspective it can and should provide on present calamities, appear primarily to inform his rhetoric.

Harrison also proves to be the mouthpiece of the providential worldview at the conclusion of the novel. When Robinson confesses, on his "deathbed," his part in forging the false will attributed to Mrs. Harris, and testifies that Amelia was her mother's substantial beneficiary in her actual will, Harrison receives these words with "Good Heaven! how wonderful is thy Providence."[29] After assisting in the apprehension of Murphy, the lawyer who masterminded the false will, Harrison races to Booth's cell, where he embraces Booth and announces, "Your Sufferings are all at an End; and Providence hath done you the Justice at last, which it will one day or other render to all Men."[30] Harrison's breathless congratulation does not keep him from adding that what Booth experiences in this world, all will experience in the future life. The doctor returns to this point in the calm of the following morning, quoting Homer's *Iliad* on the point that Jupiter always eventually executes his vengeance, so that transgressions are ultimately visited upon the transgressors and even upon their children. "I wish," Harrison concludes, "you would read a little in the Delphin *Aristotle,* or else in some Christian Divine, to learn a Doctrine which you will one Day have a Use for, I mean to bear the hardest of all human Conflicts, and support with an even temper and without any violent Transports of Mind, a sudden gust of Prosperity."[31]

Harrison's "great, useful, and uncommon Doctrine" is far more declarative than that its counterpart in *Tom Jones.* The world is such that all human creatures will experience the vagaries of circumstance. All, without exception, will experience evil in some form. A fortunate few will experience happiness in this life. The good that happens to these few in the world is indeed a witness to providence, but primarily it signals to all the nature and promise of the one truly secure providential moment, the final judgment. With this comes a plea for perspective. Those who enjoy providence in this life need to recall its rarity, and the fact that evil will inevitably be part of their lot as well. Those whose unhappy lot goes unrelieved should look to the future state for consolation, and know that the almighty justice shall there reign undeterred.

If Harrison's doctrine is clear, is it the doctrine of *Amelia?* Two cardinal reasons argue that it is not. First, it does nothing to reduce the force of Amelia's laments earlier in the novel. We do not finish the novel less aware of, or mollified—theologically or otherwise—about the extent of her predicament. The sense of the ending in *Amelia* is not one in which her concerns are made irrelevant, and Harrison's pronouncements do nothing to suggest that they can be. Taken as a whole they in fact do the opposite: Amelia's plight is, by implication, typical and to be anticipated, and our only recourse is the stoical perspective that the transgressors will eventually get it, if not in this world than in the next. Fielding ensures that the reader understands concretely the implication of Harrison's creed, so that the creed never permits a sanguine perspective, much less a celebratory euphoria.

It is also the case that to make Harrison's doctrine the doctrine of *Amelia* would make him the novel's mouthpiece. But the novel presents no single spokesperson: Amelia performs that role as much as Harrison, and indeed throughout the novel different characters do so at select moments. Harrison represents Christian doctrine in *Amelia,* but his are not the novel's final words about its world.[32] He represents Christianity at its effective limits, challenged by the problem of evil and made shrill in its affirmations. *Amelia,* however, is no more an endorsement of Harrison's viewpoint than *Tom Jones* is of Allworthy's, or *Joseph Andrews* of Parson Adams's. At the end of the novel the force of Amelia's laments stands. This is manifest despite the absence in the novel of a powerful narrator and his interpositions. The consequence of this displacement makes the matter of viewpoint in *Amelia* more complex. It is the tension of the complex interactions of Harrison and Amelia throughout the novel that comes closest to the "doctrine" because it most fully dramatizes both sides of the contest of providence and evil. The novel's ethos, then, resides not in one voice but in at least two, and this underscores the uncertainty of the world: no single voice, no single experience can alone convey the panorama that is felt in life. The result in *Amelia* is unmistakable: the displacement of a narrator's summary viewpoint in turn allows evil to displace providence from this world into the next.

Displacement does not argue disarray. The absence of the narrator does not here dilute the force of the novel's message, delivered through the range of characters who populate the novel and pronounce, not just in words but in actions, their judgments about matters of providence and evil. Booth's anguish and frustration with the duplicities of patronage, Amelia's despair, and Harrison's insistence on the relevance of Christian virtue to our troubles all describe such judgments and reactions. While Fielding's narrator is lapsed, the reader does not need to exercise much sagacity to identify which characters and sentiments merit our sympathy, and which do not. Yet no one character presents an outlook that fully makes sense of the novel, or at least fully informs our reactions to it. Booth's endless capacity to serve as his own worst enemy qualifies any sense we have that he judges human affairs wisely. Amelia's despair occupies her whole person, and while fully sympathetic makes no pretension to a larger perspective that might offer some sense of resolution. Most telling, Harrison's orthodoxy is stretched beyond its limit by the events of the novel; he himself qualifies his closing affirmations of providence by noting implicitly that not all will be served in this world, and there is scant consolation in his assurances that those less fortunate than the Booths may take consolation in this foreshadowing of their own just desserts.

Each of these characters does work toward making *Amelia* a new kind of documentation of Fielding's grand theme of the standing tension between orthodox Christianity's stated faith in providence and the brute facts of human evil in the world. Here the sense of the ending brings forebodings about the future front and center, muting any potential *Amelia* might have for mimicking its predecessors' triumphant tones of resolution. There marriage approves the providential in a major strain; here Fielding permits no such triumphalism to accompany the Booths' narrow escape. Relief replaces triumph, and Harrison's summary pronouncements (made to parallel those of Allworthy at the conclusion of *Tom Jones*) do not so much celebrate the good that happens to the good as they glance awkwardly and knowingly at the less fortunate who must wait for the final judgment to receive their just desserts.

Booth's condition captures the shift. He later returns to London for the briefest possible visit, clearly implying that he remains vulnerable there. Given the chance, he will return to the habits that were his demise. Booth is of course older than Tom Jones, and he concludes the novel chastened by an experience more noteworthy for its documentation of his limitations than for any transformation of his character. His "conversion" from stoicism to Christianity does not carry with it the resiliency in the face of circumstance that Tom Jones displays: it is impossible to imagine Booth forgiving any one of his Blifils the way Tom does (a show that stuns even Allworthy). Events overpower characters in *Amelia,* and Booth stands admonished and diminished rather than exalted by his travails. While Tom Jones needs only prudence to get on in the world, Booth needs Christianity and a one-way ticket to the country.

Amelia, then, departs from its predecessors not in its theme but in its treatment of that theme. Rawson especially, but also in important ways Hunter, see in this departure genuine diminishment. Fielding faced a changing world with limited resources. *Amelia* presents Fielding's starker thoughts, which he avoided in the earlier novels. Those who champion *Amelia* argue for a shift in response to the changing world in which Fielding necessarily hardens his orthodoxy into a kind of theological shield against the onslaughts of modernity. In both cases Fielding is, in my judgment, enfeebled, and I want to suggest an alternative answer which, while not fully satisfying, makes *Amelia* a lesser but not totally divergent work.

While there is a case to be made for literary diminishment, it seems to me that the focus on this, or the turn among more recent critics to the celebration of new virtues in *Amelia,* can obscure the more fundamental fact that for Fielding really to refine his theme he had to write his final novel in this way. The locus of disenchantment with *Amelia*—the displacement of the narrator—is the keystone to this refinement and the index of Fielding's real artistic development. In the earlier novels, the sense of providential triumph obscures the fact that evil, however sullied and bowed, is not obliterated. The full blush of triumph can obscure a great deal, and Fielding in the earlier novels captures, perhaps more than most, the sense of such moments.

Amelia captures the obscurities of that moment. As such it is in the end an index of Fielding's artistic integrity, because it completes the full exploration of his great theme. Fielding does not here betray his art, but develops the alternative view. In this he is decisively modern, and the terms of his modernity are theological: they focus on God's providence and the claims that might be made for it.[33] The degree of shift in the novels is not ontologically immense: the same factors exist in each world. What changes is not the facts but the perspective. Whatever one's judgments about *Amelia*'s quality in comparison with its predecessors, it is decisively not divergent from them in the ways that the critical discussion suggest. In the theological context it stands closer to culmination than disruption. The novel not incidentally reminds readers of Fielding that providence in this world is finally an article of faith rather than a comprehensive empirical perception in *Joseph Andrews* and *Tom Jones*. The fuller presence of providence, through coy invocation and ultimately unattributable interposition, would not decisively answer the problems raised by *Amelia*. Limits of perception are Fielding's overarching interest when it comes to human relations, and it is the striking fact of providence that it is only perceived retrospectively. *Amelia* reminds us that the earlier novels do not fully or unambiguously affirm providence, and works out the consequences of its limits in informing human perspective.

The structural parallels of the endings of all three novels underscore the sense of progression. In each, the reader concludes with the sense that comedy has triumphed over tragedy—in this instance. It is the implication of that qualification that grows and marks Fielding's artistic maturation. Fielding always invests too much in his couples to permit their demise, but he also invests a great deal in the recognition of how fragile their happiness is. Amelia and Booth do survive and flourish, but we have a very concrete sense of what it would mean had they not done so. This dramatizes retrospectively the chance nature of their condition, and permits the narration and its reader no relief or mollification in the form of comic fun.

Amelia may be the least reread of Fielding's novels. If this is so, it testifies to its rather alarming willingness to discard the cultivated sense of hopeful anticipation and realization that makes its predecessors such wonderful exercises in the gratification of our fondest hopes. It is, then, decisively a sober book from a man whom we do not necessarily want to be sober, at least in his literary art. It reminds us of what we may earlier have missed—never an easy or welcome experience. It is the conundrum of Fielding the novelist, who so often gives the reader what she or he wants, that his decision in his final novel not to do so is itself the index of his integrity as an artist. *Amelia* is not aesthetic anticlimax, but new variation on a great theme.

Chapter 5 ∼

The Binding of Providential Narrative: Fielding, Genesis 22, and the Eighteenth-Century Religious Sensibility

Henry Fielding shared with his age the cherished hope that human happiness was the surest sign of the goodness of God's creation. In Fielding's novels the essence of such happiness is a good marriage: the union of mind, heart, and body, and the resulting family life of parents and their children. Domestic bliss becomes in his fiction the epitome of human happiness. A range of marriages in a variety of conditions take the stage in Fielding's novels, and even when an individual union's appearance bears negligible narrative consequence, the narrator will digress to sketch its character. The institution clearly distilled many things for Fielding, both personally and socially, and presented a microcosm of the social order. The moral weight of marriage in Fielding's narrative art only increases when we recognize that it served as a barometer for theological as well as social analysis. Examining the fate of a marital union—especially the fate of a marriage of two worthies like those who occupy center stage in each Fielding novel—axiomatically raised for Fielding the question of God's providential interposition in the world. Will two good people who love and deserve each other be able to live together for the rest of their lives? *Joseph Andrews* and *Tom Jones* compel the reader both to reply affirmatively in principle ("this should be so!"), and to concede that whatever should be, may nonetheless not be in fact. Pope's dictum that "Whatever is, is right" is in Fielding fraught with qualification: whatever is, nearly was not. Fielding's story resides precisely in the implications of that consideration. In *Amelia* Fielding extended the chronology, shifting the reader's attention from the prospect of marriage to its condition. The tenor of the question, however, barely alters: will two good people who love and deserve each other, and have made a lifelong commitment, be able to honor that commitment and live the modest life they envisioned and deserve for themselves and their children?

Fielding's artistic practice was firmly located in a historical context that was unmistakably religious, and in the end decisively theological, in orientation. Its question was the degree to which the human being could discern a divine influence on the ways of the world. We have seen this question, the animating force of Fielding's novels, find earlier, intense expression in a range of eighteenth-century writing: in the drama, in literary criticism, and in theological controversy. In the drama, Nahum Tate's revision of Shakespeare's *King Lear* excised over 800 lines of text and deleted its Fool while radically revising the plot and denouement to fashion a happy ending instead of a "gor'd state." The endorsement of audiences and then of Samuel Johnson lent authority to a revision that became the basis for productions throughout Fielding's lifetime and beyond, well into the nineteenth century. In addition to Johnson's endorsement, Tate's revision also spurred a debate early in the eighteenth century between John Dennis and Joseph Addison on the appropriate resolution of a tragic drama. At issue was not whether there was a providential hand, or even its location not in this world but in the final judgment; rather the two critics argued about whether or not the tragic drama itself should depict providence by intimating the final judgment. Dennis' argument in favor stemmed from his claim that the drama had a moral obligation to present, for its viewers, a vision of the future state in order to direct their behavior in the present, while Addison judged that fealty to the principle of mimesis demanded that evil stand uncorrected, since this is the way the world really is.

The deism controversy, which began in the late seventeenth century and extended well into the 1740s, the time when Fielding composed his novels, mirrored the debate about poetic justice so directly as to underscore their common theme as the unmistakable preoccupation of the age. Here again the assumption was that providence is not knowable in this world, and the question became not whether there is in fact a providential dimension of the divine activity, but where to locate it securely: in the creation, or in the final judgment? For these controversialists, the answer hinged on the degree to which evil stood as a recognized force in the world. John Toland and Matthew Tindal posited providence in the creation, and saw any further establishment of the divine activity as an unacceptable compromise of the perfection of creation. For them human life is a matter of exercising our reason, a capacity that allows us to discern the natural order and thereby secure our fate. William Law and Joseph Butler dispute this claim. Law argued from grounds of human epistemic limitations and the consequent transcendent claims of religion; Butler, from the undeniable empirical fact that while most of the time good people get their reward, this is not always the case, so it would compromise the divine justice if there were no final judgment. Law and particularly Butler, writing in the 1730s, each articulated a position that recognizes the unknowability of providence in the here and now, but stipulated that this does not have devastating consequences for traditional Christian faith in the final judgment. The appearance in the 1740s of Thomas Morgan's works, particularly *The Moral Philosopher*, and of Hume's *Enquiry* demonstrate that Law and Butler failed to close the controversy, and that the proponents of "natural religion" had taken tenacious hold of the eighteenth-century theological imagination.

These instances of dramatic, literary critical, and theological activity in eighteenth-century England underscore the age's preoccupation with the idea of providence, and establish the context in which Fielding wrote his novels. In these Fielding's chief construct is his narrator, who recounts retrospectively the relevant history of a man and woman who wish to be married *(Joseph Andrews* and *Tom Jones)* or who are in fact married *(Amelia)*. The reader is made to care about the fate of these couples, a fate that is axiomatically a matter of their surrounding circumstances. Fielding's narrators play the didactic role of teaching the reader how to read through lessons in discernment about the significance of specific events to the overarching direction of the narrative. The narrator teaches the reader to assess what claims can be made for the hand of God in the world. Through his novels Fielding asked and answered questions about the appropriate resolution of their plots and, by direct implication, about the capacities of human beings to recognize God's hand in the complex fabric of circumstance. Fielding's answers were the most nuanced of his age because they were the most carefully worked out through his series of three extended prose narratives that not incidentally combine dramatic episode, critical theory, and theological rumination.[1]

At the outset of this study I offered a structural analogy between the role of marriage in Fielding's narrative and that of conversion in Augustine's *Confessions*. We have seen that for Fielding marriage does indeed hold the status of conversion in classic Augustinian providential narrative: it is the formative existential fact of life around which he shapes his narratives. As with Augustine's conversion, the decisive question in Fielding focuses not on the whether of a marriage, but its how. This turns the reader's attention to the events surrounding the marriage—those that conduce to its realization and happiness, and those that do not—and with these scales Fielding measures the prospects of the claim that there is divinely providential interposition in this world. No detail proves too small for the sagacious reader's adjudication on these terms.

We have also seen, however, the limits to the analogy with conversion. Conversion narratives offer unambiguous testimony that God interposed providentially in the teller's life at a particular time and place. The moment of conversion is never ambiguous to its (converted) narrator. Surrounding events query the prospective convertee's readiness. God, these narratives assure their readers, is always at the ready; having established the process, the question quickly becomes one of the reader's readiness, with the proffered narrative a blueprint by which to assess the answer to that question.

Fielding's central marriages are also never ambiguous, but neither is the reader's sense that the readiness was yesterday, is now, and may not be a possibility tomorrow. The novels cultivate a sense of urgency that increases precisely as the narrative lengthens to document the detours and impediments to what should be just about everyone's desire. The constraint thus proves to be not a matter of clarity about the good, but of the cooperation of circumstance. In Fielding, then, unlike Augustine, the surrounding events do not parse so straightforwardly. The difficulties encountered, the problems that stand between people's laudatory desires and their realization, call into question precisely the readiness of God to interpose. The striking result—particularly for a writer as captivated by sex as Fielding—is the absence in his novels of anything analogous to Augustine's "Give me chastity, Lord—but not yet!" His inability at this stage of his life not to sin, his capture in the clutches of human fallenness from which even his recognition of the good cannot free him, is Augustine's point. The contrast is one of focus. Fielding indulges in casuistry about sex, but it is in fact the case that instances of malicious tampering with the fates of others exercise his narrators far more than a mutually spirited moment of sexual indiscretion. Moments when the narrators make precisely this distinction abound in his novels. As discussed in detail in chapter three, the most pointed instance occurs in the context of the scene at Upton in *Tom Jones,* when the narrator insists that Sophia's decision to leave without seeing Tom, despite the fact that she has finally found him after an arduous search, had less to do with her discovery that he was in bed with Mrs. Waters than with what she (mistakenly) took to be liberties he had taken with her name and history. Subtleties of perception here test the reader, and the narrator relates details of how Sophia lets Tom know she was there (and knows of his dalliance) to prove what he anticipates will be a controversial claim for his reader to accept.

The scene at Upton illustrates that, unlike conversion, marriage occupies the structural but not the moral or theological center of Fielding's narratives. That center, to which marriage pointed for Fielding, is the urgent question of whether we can discern the hand of God at work in the world. Infidelity, the central threat to marriage, proves less momentous in Fielding's novels than the chains of circumstantial misunderstanding in which it may partake. This is true even in *Amelia*, when the reconciliation of Amelia and Booth includes her revelation that she has known for some time about her husband's infidelity, and has already forgiven him for it. The implications of Augustine's cry for chastity are that he knows the good but wants to indulge temptation a bit longer. However astute a psychologist, Fielding's interest was instead the very different question of how events do and do not cooperate when the good is known but achieved with difficulty. Once again *Amelia* provides the most useful example, because Booth is the closest thing to an Augustinian hero in Fielding's fiction. But Booth's affair with Miss Mathews presents duress not simply of conscience, but of finance and social standing. Fielding only briefly nods at the matter of physical gratification, while lavishing considerable attention on the context that presses Booth into a half-hearted infidelity.

Fielding the novelist, then, narrates providence very differently from Augustine. He makes marriage rather than conversion the existential center of the narrative. The question addressed is no longer the readiness of the individual to convert to God, with the corollary that God stands ready to interpose. It is rather the question of whether God does interpose, with the corollary that the (unambiguously) good human situation that the marriage bespeaks is itself fragile and in need of support, whether to be consummated or sustained.

Fielding's revisionist narrative practice achieves its ultimate effect in the senses of the endings in each of his novels. It is at these moments in the reading experience that his principled diffidence achieves its distilled essence. In the worlds of *Joseph Andrews* and *Tom Jones*, and even in the benighted world of *Amelia*, the implicit design of providence finally manifests itself. Yet Fielding always pushes the odds hard enough to risk the charge of contrivance. Tom Jones and Sophia Western marry thanks largely to events beyond their control, and the Booths escape poverty and the cruelties of the city due to reasons beyond their making. They are not alone in their impotence. Such would-be forces for good as Parson Adams, Squire Allworthy, and Doctor Harrison, each introduced as a tower of goodness, succeed only in failing to promote, sometimes even to recognize, the narrative's manifest destiny. Their failure is all the more galling because Fielding places each in a position to advance the cause, only so that the reader can witness their failure to answer the call. Combinations of small circumstance and slight coincidence have more to do with the resolution: "deathbed" confessions and happenstance asides turn out to be the true allies of happy resolution.

Such slender threads to support what is ultimately quite weighty matter do not constitute a warrant for the role of providence in the world. Fielding pushes the reader, harder than is generally acknowledged, toward Hume's skepticism about claims for supernatural agency. Behind those small circumstances and slight coincidences is an insistent empiricism, closely connected with a distrust of the human habit of providential attribution. No mean rhetorician, one of Fielding's greatest rhetorical gambits is the narrator's remark, in the introductory chapter to Book XV of *Tom Jones,* that the chief objection to the usual claim of religious and moral writers—that virtue is the certain road to happiness, and vice to misery—is that it simply is not true. We risk slighting this observation's force, and its grim, felt regret, if we neglect Fielding's own, no doubt hard-earned, conviction that we simply cannot be sure about providence in the details.

If that were all Fielding had left us to say, he would be a much less interesting and compelling novelist than he is. This is half the story, or half the sense of his endings, and I discuss this half initially because it has been so easily discounted on the one hand, and exaggerated on the other. It does not go away; at the same time, Fielding is unwilling to endorse Humean conclusions about the facts of life. The desirable endings of Fielding's novels do unmistakably affirm the idea of a general providential design that takes recourse, under the pressure of this empiricism, in both the created order and, especially and increasingly, the final judgment. The paradigm of divine activity invoked in chapter one of this study—creation, providence, eschatology—affords a useful typology of the theological development of Fielding's novels. *Joseph Andrews* testifies to the sheer goodness of the creation. The sense of evil and the fallenness of humanity barely obtrude. The most serious obstacle to the happy resolution is Parson Adams, and however bumbling the great patriarch's namesake may be, the reader never doubts that he will finally close the door on Joseph and Fanny. Happy circumstances are for the most part a given, an outgrowth of the natural order of things. *Tom Jones* retains at least some of this exuberance, but offers a more searching examination of circumstance that turns into a weighing of the ways good and evil interact. As the Fielding novel that examines most minutely the middle dimension of the divine activity, it is striking that it alludes both to the goodness of the creation and, at moments, the assurances of the final judgment. *Amelia,* however, presents the results of the examination of the world, and it presents an unremittingly pessimistic assessment of any identification of a creation that is thoroughly good, or a providence that actively works for the happiness of the good. Fielding's final novel takes recourse to the final judgment as the divine moment of retribution for what the world has wrought, to set straight what the world itself cannot. Its ending is not a headlong rush to consummation, but a distress relieved.

From creation to providence to eschatology: Fielding in his novels develops a view of divine activity that moves in chronological continuity with its classical theological expression. Its heart is the idea of providence, for Fielding never fully relinquishes the cherished sense that God's plan embraces what is best for humanity in this world. Like the debaters of poetic justice and the controversialists of deism, Fielding found providence difficult to pinpoint in this world, and took recourse to the framing activities of creation and eschatology to affirm the divine plan. From this theologically based understanding of Fielding's canon, several judgments emerge. First, *Tom Jones* is Fielding's greatest novel because it most successfully balanced creation and eschatology in a minute examination of the here and now. Its assurances of tone and execution are functions of this mediatorial status. Second, *Joseph Andrews* made *Tom Jones* possible, and *Amelia* follows logically from its predecessor. Fielding's greatest artistic achievement required a predecessor effort that established as a baseline, a given, the sense of the goodness of the created order. His masterpiece spawned in turn a novel that brought into greater relief the equally deep sense of the evil that mars the world and challenges theological confidence.

This thematic movement of Fielding's novels is itself encapsulated in the endings of each individual novel, most notably in *Tom Jones* and *Amelia*. Each embodies the tension between good and evil, and each affirms in its happiness the triumph of goodness while also letting evil carry on. To edit slightly Fielding's own characterization of the religious and moral writers: virtue is indeed rewarded, but vice is not miserable and indeed is shown plotting the future even as the narrator "resolves" the plot of the novel. Fielding calibrates evil in a kind of counterpoint to the trumpets of happiness. Blifil is plotting for parliament at the end of *Tom Jones,* and the Booths' wholesale retreat from the city at the end of *Amelia* acknowledges their vulnerability. *Tom Jones* can sustain a closing reference to Parson Adams, but this is literally unimaginable at the end of *Amelia*.

Happiness is a precarious commodity, and good people enjoy no assurance of it in this world. An index of the uneasiness of Fielding's belief in happiness, and of the complications that ensue from its translation into the marital union, is the invocation and echo in his novels of what may be the greatest Scriptural challenge to that value: the story of Abraham and Isaac. Perhaps the ultimate Scriptural encapsulation of Fielding's fictional sensibility, Genesis 22 functions as a kind of coda for the novels: God gives, God appears to take away, God restores—all in the (apparent) service of teaching human beings to know better their true relation to God in the world. The story of Abraham and Isaac mirrors the dynamic of Fielding's novels: an intense desire for the realization of domestic happiness in this world; a desire to link that realization with divine sanction and protection; and a dawning, then growing recognition that the ways of God are in fact beyond our immediate comprehension, and certainly our specific attribution to this particular condition at this particular time. As such its invocation pressures the cherished ideals of Fielding and his time.

Like Fielding, other eighteenth-century writers turned, at crucial moments and in distinctive ways, to the story of Abraham and Isaac. Approaching the conclusion of *Christianity Not Mysterious,* John Toland considered the passage as a possible objection to his central claim that there is no conflict between Christian faith rightly understood and human reason. Toland argues that Abraham was not in fact irrational when he bound his son, because Isaac's existence was itself a miracle, one to which Abraham could offer eyewitness testimony. Toland concludes that because Abraham had this knowledge, he knew that if he did kill Isaac, God could—and, of course, would—perform another miracle to restore to Abraham his long-awaited progeny.

Nahum Tate's decisions in revising *King Lear* do not attest to the direct influence of Genesis 22, but they do bespeak the same anxieties. Shakespeare's play itself has decided tonal, and to some extent structural, affinities with the biblical story. It opens with Lear's disruption of the kingdom, which parallels the disruption of the divine command: why would the king willfully divide his kingdom, and why would God explicitly undo his miraculous intervention? Cordelia is herself a kind of Isaac, an unwitting and helpless pawn in the face of commissions that directly implicate her, even though they have no apparent connection to her past behavior or personal qualities. She is nearly sacrificed for her refusal to mouth filial pieties that would in that context only mock her genuine love and regard. It is no accident that Tate's self-proclaimed chief improvement of Shakespeare's version is the introduction of a love story between Cordelia and Edgar. Their courting becomes part of the play, and their union is imminent at its conclusion. It is difficult to determine what gives greater joy to Edgar: his newfound kingship or his imminent marriage. Like Fielding with *Joseph Andrews* and *Tom Jones,* Tate assumes the need for a wedding at the end of his version of *Lear* and thus utterly reverses its genre, rendering a tragic resolution comic.

In chapter three I discussed Fielding's direct appropriation of Genesis 22 in *Joseph Andrews.* Here we might recall that the episode underscores a contradiction, very nearly amounting to hypocrisy, in Parson Adams's counsel that Joseph speaks from lust in seeking an immediate marriage with Fanny. Joseph is in fact fearful for Fanny's literal safety, a fear that the events of the novel justify. Adams invokes patience and acceptance of what God delivers, only to be interrupted in his lengthy monologue by the news that his son has drowned. Fielding makes the story work by showing how speedily and unselfconsciously Adams discards the principle he has just invoked: he dissolves in inconsolable grief at the (soon discovered to be only apparent) loss of his son. Fielding's reader mistakes neither the intended moral, nor its implication: Adams reacts appropriately when he bewails the loss of the son, and understandably when he rejects Joseph's proffered consolation of the future state, and Adams is thus really a better man, because a more feeling human being, than his apparently hard-hearted counsel to Joseph implies.[2]

The story also has its echoes, especially of effect, in *Tom Jones*. A foundling, paired with the "legitimate" nephew, Blifil, Tom is adopted by Allworthy, himself a childless widower who badly wanted a son. Allworthy later obeys the voices of others in his household who tell him to banish Tom. Thrown into the world, only a series of reversals and recognitions keep Tom from realizing the reputation of his youth, that "he was certainly born to be hang'd." Tom's literal near escape from death results in his restoration with Allworthy, revealed by later events to be his uncle. This recognition legitimates the patriarchal line; Tom is thus Allworthy's legitimate heir by blood relation. What appeared to be possible, and was then rendered in appearance decisively impossible, becomes again possible through dispensation beyond expectation.

The emergence of this story, whether explicitly or as echo, bespeaks anxieties about the divine communication with the world. Missing throughout is the voice of God. Parson Adams learns of his son's death, and then that his son has been spared, from unidentified lookers-on, at least one of whom would appear to be an eighteenth-century ambulance chaser. Allworthy's counsel to banish Tom comes from his hired tutors, Thwackum and Square, and Tom's peer and rival, Blifil. None provides even a passing imitation of the voice of God, nor is there even the suggestion that one of them might. Absent the divine voice, there is also no divine command: Fielding chooses not to make either Adams or Allworthy the potential agent of his progeny's demise. That commission is displaced onto nature (*Joseph Andrews*) or circumstance (*Tom Jones*).

For all the parallels, the contrast is striking: Abraham's commission comes directly from God, and it commissions Abraham to kill his son. Revisions of the story in the eighteenth century, particularly those by Fielding, in some sense eliminate its gut while retaining its skeleton. The historical significance of this revision is that it eliminates direct divine communication, and by default absolves humans of responsibility for attending to such communication. The key point is that in doing so, it does not revise away the idea of God—a God who creates and who finally and decisively concludes the creation. It rather makes the strong epistemological claim for the human inability to capture with precision the divine activity—providence—in specific worldly events. God is silent, and one consequence of this fact is our inability to attribute confidently the events of the world to the hand of God.

This is more than a version of the Augustinian marvel at the mysteriousness of the divine ways. It is instead a fundamental epistemological bracketing of what the believer can know of the ways of God in the world. Here

Fielding shades much more toward Faulkner and away from Augustine: he documents the limits of human knowledge, the incapacity to discover the divine answer to the human question in this world. This is itself the eighteenth-century binding of providential narrative as practiced by Augustine and his successors: the pervasive injection into such narratives of a radically skeptical epistemology that implicates not just the development of its plot but pervades its sense in ending. Augustine has his uncertainties, to be sure, but these narratives simply do not hear the voice of God. Their characters respond to human, rather than divine, commands. To the degree that they yearn after such a voice, and such commands, those yearnings go unsatisfied. Providential narrative is in effect held down, tied up by this limitation, so that it can no longer affirm that this specific detail, that particular incident, may be attributed to God's interposition in human affairs. In this respect Fielding's revision of Augustine itself replicates the binding of Isaac, where Isaac is understood as Augustinian providential narrative, the reader is Abraham, and Fielding's narrator stands as Yahweh. This is most explicit in *Tom Jones,* where the narrator (Yahweh, speaking in magisterial tones) enjoins the reader (Abraham, who has been given the text and taught to love it and hope for it) through the introductory chapters to honor the interpretive boundaries of the narrative account (Isaac). As Isaac must die, so must the idea that specific events of the narrative testify to the providential hand of God.

In the end Yahweh spares Isaac, and Fielding spares the genre of providential narrative by providing a happy ending and an invocation of the future state. But just as Isaac must have changed utterly from the experience, so providential narrative has also changed. No longer does even the largest detail testify directly and unambiguously to providence.

Fielding's binding of providential narrative, and its less worked out but unmistakable intimations in the writings of other eighteenth-century figures, raises a serious question about the historical tenability of any attribution of a "precritical" sensibility to them. In fact Fielding's narrators sowed the seeds of the story-telling principles and practices that bred the Quentin Compsons of the twentieth century. Fielding's narrators are decidedly not "comic analogue(s) of the true believer's reliance on a benign providence in real life"[3] but self-described historians working through processes of order and selection to illustrate what human beings can and cannot know. As such they are prototypical eighteenth-century intellectuals, probing events for clues to the hand of the deity. The recourse to Genesis, rather than the synoptics, tells much about the degree of qualification here. The difficulties that such Enlightenment stalwarts as Voltaire and Thomas Jefferson encountered with the Gospel accounts of miraculous activity have precise parallels in Fielding's novels. He was as much a creature of the Enlightenment as were they.

The impetus of Fielding's religious sensibility clearly points in certain respects toward such nineteenth and twentieth century figures as Feuerbach and Faulkner, and away from his fourth century progenitor, Augustine. Demonstrably wary of the religious mechanism of wishful thinking, Fielding took pains to expose and correct it. On this point he is systematic in both narrative commentary and characterization. There is the subtle but ongoing disjunction, mounting to a crescendo as the reader approaches the denouement, between his characters' comparably free invocations of providence and his narrator's scrupulous avoidance of such language. Less gently and sympathetically, the hypocrisies of the Parson Thwackums of the world appear in stark relief. And there is "that set of Religious, or rather Moral Writers" whose decidedly mistaken notions about the connection between virtue and happiness epitomize what Fielding's novels debunk.

Systematic attacks on wishful thinking do not, however, preclude for Fielding an equally steady commitment to the classical triad of divine activity. His qualification focuses on the capacity of the human to know, and exposes the false foundation of providential attribution. The endings of the novels and their overarching frame of reference bespeak complete confidence in the secure foundation of the divine moments of creation and the final judgment. In this context it is not the case that there can be no providence in the world; rather it is that the providence that must exist is inaccessible to human perception in ways that were once traditionally acceptable. To the degree that his novels do collapse providence into eschatology, then, Fielding offers evidence of a theological mind seeking to maintain its integrity through the discipline of narrative art.

Behind this resides a distinction that testifies not to an enfeebled intellect, but rather to a superior combination of honest ratiocination and deeply held faith. Fielding's narratives move toward Humean skepticism about what we can know, but they draw their line there: it is far from clear to Fielding that such epistemological limitations in the here and now fully compromise faith in either the goodness of the created order, or the plausibility of the final judgment. It is rather the case, in Fielding's considered narrative judgment at least, that epistemological skepticism collapses providence into eschatology for our present apprehension, while allowing us to continue to affirm the presence of God in the world, however unapprehended by us. The world becomes a theater of divine providence for which there is no playbill; hence Fielding in some ways anticipates Beckett's *Waiting for Godot* in recognizing the absurdity of that situation. It is an index of his time, however, that Fielding could make that distinction without the absurdist consequences that a character like Estragon so tellingly articulates. It is perhaps an index of ours that we find it so difficult to recognize why Fielding never became Estragon.

Providence has always been the most retrospective of theological doctrines; the Christian never fully recognizes the hand of God until after the fact. Fielding's version of the narrative quality of experience honors that fact and takes from it the precise perspective that informs and shapes his narrative art. The resulting self-conscious retrospection aligns him most closely with his contemporaries William Law and Joseph Butler, each of whom judged Christianity to encompass both relative ignorance about the larger ways of this world and faith in the Christian God. This renders him a narrative theologian in the Christian tradition who, for all their differences, does indeed follow Augustine's theme of life as a path on which we are led unknowingly, that we might knowingly be led. The difference in the end is one of degree: for Fielding, the knowingness would come later, in the future state, and the resulting lengthier trial provided a deeper, at times more anguished, preparation for the ultimate human reunion with the divine. To the degree that his narrative art could express that truth, it was intended as a bulwark for his own and his readers' days—a consolation and an inspiration to go forward with confidence into a future that the present could only dimly perceive.

Notes

Chapter 1

1. C. J. Rawson, *Henry Fielding and the Augustan Ideal Under Stress* (London: Routledge & Kegan Paul, 1972), and J. Paul Hunter, *Occasional Form: Henry Fielding and the Chains of Circumstance* (Baltimore: Johns Hopkins University Press, 1975).

2. See, for instance, Stephen Crites, "The Narrative Quality of Experience," *Journal of the American Academy of Religion* 39 (1971), 291–311. A significant body of work, spurred by Hans Frei and George Lindbeck, addresses these issues with specific reference to the hermeneutics of biblical interpretation (often absent sustained textual reference, as in Crites); useful and illustrative collections include Garrett Green, ed., *Scriptural Authority and Narrative Interpretation* (Philadelphia: Fortress Press, 1987), and Stanley Hauerwas and L. Gregory Jones, eds., *Why Narrative? Readings in Narrative Theology* (Grand Rapids, MI: William Eerdmans Publishing Co., 1989). An excellent example of work in this tradition that most emphatically engages in extensive textual analysis is Eric Ziolkowski's *The Sanctification of Don Quixote: From Hidalgo to Priest* (University Park: Penn State University Press, 1991).

3. Examples extend as far back as the novel's initial reception. See the entries in Ronald Paulson and Thomas Lockwood, eds., *Henry Fielding: The Critical Heritage* (New York: Barnes & Noble, 1969). Twentieth-century versions of this judgment appear as early as Aurelien Digeon, *The Novels of Fielding* (New York: E.P. Dutton & Co., 1925), esp. 220–221, and include many of Fielding's most distinguished interpreters: Robert Alter, *Fielding and the Nature of the Novel* (Cambridge: Harvard University Press, 1968), esp. 141 ff.; C. J. Rawson, op. cit.; and J. Paul Hunter, *Occasional Form*, 206 ff. Martin Battestin lauds and condemns, arguing simultaneously for *Amelia* as Fielding's "maturest thinking about human nature and about the grounds of order in society" and against it as "itself the expression—in some respects, the embodiment—of a theory of human nature virtually indistinguishable from the psychology it ostensibly repudiates" ("The Problem of *Amelia*: Hume, Barrow, and the Conversion of Captain Booth," [*English Literary History* 41

(1974), 635]). In contrast, Eric Rothstein's stimulating *Systems of Order and Inquiry in Late Eighteenth-Century Fiction* (Berkeley: University of California Press, 1975) is of note precisely because of its minority status: it champions *Amelia* as nothing less than an organizational and thematic tour de force.

4. See Angela Smallwood, *Fielding and the Woman Question: The Novels of Fielding and Feminist Debate 1700–1750* (New York: St. Martin's Press, 1989), and a host of articles: Mary Anne Schofield, "Exploring the Woman Question: A Reading of Fielding's *Amelia*," *Ariel* 15 (1985), 45–57; John Richetti, "Voice and Gender in Eighteenth-Century Fiction: Haywood to Burney," *Studies in the Novel* 19 (1987), 263–272; Patricia Howell Michaelson, "*The Wrongs of Woman* as a Feminist *Amelia*," *Journal of Narrative Technique* 21 (1991), 250–261; Mona Scheuermann, "Man Not Providence: Fielding's *Amelia* as a Novel of Social Criticism," *Forum for Modern Language Studies* 20 (1984), 106–123; Cheryl Wanko, "Characterization and the Reader's Quandary in Fielding's *Amelia*," *Journal of English and German Philology* 90 (1991), 505–523; and Dianne Osland, "Fielding's *Amelia*: Problem Child or Problem Reader?" *Journal of Narrative Technique* 10 (1980), 56–67. For a demurrer from the valuation of Fielding on this theme, see Nancy Armstrong, *Desire and Domestic Fiction: A Political History of the Novel* (New York: Oxford University Press, 1987).

5. An impressive example of such a claim on the basis of gender, pursued with reference not only to the novels but to the full Fielding corpus, is provided by Jill Campbell in *Natural Masques: Gender and Identity in Fielding's Novels and Plays* (Stanford, CA: Stanford University Press, 1995).

6. Robert Alter, *Fielding and the Nature of the Novel* (Cambridge: Harvard University Press, 1968), 146.

7. Dianne Osland, for example, argues that "[w]hatever the ultimate truth of the situation might be, in the immediate consideration [Harrison's] argument is made irrelevant by the novel's inescapable emphasis on the worldly dimension" ("Fielding's *Amelia*: Problem Child or Problem Reader?" *Journal of Narrative Technique* 10 [1980], 63).

8. The most comprehensive expression of his view may be found in Battestin's *The Moral Basis of Fielding's Art* (Middletown, CT: Wesleyan University Press, 1959) and *The Providence of Wit: Aspects of Form in Augustan Literature and the Arts* (Oxford: Clarendon Press, 1974), and also in the notes to the Wesleyan editions of the works of Henry Fielding, particularly those to the introductory chapters of *Tom Jones*. Battestin's work has elicited much response. Hunter endorses the claim for ethics (see *Occasional Form*, esp. 78 ff.), but finds less evidence of dogmatic confidence. Rawson directly critiques Battestin's position in *The Augustan Ideal*, emphasizing the inevitable slipperiness of attributions of influence. See also Donald Greene's critique of R. S. Crane's work on latitudinarian thought, and its appropriation by Battestin and others ("Latitudinarianism and Sensibility: The Genealogy of the 'Man of Feeling' Reconsidered," *Modern Philology* 75 [1977], 159–183), and the interpretation offered by Aaron Schneider in "Hearts and Minds in

Joseph Andrews: Parson Adams and a War of Ideas," *Philological Quarterly* 66 (1987), 367–389, esp. 383–384.

9. "Fielding's Muse of Experience," in J. Paul Hunter and Martin Battestin, *Henry Fielding in His Time and Ours,* with an introduction by Andrew Wright. Papers presented at the William Andrews Clark Memorial Library Seminar at the University of California at Los Angeles, May 14, 1983 (Pasadena, CA: Castle Press, 1987), 43. The fact that in 1696 John Toland, a notorious deist, could choose an epigraph from Tillotson for *Christianity Not Mysterious* and successfully insinuate the accord of his proposal with the philosophy of John Locke suggests that Fielding inherited a more fluid situation than Battestin's dichotomy allows.

10. Rawson questions the tenability of Battestin's historical attribution of latitudinarian influence; see his extended review of *The Providence of Wit* in *Order from Confusion Sprung: Studies in Eighteenth-Century Literature from Swift to Cowper* (London: George Allen & Unwin, 1985), esp. 384 ff.

11. The earliest instance of this is the work of R. S. Crane, whose seminal essays on "The Plot of *Tom Jones* " (in Henry Fielding, *Tom Jones,* ed. Sheridan Baker [New York: W.W. Norton & Co., 1973]) and "Suggestions Toward a Genealogy of the 'Man of Feeling'"(*English Literary History* 1 [1934], 205–230) willfully refuse to inform each other. Sheldon Sacks underscores the ghostly power of Crane's influence even thirty years later:

> The first of my critical ghosts insisted that Fielding was "not writing a system, but a history" (i.e., what we now call a novel). He pointed out that not only had I made extensive use for my own purposes of a particular critical analysis which relates all parts of the novel to a defined artistic end, but that I had agreed in all essentials both with such concrete analyses and, so far as I was capable of understanding them, with the aesthetic assumptions on which concrete analyses depend. Since I had agreed that all the elements of novels—including what I termed "value judgments"—were dictated by and organized to achieve an artistic end, such judgments may have only the most tenuous relation to authorial beliefs; the answer to my detailed question must be a hearty "Nothing"; though I might define such classes, the judgments whose presence they insured were controlled by the artistic end of the work, and I could make no significant inferences from them. Biographers and historians, this ghost argued, had better confine their activities to biography and history and let literary critics perform feats of literary criticism. As it was not likely that novelists would have to believe anything in particular in order to evaluate characters, actions, and thoughts in a given way, my general question was unanswerable or, worse yet, capable of eliciting a set of thoroughly misleading answers [Sheldon Sacks, *Fiction and the Shape of Belief* (Berkeley and Los Angeles: University of California Press, 1964), 233].

12. Leo Braudy, *Narrative Form in History and Fiction: Hume, Fielding, and Gibbon* (Princeton, NJ: Princeton University Press, 1970). Braudy builds on the claims of *Narrative Form*, extending them without revision, in "Providence, Paranoia, and the Novel," *English Literary History* 48 (1981), 619–637.

13. Ibid., 163.

14. Campbell's *Natural Masques* offers a brilliant revisionist reading of Fielding that winnows gender (mis)constructions in both Fielding's works and the subsequent critical commentary. The result captures another version of principled diffidence with reference to sexuality. Yet Campbell's work also falls decidedly into the camp of the stigmatic deniers: her often-invoked sets of changing institutions in Fielding's time always include politics, government, economics, and literature—but never religion.

15. Ian Watt, *The Rise of the Novel: Studies in Defoe, Richardson and Fielding* (Berkeley: University of California Press, 1957). See also his "Serious Reflections on *The Rise of the Novel*," in *Novel* I, no. 3 (1968), 205–218. Watt's influence is evident throughout subsequent studies: See, for example, Leopold Damrosch, *God's Plot and Man's Stories: Studies in the Fictional Imagination from Milton to Fielding* (Chicago: University of Chicago Press, 1985), esp. 1–17. Hunter offers the most explicit acknowledgment and captures the way that all roads have seemed to lead to Watt: "Everyone in the past thirty years who has written about the beginnings of the English novel has been engaged in rewriting Watt and, in so doing, renewing him" (*Before Novels,* xx). John Richetti argues that his successors extend Watt's work in useful ways without superseding it; see "The Legacy of Ian Watt's *The Rise of the Novel*" in *The Profession of Eighteenth-Century Literature: Reflection on an Institution,* ed. Leo Damrosch (Madison: University of Wisconsin Press, 1992).

16. "There is a curious antinomy here. On the one hand, Defoe and Richardson make an uncompromising application of the realist point of view in language and prose structure, and thereby forfeit other literary values. On the other hand, Fielding's stylistic virtues tend to interfere with his technique as a novelist, because a patent selectiveness of vision destroys our belief in the reality of report, or at least diverts our attention from the content of the report to the skill of the reporter. There would seem to be some inherent contradiction between the ancient and abiding literary values and the distinctive narrative technique of the novel" (*The Rise of the Novel,* 30).

17. See, for example, Alter, *Fielding and the Nature of the Novel,* 6–25, and Meir Sternberg, *Expositional Modes and Temporal Ordering in Fiction* (Baltimore: Johns Hopkins University Press, 1978), 17–18.

18. Lennard Davis makes Watt's assumption explicit in *Factual Fictions: The Origins of the English Novel* (New York: Columbia University Press, 1983), 111.

19. See the important, now classic corrective to this problem in Wayne Booth, *The Rhetoric of Fiction,* 2nd ed. (Chicago: University of Chicago Press, 1983), 23–64.

20. Michael McKeon, *The Origins of the English Novel 1600–1740* (Baltimore: Johns Hopkins University Press, 1987), esp. 1–3.

21. *Origins of the English Novel,* 124.
22. See, for example, Michael Goldberg, "God, Action, and Narrative: *Which Narrative? Which* Action? *Which* God?" *Journal of Religion* 68 (1988), 39–56.
23. Hans W. Frei, *The Eclipse of Biblical Narrative: A Study in Eighteenth and Nineteenth Century Hermeneutics* (New Haven and London: Yale University Press, 1974). Frei acknowledges in his preface the problem of the canonical leapfrog, but judges that the story he has to tell is the essential prelude to such interpretive work. The danger of this decision is, however, the resulting brief use of Fielding as essentially a one-dimensional prooftext for Frei's theory. See also Samuel Preus, "Secularizing Divination: Spiritual Biography and the Invention of the Novel," *Journal of the American Academy of Religion* 59 (1991), 441–466, who argues for a connection between Puritan conversion narrative (e.g., Bunyan) and the early novel in England (e.g., Defoe). Preus endorses "formal realism," but only alludes to Richardson and Fielding.
24. Ibid., 13–14.
25. Ibid., 14.
26. Ibid., 146.
27. Kathryn E. Tanner usefully amplifies and clarifies Frei's position in "Theology and the plain sense," in *Scriptural Authority and Narrative Interpretation,* 59–78.

Chapter 2

1. Ronald Paulson and Thomas Lockwood, eds., *Henry Fielding: The Critical Heritage* (New York: Barnes & Noble, 1969), 236.
2. Henry Fielding, "Examples of the Interposition of Providence in the Detection and Punishment of Murder," (London, 1752), 8–9.
3. Fielding's library included two volumes of Toland's miscellaneous works and a separate copy of *Christianity Not Mysterious;* Anthony Collins's *A Discourse of the Grounds and Reasons of the Christian Religion;* the complete works of John Locke and Samuel Clarke; Shaftesbury's *Characteristics;* Middleton's *Enquiry into the Miraculous Powers of the Christian Church;* Hume's *Essay on Human Understanding;* Newton's *Observations on Daniel and the Apocalypse;* the complete works of Spinoza; Skelton's *Deism Revealed; The Spectator* in eight volumes; and John Dennis's letters and collected works. See Frederick G. and Anne G. Ribble, eds. *Fielding's Library: An Annotated Catalogue* (Charlottesville, VA: Bibliographical Society of the University of Virginia, 1996).
4. Michael McKeon, *The Origins of the English Novel 1600–1740* (Baltimore: Johns Hopkins University Press, 1987), 125. See also his "Origins of Interdisciplinary Studies," *Eighteenth Century Studies* 28 (Fall 1994), esp. 24–26, where the notion of a "superintending divinity" appears to be at most a metaphor with vague ethical implications. McKeon offers the most formidable case against the following argument, but arguments that religion was alive and well in the eighteenth century can also engender

disparaging incredulity: see, for example, Arthur H. Scouten on Aubrey Williams, "Recent Interpretations of Restoration Comedy of Manners," in *Du Verbe au Geste: melanges en l'honneur de Pierre Danchin* (Nancy: Presses Universitaires de Nancy, 1986), 99–107.

5. For surveys of the term and its uses in literature and in literary criticism, see M. A. Quinlan, *Poetic Justice in the Drama: The History of an Ethical Principle in Literary Criticism* (Notre Dame, IN: Notre Dame University Press, 1912), and Wolfgang Zach, *Poetic Justice: Theorie und Geschichte einer literarischen Doktrin: Begriff—Idee—Komödienkonzeption* (Tübingen: Max Niemeyer Verlag, 1986). Clarence C. Green's *The Neo-Classic Theory of Tragedy in England During the Eighteenth Century* (Cambridge: Harvard University Press, 1934) includes a chapter, "Poetic Justice," which focuses on the conflict between Addison and Dennis. The most recent discussion focusing on Rymer and Tate is Scott Cutler Shershow, "'Higlety, Piglety, Right or Wrong': Providence and Poetic Justice in Rymer, Dryden, and Tate," *Restoration Studies in English Literary Culture 1660–1700* 15 (1991), 17–26.

6. "M. H. Abrams, *A Glossary of Literary Terms,* 3rd ed., Rinehart English Pamphlets (New York: Holt, Rinehart & Winston, 1971), 132.

7. *The Critical Works of Thomas Rymer,* ed. Curt A. Zimansky (New Haven: Yale University Press, 1956), 22–23. This is excerpted from Rymer's essay, "The Tragedies of the Last Age consider'd and Examin'd by the Practice of the Ancients, and by the Common Sense of all Ages, in a Letter to Fleetwood Shepheard, Esq."; it was first published in 1678.

8. Shershow attributes a "theological urgency" to Rymer's account ("'Higlety, Piglety, Right or Wrong'"), 17.

9. Ibid., 23.

10. Jeremy Collier, *A Short View of the Immorality, and Profaneness of the English Stage* (London, 1698).

11. On Collier, see the excellent treatment in Aubrey Williams, *An Approach to Congreve*, 58–90.

12. *A Short View,* 2.

13. Ibid., 14–15.

14. Ibid., 64, where Collier quotes Lady Plyant and Sr. Paul Plyant in the *Double Dealer.* The implication of their smutty talk "must be that *Providence* is a ridiculous supposition, and that none but Blockheads pretend to Religion."

15. Ibid., 68. Collier published a sermon of thirty-three pages addressing the condition of the body during the inevitable interim between death and the final judgment, when it would rejoin the soul in a state superior to its earthly one.

16. Ibid., 140.

17. *A Short View,* xx.

18. In a subsequent rejoinder, Collier gives no quarter and reiterates these themes ("If there must be Strumpets, let *Bridewell* be the *Scene.* Let them come not to Prate, but to be *Punish'd.*"), and even anticipates Sherlock by tracing a direct causal line between atrocities in England and its immoral

drama (*A defence of the Short View of the Profaneness and Immorality of the English Stage & c.; Being a Reply to Mr. Congreve's Amendments, & c. And to the Vindication of the author of The Relapse* [10]).

19. Ibid., 24.

20. For an excellent general discussion, including numerous references to Nahum Tate, see Jean I. Marsden, *The Re-Imagined Text: Shakespeare, Adaptation, and Eighteenth-Century Literary Theory* (Lexington: The University Press of Kentucky, 1995).

21. "Shakespeare, Tate, and Garrick: New Light on Alterations of *King Lear*," *Theatre Notebook* 36 (1982), 17.

22. Tate regarded this as his chief improvement on the implausibilities of Shakespeare's plot: "'Twas my good fortune to light on one expedient to rectify what was wanting in the regularity and probability of the tale, which was to run through the whole a love betwixt Edgar and Cordelia, that never changed words with each other in the original. This renders Cordelia's indifference and her father's passion in the first scene probable. It likewise gives countenance to Edgar's disguise, making that a generous design that was before a poor shift to save his life" (Nahum Tate, *The History of King Lear*, ed. James Black [Lincoln: University of Nebraska Press, 1975], 2).

23. Ibid., lines 126–160, pp. 94–95. Shershow nicely captures the tenor of Tate's dialogue: "The characters of this play are hardly moral agents at all: they are moralistic examples to adorn the stage. Thus the play, in effect, is *about* convincing the world that providence does prevail" ("'Higlety, Piglety, Right or Wrong,'" 24).

24. William Shakespeare, *King Lear*, ed. David Bevington (Toronto: Bantam Books, 1980), lines 329–332, p. 134.

25. For what follows concerning the history of the reception of Tate's version, I am indebted to Bevington's informative brief essay, "*King Lear* in Performance," op. cit., xxix-xxxvi.

26. Garrick's renown for returning to Shakespeare's version probably overstates the case. His 1756 production of *Lear*, for example, restored only ten lines from Shakespeare's production ("Shakespeare, Tate, and Garrick," ibid.)

27. Productions of Shakespeare's plays today cope with *Lear* in similar ways. See Gordon P. Jones, "Nahum Tate is Alive and Well: Elijah Moshinsky's BBC Shakespeare Productions," in Bulman, J.C., ed., *Shakespeare on Television: An Anthology of Essays and Reviews* (Hanover, NH: University Press of New England, 1988), 192–200. Doris Adler notes that many productions still adopt Tate's reordering of the scenes and emerge with a hybrid Cordelia who is part Shakespeare's tragic heroine and part Tate's romantic ingenue ("The Half-Life of Tate in *King Lear*," *Kenyon Review* 7 [1985], 52–56).

28. Nancy Klein Maguire offers a nuanced interpretation of the political purposes that informed Tate's revision; see "Nahum Tate's *King Lear*" in Jean Marsden, ed., *The Appropriation of Shakespeare: Post-Renaissance Reconstructions of the Works and the Myth* (New York: Harvester Wheatsheaf, 1991), 29–42.

29. Arthur Sherbo, ed., *Johnson on Shakespeare,* with an introduction by Bertrand H. Bronson, "The Yale Edition of the Works of Samuel Johnson" (New Haven: Yale University Press, 1968), 8:704.

30. Joan E. Klingel argues that, contrary to the received tradition, Johnson was not in fact inconsistent about his views concerning poetic justice: he simply cared about it when he cared about the characters and their fates, and otherwise did not concern himself with it ("Reconciling Johnson's Views on Poetic Justice," *Rocky Mountain Review of Language and Literature* 37 [1983], 195–205).

31. So Black, in his introduction, esp. xviii-xx, and Bevington, xxix-xxx.

32. Green, *Neo-Classic Theory,* usefully identifies the appeal of Tate's version while perhaps doing less than full justice to the capacities of Dr. Johnson and others to recognize the true horror of Shakespeare's tragedy. Tate's version, he writes, "observed poetic justice to the letter. It became a balm to the easily tortured feelings of the eighteenth century" (146).

33. Ibid.

34. Donald F. Bond, ed., *The Spectator,* with an introduction and notes by Donald F. Bond (Oxford: The Clarendon Press, 1965), 1:168–169.

35. Ibid., 1:170.

36. E. N. Hooker, ed., *The Critical Works of John Dennis* (Baltimore: Johns Hopkins University Press, 1939), vol. 2, 18–22.

37. Ibid., 20–21.

38. Ibid., 463–464.

39. Ibid., 465.

40. E. N. Hooker argues that the conflict is in fact chimerical: Dennis advocates simple distributive justice, punishing evil and rewarding good, but Dennis was interested in the moral effect of the tragedy where Aristotle was interested in the psychological. Such a separation of the psychological and the moral, however, was foreign to Addison; it is precisely the psychological effect of the tragedy which Addison catalogues in terms of its moral attributes. Both interested in the moral effects of the tragedy, Addison and Dennis differ in where emphasis ought to be placed: on the fact of evil in the present world (Addison), or on the fact of just desserts in the next (Dennis). In "The Argument on Poetic Justice (Addison *versus* Dennis)," *Indian Journal of English Studies* 3 (1962), 61–77, Amrik Singh regards the debate as a pseudo-argument because Dennis wants to reward the virtuous and punish the wicked, and Addison says little about this. The debate, however, is not about the fact of such rewards and punishments but their location in this world or the next. Like Singh, Richard Tyre ("Versions of Poetic Justice in the Early Eighteenth Century," *Studies in Philology* 54 [1957], 29–44) argues that as Christians Addison and Dennis share the same view of salvation history and thus saw poetic justice as divinely sanctioned. But this consensus could not resolve their disagreement about where to locate the providential moment, and the consequences—whether reassuring or misleading—for its location in the "tragic" denouement.

41. Cf. *The Spectator* no. 7, esp. the following: "I know but one way of fortifying my Soul against these gloomy Presages and Terrours of Mind, and that

is, by securing to my self the Friendship and Protection of that Being, who disposes of Events, and governs Futurity. He sees, at one View, the whole Thread of my Existence, not only that Part of it which I have already pass'd through, but that which runs forward into all the Depths of Eternity. When I lay me down to Sleep, I recommend my self to his Care; when I awake, I give my self up to his Direction. Amidst all the Evils that threaten me, I will look up to him for Help, and question not but he will either avert them, or turn them to my Advantage. Though I know neither the Time nor the Manner of the Death I am to die, I am not at all sollicitous about it, because I am sure that he knows them both, and that he will not fail to comfort and support me under them" (ibid., 34–35).

42. See, for example, *The Spectator* no. 293: "Those who believe a future State of Rewards and Punishments act very absurdly, if they form their Opinions of a Man's Merit from his Successes. But certainly, if I thought the whole circle of our Being was concluded between our Births and Deaths, I should think a Man's Good-Fortune the Measure and Standard of his real merit, since providence would have no Opportunity of rewarding his Vertue and Perfections, but in the present Life" (ibid., vol. 3, 43).

43. See, for example, no. 237: "In our present Condition, which is a middle State, our Minds are, as it were, chequered with Truth and Falsehood; and as our Faculties are narrow and our Views imperfect, it is impossible but our Curiosity must meet with many Repulses. The Business of Mankind in this Life being rather to act than to know, their Portion of Knowledge is dealt to them accordingly" (ibid., 421). And in the same number: " . . . it is to be consider'd that providence in its Oeconomy regards the Whole System of Time and Things together, so that we cannot discover the beautiful Connexions between Incidents which lye widely separated in Time, and by losing so many Links of the Chain, our Reasonings become broken and imperfect" (ibid., 422). This emphasis on the inherent uncertainty in moralizing on individual worldly fates as examples of direct providential interposition finds explicit expression in Addison as a kind of misplaced, overzealous form of poetic justice: "We cannot be guilty of a greater act of Uncharitableness, than to interpret the Afflictions which befall our Neighbors, as *Punishments* and *Judgments*. . . . The Folly of ascribing Temporal Judgments to any particular Crimes, may appear from several Considerations. I shall only mention two: First, that, generally speaking, there is no Calamity or Affliction, which is supposed to have happened, as a Judgment, to a vicious Man, which does not sometimes happen to Men of approved Religion and Virtue" (ibid., 211, 213).

44. Hooker, 148.

45. Ibid., 162.

46. See, for example, the following from "The Usefulness of the Stage, to the Happiness of Mankind, to Government, and to Religion" (1698): " . . . if the Stage were arriv'd to that Degree of Purity, to which in the Space of some little time it may easily be brought, the frequenting our Theatres would advance Religion, and, consequently, the Happiness of Mankind,

and so become a Part of the Christian Duty, which I shall demonstrate when I come to speak of Religion" (ibid., 162–163).

47. Ibid., 263. Dennis continues: "And as the True Religion must not only propound the Happiness of its Professors, but must really effect it; and as that alone is the True Religion, which makes the best Provision for the Happiness of those who profess it; so that must be the best and the noblest Art, which brings the greatest Felicity with it."

48. Samuel Richardson quotes *Spectator* no. 40 at length in his discussion of the denouement of *Clarissa*.

49. Gotthard Victor Lechler, *Geschichte des Englischen Deismus* (Stuttgart und Tübingen: J. G. Cottascher Verlag, 1841) and Sir Leslie Stephen, *History of English Thought in the Eighteenth Century* 2 vols. (New York: Peter Smith, 1949) have stood the test of time and remain useful for their proffered wealth of detail. Gerald R. Cragg offers a helpful synoptic overview in *The Church and the Age of Reason: 1648–1789* (New York: Penguin Books, 1970) and *Reason and Authority in the Eighteenth Century* (New York: Cambridge University Press, 1964). In *John Toland and the Deist Controversy: A Study in Adaptations* (Cambridge and London: Harvard University Press, 1982), Robert E. Sullivan eschews the panoramic for the particular: his chapter "The Elusiveness of Deism" offers a persuasive rationale for this approach, and a near-scathing critique of those who would generalize about deism. Two recent efforts offer generalizations about deism in the service of understanding its influence in subsequent religious thought: in *Natural Religion and the Nature of Religion: The Legacy of Deism* (London and New York: Routledge, 1989), Peter Byrne provides an overview of deism in England to suggest its enduring influence on theories of religion to the present, while Peter Harrison focuses on the emerging awareness of religious diversity, and the corresponding shift from sacred to natural history, in *'Religion' and the Religions in the English Enlightenment* (Cambridge, UK: Cambridge University Press, 1990).

50. *Toland and the Deist Controversy*, 233.

51. John Toland, *Christianity Not Mysterious*, Faksimile-Neudruck der Erstausgabe London 1696 mit einer Einleitung von Gunter Gawlick und einem textkritischen Anhang (Stuttgart-Bad Cannstatt: Friedrich Frommann Verlag [Gunther Holzboog], 1964). Stephen describes it as "the signal-gun which brought on the general action . . ." (*History of English Thought*, 105).

52. For the view that Locke's position was in fact genuinely distinct from that of Toland and Tindal, see Alan P. F. Sell, *John Locke and the Eighteenth-Century Divines* (Cardiff: University of Wales Press, 1997).

53. Sullivan establishes that Toland's larger project, of which *Christianity Not Mysterious* was only the first part, was to fashion an acceptable civil religion for eighteenth-century England. The project's success would, he hoped, lead to the preferment he (like Fielding) so ardently yet unsuccessfully cultivated throughout his life. The reaction to the book, however, effectively dashed its author's grand scheme: Toland's book was condemned by both the English and the Irish parliaments, and Toland himself was declared persona non grata in Ireland. *Christianity Not Mysterious* also inspired the new blasphemy

laws of 1697 (see Harrison, *'Religion' and the Religions in the English Enlightenment,* 87–88).

54. Sullivan, *Toland and the Deist Controversy,* 51. South's reputation as an authority on Christian belief almost equaled Tillotson's. Martin Battestin has decisively demonstrated Fielding's admiration for Tillotson, South, and especially Isaac Barrow, and has suggested ways in which their sermons figure in the novels; the most prominent example is, of course, Booth's conversion in *Amelia,* in which Booth discards his beloved classics for Barrow's sermons.

55. *Christianity Not Mysterious,* ix.

56. Ibid., xxx.

57. Ibid., 6.

58. Ibid., 20.

59. Ibid., 34–35.

60. On the relation of revelation and reason, " . . . revelation was a means of communication while reason provided the grounds of belief" (Harrison, *'Religion' and the Religions in the English Enlightenment,* 164).

61. Ibid., 43.

62. Ibid.

63. Ibid., 44. Stephen remarks: "Perhaps . . . it was pardonable in divines to look with a certain distrust upon a theory which contemplated the propriety of occasionally cross-examining an archangel" (*History of English Thought,* 107).

64. Ibid., 46. Toland's hermeneutic is hardly idiosyncratic; see, for example, the following from Thomas Morgan's *The Moral Philosopher* forty years later: "And this Effect the Miracles of Christ and the Apostles plainly had upon the People, to convince them that they were no Enemies to God, or their Country; and consequently, to dispose them to consider coolly and soberly, the Nature and Tendency of the Doctrines they had to propose to them, and not to take up implicitly with what the Priests and Rulers thought or said of it. . . . Miracles, therefore, are perhaps the most effectual Means of removing Prejudices and procuring Attention to what is deliver'd; but can never be taken for the proper Evidence or Proof of the Doctrines themselves, without quitting the only certain Mark or Criterion of divine Truth, and exposing ourselves to all the Enthusiasm and Imposture in the World" (Thomas Morgan, *The Moral Philosopher* [London: Routledge and Thoemmes, 1995], 98–99).

65. Ibid., 108.

66. Ibid., 64.

67. Ibid., 136–137.

68. While at least in principle friendlier to revelation, Fielding's Parson (Abraham) Adams in *Joseph Andrews* would appear to have read Toland with approval on this particular exegetical point. See chapter three for a discussion of Adams's sermon to Joseph on serenity in the face of (apparent) affliction.

69. Ibid., 176.

70. Thomas Morgan also invokes the triumvirate of deism, atheism, and Christianity in the service of a similar claim: " . . . the Question here, is not whether God governs the World by general Laws, but whether the World does not support and govern itself by certain inherent, essential Powers and

Properties in the Things themselves? And this, in Truth and Reality, is the Question between Deists and Atheists, and not between Christians and Deists, as has been foolishly and most absurdly supposed" (*The Moral Philosopher*, 185).

71. Matthew Tindal, *Christianity As Old As the Creation*, (Faksimile-Neudruck der Ausgabe London 1730), herausgegeben und eingeleitet von Gunter Gawlick (Stuttgart-Bad Cannstatt: Friedrich Frommann Verlag [Gunther Holzboog], 1967). To move from Toland to Tindal, of course, leaves undiscussed such writers as Wollaston and Clarke. While this selection risks a depiction of the deism controversy as neat and orderly when it was not, it is inevitable, and *Christianity as Old as the Creation* is indisputably among the most important texts of the controversy. For many students of deism, it marks the apex of deistic expression in England. "In 1730 appeared a book, which may be said to have marked the culminating point of the whole deist controversy" (Stephen, *History of English Thought*, 134). See also Byrne, *Natural Religion*, who argues persuasively that the "Tindal-like perspective" is in fact characteristic of deism. Craig, *The Church and the Age of Reason*, also moves in his account from Toland to Tindal, thus bypassing in chronology the writings of Wollaston and Clarke.

72. *Christianity As Old As the Creation* was described in some circles as "the Bible of the Deists" and eclipsed *Christianity Not Mysterious* as the principal object of attack in the controversy (Rupp, *Religion in England 1688–1791*, 267–268).

73. Ibid., iii-iv.

74. Ibid., 4.

75. Ibid., 5, 6.

76. Ibid., 20–21. Compare Thomas Morgan for an even more direct parallel to Smith: "Let our Moralist now look without him . . . and here on this Globe in which he lives, he will see an innumerable Family of Cretures raised up and provided for, by an unseen Hand . . ." (*The Moral Philosopher*, 422).

77. Ibid., 24. Cf. also the following, (ibid. 191): "If You allow, that Men by their reasoning faculties are made like unto God, and framed after his Image; and that Reason is the most excellent gift God can bestow; do they not destroy this Likeness, deface this Image, and give up the Dignity of human Nature, when they give up their Reason to any Person whatever?"

78. Ibid., 26.

79. Ibid., 28. Tindal cites, among others, Barrow and Tillotson to support this statement.

80. Ibid., 40, 44.

81. Ibid., 60. Harrison remarks that "Tindal's project, if passé, nonetheless represents another stage in the erosion of the exclusive claims of Christianity" ('Religion' and the Religions in the English Enlightenment, 167).

82. Ibid., 131. Tindal shares Toland's contempt for the view that posits church history as the source of true Christianity: "And what Disturbances have not your *Beckets, Lauds, &c.* created here, when they got into Power, and became then as insolent, as before they were submissive. . . . And before the happy

Revolution, the Spirit of Persecution was so outrageous, that *Protestants* ruined *Protestants* upon the Account of Rites, Ceremonies, Habits, *&c.* to the great Joy of the common Enemy" (ibid., 154–156).

83. Ibid., 196.

84. Ibid., 246. Tindal's suspicion about tradition and the external marks of Scripture would in at least one instance warm the hearts of feminist interpreters: "What other Reason can be assign'd, why . . . *Rom.* 16.I. is not rendered *Deaconess,* as well as elsewhere *Deacon;* but *Servant of the Church;* except it be to hinder the People from perceiving, that there was in the Days of the Apostles, an *Order of Women,* who had something more to do in the Church than to sweep it; and who, even at the Council of *Nice* (*Can.* 19) are reckon'd among the Clergy?" (ibid., 320).

85. Ibid., 338–339.

86. Ibid., p. 342: "I am so far from thinking the Maxims of *Confucius,* and Jesus Christ to differ; that I think the plain and simple Maxims of the former, will help to illustrate the more obscure Ones of the latter, accommodated to the then Way of speaking."

87. Ibid., 363.

88. Ibid., 384.

89. William Law, *The Case of Reason, or Natural Religion, Fairly and Fully Stated. In answer to a Book, entitled, Christianity as Old as the Creation* vol. 2 of *The Works of William Law* (London: Printed for J. Richardson, 1762 and reprinted for G. Moreton, 1892).

90. *The Case of Reason,* 66.

91. "Law continues and even extends the range of Boehme's polemic against what he called 'Babel', which for him arose out of his own bitter persecution by learned obscurantists. Reason for both men is part of fallen human nature, and becomes the text for a continuing onslaught by Law against Christian scholarship, Biblical critics and commentators, and all Christians who devote their energies to the study of the pagan classics" (*Religion in England 1688–1791,* 238).

92. *The Case of Reason,* 88.

93. Although how obdurate to Law is a nice question. It is a question, however, that Toland's account cannot easily raise. Fielding can and does raise it in *Joseph Andrews,* as discussed specifically in chapter three, and with attention to comparative implications in chapter five.

94. Ibid., 89.

95. Ibid., 99.

96. Ibid., 134.

97. Joseph Butler, *The Analogy of Religion Natural and Revealed to the Constitution and Course of Nature* (Hartford, CT: Samuel E. Goodrich, 1819).

98. "Butler . . . does not challenge the view that reason must be our final court of appeal. His strategy is rather to question whether that precludes anything new being disclosed by revelation. Tindal, the immediate object of Butler's attack, had excluded such a possibility" (David Brown, "Butler and Deism," in Cunliffe, ed., *Joseph Butler's Moral and Religious Thought,* 17).

99. John Vladimir Price provides a useful introduction to Morgan's life and work in *The Moral Philosopher*, v-xvii. J. Paul Hunter first brought Morgan to the attention of scholars of eighteenth-century literature in *Occasional Form: Henry Fielding and the Chains of Circumstance* (Baltimore: Johns Hopkins University Press, 1975), 101–104.
100. *The Moral Philosopher*, 198. Morgan subsequently characterizes this as "the first and great Principle of Christianity."
101. Martin Battestin suggests a connection between Hume and Fielding in "The Problem of *Amelia*: Hume, Barrow, and the Conversion of Captain Booth," *English Literary History* 41 (1974), 613–648.

Chapter 3

1. This general claim can be extended to Richardson's *Pamela* (1740) and *Clarissa* (1748), which also focus on issues of "virtue rewarded" (the subtitle of the former) and human malice.
2. I use the term "historian" to distinguish my interpretation from those that characterize Fielding's narrators as divine figures whose resolutions of his creations are themselves providential. Their number is legion. In addition to Booth as cited in chapter one, see, for example, Meir Sternberg, *Expositional Modes and Temporal Ordering in Fiction* (Baltimore: Johns Hopkins University Press, 1978), 266: " . . . the omnipotent narrator, replacing the supernatural agents of earlier fiction, will play Providence in the end . . ." Simon Varey collapses Fielding and his narrator to a similar end in writing about *Joseph Andrews* (*Henry Fielding* [New York: Cambridge University Press, 1986], 56–57): "As onlookers, we can see that the author . . . acts the part of Providence." Rebecca West also makes this claim for Fielding's narrators in *The Court and the Castle: A Study of the Interactions of Political and Religious Ideas in Imaginative Literature* (London: Macmillan & Co., 1958), 87: "Fielding's aim was to give an objective picture of his characters, a god's-eye view." Attribution of divinity seems to me clearly inaccurate, and suggests an unqualified endorsement of providence not to be found in the novels.
3. Christine van Boheemen argues that *Tom Jones* is a reworking of the Book of Genesis, a "plot of patriarchy" in which "Fielding tries to justify the ways of God to man, as well as to legitimize the natural presence of man as always already secretly related to God." She argues that Fielding ultimately fails because the task is untenable: the crucial point is that the unified image of the (male) self rests ultimately on the questionable orthodoxy concerning the unity of one God who is simultaneously all-good, all-knowing, and benevolent, yet not implicated by the fact of evil in His created order. While my own assessment is that Fielding's theological aims are in fact less Miltonic than van Boheemen suggests, her emphasis on the theological angle of Fielding's artistic vision leads her to very helpful insights regarding, for example, the character of Allworthy and the role of evil in the novel's resolution. See

The Novel as Family Romance: Language, Gender, and Authority from Fielding to Joyce (Ithaca: Cornell University Press, 1987), esp. 55 ff.

4. While the role and efficacy Fielding accords evil in *Joseph Andrews* and *Tom Jones* has received little explicit attention, what has been seen as the ambiguity of his affirmation has been widely discussed. J. Paul Hunter finds in Fielding's novels an author "between eras, a reactionary pioneer" whose writing reflects inconsistencies and uncertainties "related to retreating ontological certainties and the demands of time" (*Occasional Form*, xi, 7). Hunter's retreating certainties include religious but highlight political, sexual, and moral concerns. C. J. Rawson argues in *Henry Fielding and the Augustan Ideal Under Stress* (London: Routledge & Kegan Paul, 1972) that "even these more limited harmonies were felt to be under threat . . . disruptive pressures and radical insecurities became evident in some of the seemingly most confident, and some of the most conservative, writing of the period. It is this which I seek to convey . . . a sense of beleaguered harmony, of forms preserved under stress, of feelings of doom and human defeat ceremoniously rendered" (ix). In what follows I seek to suggest that these certainties can be at least partially identified by reading the novels as discussions of the contention of ideas about providence and the recognition of human evil. At the same time I hope to argue against the implication that Fielding was himself entirely chained by his circumstances.

5. This is not to deny that Fielding's narrators are manipulative. Indeed, much of Fielding's rhetorical skill resides in his capacity to have it both ways: to present a historical account, and then to suggest to the reader its uncertainties, ambiguities, and irresolutions. The phrase "so matters fell out" (later to be discussed with respect to the scene at Upton in *Tom Jones*) deserves equal weight with "I would not have the reader think" in any rendering of Fielding's artistry.

6. Henry Fielding, *The History of Tom Jones, A Foundling*, ed. Fredson Bowers, intro. Martin C. Battestin (Middletown, CT: Wesleyan University Press, 1975), 32.

7. J. Paul Hunter has argued persuasively against the political and aesthetic agendas that obscure Fielding's true purpose: "reader-response criticisms seem ultimately after larger game, preferring aesthetic, or sometimes political, concerns to issues involving basic and simple human needs to know about the world and to pursue that need in the reading of novels. But novels do minister to such simple, lowbrow needs, often openly. Part of Fielding's point is demonstrably to help his readers sharpen their judgment and refine their sense of how to read character through the careful observation of human conduct. The guidance provided by the narrator in *Tom Jones*, often in ironic or otherwise indirect ways but nevertheless always firmly toward a systematic examination of how the faculty of judgment works, offers the reader practical experience in epistemology" ("Novels and 'the Novel': The Poetics of Embarrassment," *Modern Philology* 86 [May 1988], 495).

8. Martha C. Nussbaum, in *The Fragility of Goodness: Luck and Ethics in Greek Tragedy and Philosophy* (Cambridge, MA: Cambridge University Press, 1986), herself suggests the parallel in setting out the interests she aims to pursue: "There are of course several other post-classical views that would significantly affect the appreciation of these questions: for example Stoic and Christian views concerning divine providence and Christian views concerning the relationship between human goodness and divine grace" (4).

9. Henry Fielding, *Joseph Andrews*, ed. Martin C. Battestin, intro. Fredson Bowers (Middletown, CT: Wesleyan University Press, 1967), 168.

10. Ibid., 235.

11. Ibid., 246.

12. Ibid., 280.

13. Ibid., 289.

14. Ibid., 344.

15. Ibid., 48.

16. Ibid., 68.

17. Ibid., 271.

18. Ibid., 291.

19. Charles A. Knight usefully discusses religious and political limits of the narrator's authority in *"Joseph Andrews* and the Failure of Authority," *Eighteenth-Century Fiction* 4 (1992), 109–124.

20. Carl A. Kropf argues that Fielding's style in *Joseph Andrews* is heteroglossic and "therefore harbors conflicting value systems" best seen through the interpolated tales that reflect in microcosm the more general tendencies of the narrative voices that tell the central story of Joseph, Fanny, and Adams ("Dialogical Engagement in *Joseph Andrews* and the Community of Narrative Agencies," in Kevin L. Cope, ed., *Compendious Conversations: The Method of Dialogue in the Early Enlightenment* [Frankfurt: Peter Lang, 1992], 206–217, esp. 211 ff). For a different understanding of Bakhtin's theory of narrative voice and the function of heteroglossia, see Gary Saul Morson, *Narrative and Freedom: The Shadows of Time* (New Haven: Yale University Press, 1994). Jeffrey M. Perl's earlier argument, in "Anagogic Surfaces: How to Read *Joseph Andrews*," (*The Eighteenth Century: Theory and Interpretation* 22 [1981], 249–270), argues that *Joseph Andrews* is a boy-loves-girl story written ironically to destroy cultural accretions, traced to Richardson, which would tend to make the story something else. It is thus explicitly constructed to avoid the sort of heteroglossic disparity Kropf advocates; Perl maintains that the novel resists criticism precisely because its meaning is so thoroughly on the surface, and is not usually appreciated by approaches that privilege depth. The narrator of *Joseph Andrews*, Perl writes, shows "a preference for the theodicean implications of comedy" (265).

21. *Joseph Andrews*, 48.

22. Robert Alter nicely captures the kinds of judgment entailed in reading Fielding, although he does not emphasize the language of sagacity and discernment. See *Fielding and the Nature of the Novel*, esp. 21 ff.

23. Richard Dircks presents the alternative view in *Henry Fielding* (Boston: Twayne Publishers, 1983), when he argues that the characters in *Joseph Andrews* are "distortions of reality as the ordinary reader would perceive the world" (64).

24. At times, of course, the narrator acknowledges the limits of readerly sagacity and simply asserts that something is the case. One example is the brief digression on the way that Parson Adams and *Joseph Andrews* play Alphonse and Gaston concerning who will walk, and who ride, to their next destination (ibid., 272–273). Even here, however, the narrator takes pains to juxtapose *judgments* of the scene: those who would regard it as deference masking desire, and the (much rarer) assessment that the two parties were earnest in their deferral to each other. The narrator resolves the matter by fiat (Joseph and Adams really are as good-natured as the narrator alleges!), but even in doing so stresses the issue as one of discerning underlying motive.

25. Iser remarks that "The very character who is possessed of the highest degree of integrity is devoid of the faculty emphasized in Fielding's preface as the intention of the novel: seeing through hypocrisy" (*Implied Reader,* 43).

26. Adams most closely approximates Voltaire's Pangloss, yet the distance between the two remains considerable because Adams is the epitome of the good-natured human being, and proves it regularly by active physical intervention. However significant, even his most obdurate failings do not alienate him from the reader, and he cannot be made the butt of sustained satire.

27. Ibid., 176–177.

28. Adams's defenders cite his good nature as the source of his difficulties. James J. Lynch argues that "Adams is not insane; his idealism is not based on a misperception of the real world, but on a belief that people are better than they act" (*Henry Fielding and the Heliodoran Novel* [Cranbury, NJ: Associated University Presses, 1986], 65). In a novel so devoted to accurate perception, however, such a belief is manifestly a source of misperception and hardly an excuse: Adams assumes people are better than they act, so he decisively misperceives the world. Richard Dircks argues that "Adams is victimized not so much by his lack of awareness, as by his giving the benefit of the doubt to others. He offers the open hand of friendship, and, if it is accepted, as it often is, he acts with the charitable humility proper to his role as a parson. When it is rejected, he reacts with an exaggerated dignity and excusable vanity. In the eyes of the worldly pragmatist he is a comic figure and the butt of malicious humor; but such vulnerability is inevitable for the man of the cloth who cannot accept cynical protective devices that might shield him from insult" (*Henry Fielding,* 51). This has the effect of distancing too much the reader's reaction from the narrator's: both are surely closer to "worldly pragmatism," and hence to some criticism of Adams, than Dircks here suggests. Simon Varey argues that Adams is the repository of "almost all the positive values of the novel" and a source of instruction to the reader in his opposition to the vices that Fielding seeks to expose. If Adams were effective in his obstruction, this would be persuasive; in fact, his actions are most successful in obstructing the marriage of Joseph and Fanny, the highest good the novel presents.

29. Ibid., 308–310.

30. Wolfgang Iser sees in the scene an invitation to look inside the Parson: "When, toward the end of the novel, Adams holds in his arms the son whom he had presumed to be drowned, his overwhelming joy causes him to forget the virtues of moderation and self-control that he has always preached . . . The reader is shown the event and the outer appearance, but he is invited, almost exhorted, to penetrate behind that appearance, and finally to thrust it aside altogether, by conceiving the idea *within*. This is an almost direct statement of the role of the reader in this novel. From the given material he must construct his own conception of the reality and hence of the meaning of the text" (*Implied Reader*, 40). In my judgment, arrangement and language play a far stronger role in determining the reader's appropriate response.

31. The extensive commentary on this scene is largely devoted to the defense of Adams. Martin Battestin, in *The Moral Basis of Fielding's Art*, comments: " . . . though the impractical side of his Christian stoicism is amusingly revealed in the episode of his son's 'drowning' (IV, 8), Adams' inability to follow his own advice on this occasion only sharpens our awareness of his compassionate nature" (108–109). As I have tried to show, however, the compassion here emerges precisely at the expense of the sermon's message, and can only qualify our sense that Adams's pontifications serve as the center of the novel's moral universe. Often defenses describe Adams as a holy fool. In "The World According to Paul: Comedy and Theology in *Joseph Andrews*," (*Ariel* 15 [1984], 45–56), James E. Evans argues that Adams's behavior to Joseph is "forgivable" because "it results from teaching the ways of God that he is too imperfect to practice completely" (53). K. J. H. Berland claims that "Adams demonstrates that the deceitful, self-aggrandizing, thriving way of life and pursuit of immediate pleasure is not successful on its own terms" ("Satire and the *Via Media:* Anglican Dialogue in *Joseph Andrews*," in John D. Browning, ed., *Satire in the Eighteenth Century* [New York: Garland, 1983], 98). Mitchell Kalpakgian is of two minds about Adams: he is at one point the apparent fool who is in fact wise, and at another the possessor of "naive beliefs" who practices "fideistic religion" (*The Marvellous in Fielding's Novels*, 36, 153). C. J. Rawson contends that "The character of Adams . . . defines the moral outlook of the book. The *comedy* of Adams's eccentricity does not diminish this, but, if anything, enriches it: it is not a dismissive comedy, but a comedy of warm sympathetic endorsement" (*Henry Fielding* [New York: Humanities Press, 1968], 5). Two points about Rawson's contention merit comment. The terms in which he assesses Adams—comedy, eccentricity, warmth, sympathy, endorsement—seem to me correct. The claim, however, that Adams defines the moral outlook of *Joseph Andrews* displaces the center of sensibility from the narrator to a character, and renders it far less stable than it actually is. Adams is too often at odds with himself to function as the novel's moral center.

32. For a brilliant exposition of Joseph in counterpoint, see Campbell, *Natural Masques*, 109–117.

33. While the passage shows Parson Adams to real disadvantage, it is not the case, as Simon Varey claims, that his message is simply displaced onto the narrator (in a kind of inversion of Rawson's perspective): "There is no divine interposition; all that is needed to 'save' Adams is to tell him that the first report was false, to disclose the right information. This is not Providence's function, but the author's. By being omniscient and also omnipotent as the controller of the fiction, the author is the instrument of Providence for his characters" (*Henry Fielding,* 57–58).

34. Against the claim that Adams's contradictions are enduring and irresolvable, and actually point to a synthesis of passion and reason, see Aaron Schneider, "Hearts and Minds in *Joseph Andrews:* Parson Adams and a War of Ideas," *Philological Quarterly* 66 (1987), 367–389.

35. Robert Alter remarks that "the whole passage ought to be compared with an earlier one—here again Fielding must be read backward as well as forward— in which Adams and Joseph are tied back to back, unable to extricate themselves, while Fanny is being hurried to the malicious squire's house by his henchmen to submit to his sexual pleasure (III, ii). Joseph of course is in agony, and Parson Adams tries to bring him to a sense of his duty to accept with equanimity the just decrees of Providence. . . . Especially in the light of Adams' subsequent failure to take physic himself in the needed hour, the high homiletic tone he adopts here toward Joseph, for all the piety and even benevolence of its motives, looks peculiarly unfeeling: it is a rare moment when Adams is less than attractive, his pious principle cutting him off from empathy with his young friend" (*Fielding and the Nature of the Novel,* 83). This is exactly right, although the scene serves as dramatic confirmation of what sagacious readers like Alter already suspect to be the case.

36. James Lynch asserts the contrary: "It is through Parson Adams that Fielding advances the principal theme of the novel: that Christian benevolence emanates from the integrity of a good-natured heart, even though that goodness often seems out of place in the world" (*Henry Fielding and the Heliodoran Novel,* 65).

37. Wolfgang Iser interprets Adams as a quixotic counterhero whose idealism blinds him to the world, but he places the onus for sorting out the claims of Adams's idealism and its alternative, "worldly-wise" cynicism, entirely on the shoulders of the reader: "The reader . . . must apply the author's remark to his novel, but the text will not tell him how to do this. The application will coincide largely with the realization" (*The Implied Reader,* 35). I concur with Iser's description of the reader's problem but suggest that Fielding's narrator clearly offers a solution.

38. Glenn Hatfeld nicely captures the sense of the ending of *Joseph Andrews,* though not in these terms: "In *Joseph Andrews* it is precisely this comfortable doctrine of 'Virtue Rewarded' (as Richardson's subtitle to *Pamela* has it) that provides Fielding with an ironic point of departure for a thoroughgoing redefinition of the word 'virtue.' Not only is Joseph *not* rewarded for the same kind of virtue which had made Pamela's fortune: he positively suffers as a result of

it; and the pointed artificiality of the novel's happy ending, far from being a flaw, drives home the moral that there is no necessary cause-and-effect connection between virtue and worldly happiness or prosperity" (*Henry Fielding and the Language of Irony* [Chicago: The University of Chicago Press, 1968], 173).

39. In this respect, then, the cumulative effect of the religious sensibility in *Joseph Andrews* does not encourage submission to the status quo, and does not simply reinforce social standards. For the opposing view, see Brian McCrea, "Rewriting *Pamela:* Social Change and Religious Faith in *Joseph Andrews,*" *Studies in the Novel* 16 (1984), 137–149.

40. I agree with Robert Alter on this point: "Broadly speaking, one may say that virtually everything realized in the art of *Tom Jones* is at least implicit in *Joseph Andrews,* is sometimes merely a simple variation of principles first developed in the earlier novel" (*Fielding and the Nature of the Novel,* ix). So also A. Digeon: "*Tom Jones* resumes the great road of *Joseph Andrews,* and this time Fielding's genius carries him as far along it as he can go" (*The Novels of Fielding* [New York: E. P. Dutton & Co., 1925], 130).

41. No one disputes the judgment that Fielding's narrative voice achieves its richest tenor in *Tom Jones,* yet no one gives the structural complement of this judgment, the introductory chapters, sustained critical attention. R. S. Crane ignores them (and indeed all the authorial commentary in *Tom Jones!*) in his famous discussion of Fielding's plot ("The Plot of *Tom Jones,*" in *Henry Fielding, Tom Jones,* ed. Sheridan Baker [New York: W.W. Norton, 1973], 844–869). Those who acknowledge them do so in a general way that endorses vaguely while begging questions about implication. J. Paul Hunter traces in Fielding a double consciousness about such chapters in general as both necessary and absurd, but does not examine them in *Tom Jones* in any detail (*Occasional Form,* 34). Ronald Paulson restricts the utility of the commentary: "Fielding shows less interest in his commentators as attitudes or points of view than simply as devices for establishing the objective meaning of an action" (*Satire and the Novel in Eighteenth-Century England* [New Haven: Yale University Press, 1967], 95). C. J. Rawson notes that these chapters "contribute massively towards the establishing of this authorial 'presence'. But this presence serves to establish a highly-charged intimacy with the action, but a firm and decorous distance. Fielding's many ironic inflections, his mock-heroic procedures, and the rest, contribute a deliberate atmosphere of aloofness and authority. Things are not allowed to become unduly emotional, although we often know that Fielding feels very strongly indeed" (*Henry Fielding,* 7). In reaction partly to reader-response interpretations, some recent work has reasserted the narrator's aggressive didacticism in *Tom Jones.* In addition to Hudson, "Fielding's Hierarchy of Dialogue," see James J. Lynch, "Moral Sense and the Narrator of *Tom Jones,*" *Studies in English Literature* 25 (1985), 599–614; and Robert L. Chibka, "Taking 'The Serious' Seriously: The Introductory Chapters of *Tom Jones,*" *The Eighteenth Century: Theory and Interpretation* 31 (1990), 23–45.

42. J. Paul Hunter remarks that "it is useful to know that real deists and theologians spoke and fought like Square and Thwackum," and argues for historical models for the two: Square was modeled on Thomas Chubb, and Thwackum on Joseph Horder (*Occasional Form,* 129). Digeon notes the parallel between the debates of Square and Thwackum and the deism controversy: " . . . he nails theologian and deist to the same pillory. . . . In *Tom Jones* the hardest blows seem to be reserved for the deist Square, but his enemy is not spared. On either side of Squire Allworthy, each appears as a pendant to the other, a little after the manner of Pangloss and Martin in *Candide;* and on every occasion they give opposite justifications for the same pharisaical morality" (*The Novels of Fielding,* 152).

43. Lance St. John Butler, in "Fielding and Shaftesbury Reconsidered: The Case of *Tom Jones,*" in K. G. Simpson, ed., *Henry Fielding: Justice Observ*ed (London and Totowa, NJ: Barnes & Noble, 1985), 56–74, nicely captures the effect of Allworthy's rationale on the reader: "One might guy Shaftesbury by aligning him with Square, but only at the expense of guying Christianity by aligning it with Thwackum" (65–66).

44. *Tom Jones,* 127.

45. The favored opprobrium to heap upon a deist was to suggest the affinity of such thought (not to say its identity) with atheism. See Sullivan, *Toland and the Deism Controversy,* and the distinction of Leslie Stephen between "deism" and "constructive deism." When they invoked natural religion and reason, Toland and Tindal were understood to favor ancient Greek thought, which their opponents placed in opposition to Christianity.

46. Sullivan usefully discusses the role of preferment in Toland's decisions to write, with particular reference to his relationship to John Locke.

47. Ibid., 128–129. Nicholas Hudson argues that the function of the Square-Thwackum debates "is only apparently to invite self-reflective judgment; their true function is to deploy the *delusion* of self-reflection" ("Fielding's Hierarchy of Dialogue: 'Meta-Response' and the Reader of *Tom Jones,*" *Philological Quarterly* 68 [1989], 177–194), 180. Here, at least, Hudson's useful general point—to reestablish the didacticism of Fielding's narrator against the tendency of reader-response critics, who can imply that the reader straightforwardly wins that wrestling match—seems to me to lead to overstatement. In this passage, the narrator's judgment is nuanced and elicits, even demands, further reflection by the reader.

48. Ibid., 651–652.

49. John Preston argues that the farcical sequences of events are meant to demonstrate that fortune rules the human condition, so that the "great, useful, and uncommon Doctrine" consists in the "absurdity of trying to adjust our behavior to a system of cause and effect" (*The Created Self,* 107). While fortune plays its role and traditional systems have limited purview, this would render the narrative commentary in large part superfluous.

50. In *The Art of Telling* (Cambridge: Harvard University Press, 1983), 26.

51. Ibid., 271.

52. On didacticism in eighteenth-century fiction and its progenitor literary forms, and the disjunction between didactic sensibilities and those of the present day, see J. Paul Hunter, *Before Novels: The Cultural Contexts of Eighteenth-Century English Fiction* (New York: W.W. Norton & Co., 1990), esp. 226 ff.

53. Henry Knight Miller argues that the claim to exterior reference is nugatory: "Whether we happen, outside the world of the narrative, to 'believe' in his order is very nearly irrelevant. But having engaged in a contract to believe in his fictional world, we discover through the author not only that his cosmos is comic; of equal significance is the fact that the author assures us of an ideal order of existence—without which the comic action could be merely farcical or grotesque" ("Some Functions of Rhetoric in *Tom Jones*," *Philological Quarterly* 45 [January 1966], 232). Hudson, "Fielding's Hierarchy of Dialogue," argues that this passage "ingeniously attribute(s) to the subjectivity of the reader what has in fact been produced through rhetorical manipulation . . ." (180). I argue, to the contrary, that Fielding is at his most explicitly and concretely referential in this passage: he means quite literally that the reader who lacks this experience of life will not be able to understand the action of *Tom Jones,* and he means to encourage precisely the sort of self-reflection that is, of necessity, independent of rhetorical manipulation.

54. Bernard Harrison, in *Henry Fielding's "Tom Jones": The Novelist as Moral Philosopher* (London: Chatto & Windus, 1975), argues, in the course of presenting his constructive case for Fielding's moral position, both for and against such privileged perspective. On the one hand, no viewpoint can be privileged in a novel so much of which is devoted to documenting shifting perspectives on the same scene (paradigmatically, that of the lost bird in Book IV). On the other, in the introductory chapter just discussed "Fielding was . . . quite serious . . . he was writing only for the reader who could read *Tom Jones* as a complex dramatic demonstration of a theoretical outlook in morals" (101). Harrison also stresses the critical role of authorial omniscience to the privileged viewpoint which allows us to know the facts, and to read assured that they are relevant. I prefer Harrison's reading to the alternative moral interpretation offered by Battestin—a strong denunciatory mode that makes deism the villain and providence the world's bulwark against evil. Both, however, must find ways to account for a narrator who, for all his moral concerns, primarily explores what can and cannot be claimed for divine governance of the world.

55. Ibid., 135.

56. Van Boheemen argues that Allworthy is benevolent patriarchy incarnate. In a sweet inversion of Battestin's famous essay on Sophia Western, she describes Allworthy as "the emblem of the idea of patriarchy": "The dubious duplicity of Allworthy's character is the effect of a structural necessity. In depicting origin as singular, self-identical, and benevolent, Fielding runs into the same problem that has baffled Christian theologians" (*The Novel as Family Romance,* 90–91). I demur in two respects. He is gullible, but not du-

plicitous. Also, this view assumes that *Tom Jones* possesses no perspective on Allworthy; van Boheemen presents him as the icon of virtue, while I would argue that his limitations are not the result of orthodox theological fissures, but of Fielding's strong sense that even people endowed with the best of nature and fortune can be and sometimes are misled. The narrator offers nothing like an endorsement of his handling of affairs.

57. Harrison aptly remarks: "Although Allworthy's goodness has something of the infuriating quality of Houyhnhnm goodness about it, it is still undoubtedly goodness" (68). Sheldon Sacks summarizes Allworthy's problem with the hermetic (but accurate) remark that he never read *Tom Jones* (*Fiction and the Shape of Belief: A Study of Henry Fielding with Glances at Swift, Johnson and Richardson* [Berkeley: University of California Press, 1964], 114).

58. Battestin's view is most powerfully presented in *The Providence of Wit* 176 ff. For two critiques of Battestin's interpretation on this point, see Frederick G. Ribble, "Aristotle and the 'Prudence' Theme of *Tom Jones*," *Eighteenth-Century Studies* 15 (1981), 26–47; and Hudson, "Fielding's Hierarchy of Dialogue."

59. *Tom Jones*, 395.

60. See Battestin's helpful discussion in the notes to *The History of Tom Jones, A Foundling*, pp. 395 ff.

61. Ibid., 401–2.

62. Ibid., 407.

63. J. Paul Hunter identifies Fielding's discussion of the marvelous as one of three traits of eighteenth-century novels that embarrass modern critics who operate from post-Jamesian assumptions ("Novels and 'the Novel,'" 481 ff.). The novel that features the marvelous, Hunter argues, presents a world in which "the fine line of likelihood is everywhere walked precariously," and where coincidences reign that no reader would wish to have to depend on in real life. At the same time, "There are no supernatural agents in Fielding (if we except Fielding himself), and no actual violations of nature's steady and discoverable laws" (482). Hunter concludes that "Fielding has it both ways: he is a faithful historian of the world of everyday reality which is governed by predictable laws, but he also loves the sense that life is made interesting and significant by unexpected events that are surprising and wonderful" (481). This captures Fielding's genuine ambiguities about providence, but providence in *Tom Jones* claims more than authorship of the unexpected, surprising, and wonderful: it is the agent of happiness that is beyond strict human causation.

64. Ibid., 783.

65. Ibid., 784.

66. Ibid., 916.

67. The evocation of the incest theme, while ultimately satirical, does underscore certain natural affinities between Sophocles's use of fate and Fielding's use of providence, and between the usage of the chorus to divulge the workings of fate in Greek tragedy and Fielding's use of the narrator's discursive prefaces. I am indebted to Eric Ziolkowski for this observation.

68. Ibid., 920.
69. Ibid., 924.
70. Ibid., 933.
71. Harrison nicely captures the tenor of the conclusion, but slights the possibility of providential attribution: "... the deliberate theatrical implausibility of the happy ending drives it home: in real life, we are to understand, Blifil and not Tom would have ended as master of Paradise Hall and of Sophia" (38); "Fielding wishes us, while rejoicing at Tom's success, to be uncomfortably conscious of the fact that he owes it to the Providence which reigns over comedy: that in real life Blifil would have ended as master of Paradise Hall and husband and gaoler of Sophia" (122).
72. Ibid., 947.
73. For a discussion of the parallel theme in Cervantes's *Don Quixote,* where the discrepancies between fortune and providence become the subject of dialogue between knight and squire as the novel moves toward its conclusion, see Eric J. Ziolkowski, "Don Quijote's Windmill and the Wheel of Fortune," *The Modern Language Review* 86 (1991), 885–897. A great admirer of Cervantes, Fielding's subtitle for *Joseph Andrews* was "Written in Imitation of Cervantes."

Chapter 4

1. In addition to the works cited in chapter one, see Peter Sabor, "*Amelia* and *Sir Charles Grandison:* The Convergence of Fielding and Richardson," *Wascana Review* 17 (Fall 1982), 3–18, and Margaret Lenta, "Comedy, Tragedy, and Feminism: The Novels of Richardson and Fielding," *English Studies in Africa* 26 (1983), 13–25.
2. Sabor, "*Amelia* and *Sir Charles Grandison,*" 12.
3. Some contend that the virtue of *Amelia* is precisely its more barefaced assertion of "the Christian message." James A. Work understands *Amelia* as simply the blunt expression of Fielding's lifelong religious commitments: "... by the time he wrote *Amelia* Fielding felt that his readers needed stronger medicine than mere benevolence, so he gave them a conversion and Dr. Harrison on the hope and fear of heaven and hell" ("Henry Fielding, Christian Censor," in Frederick W. Hilles, ed., *The Age of Johnson: Essays Presented to Chauncey Brewster Tinker* [New Haven: Yale University Press, 1949], 147). Richard Dircks carries forward this viewpoint when he argues that *Amelia* differs from the earlier novels only to the degree that Fielding's own Christian resolve was firmer when he wrote it (*Henry Fielding* [Boston: Twayne Publishers, 1983], 118). While I seek to highlight the theological continuities shared by the novels, both the substance and the implication of my position differ from Work and Dircks: I argue that *Amelia* modifies rather than completes a traditional Christian affirmation of providence, and that its displacement of providence from this world to the next is recognizably a strain in the senses of the endings *Joseph Andrews* and *Tom Jones* that easily goes unrecognized apart from a reading of the youngest sibling.

4. Henry Fielding, *Amelia*, ed. Martin C. Battestin, with a textual introduction by Fredson Bowers (Middletown, CT: Wesleyan University Press, 1983), 15.

5. Alter suggests that this involves a shift of epic antecedents: where *Joseph Andrews* and *Tom Jones* draw on Homer's *Odyssey* and so stress the comic rendering of the arduous voyage, *Amelia* turns instead to Virgil's *Aeneid* and so stresses the rendering of duty (*Fielding and the Nature of the Novel,* 142).

6. Donald Fraser, "Lying and Concealment in *Amelia,*" in K. G. Simpson, ed., *Henry Fielding: Justice Observed* (London and Totowa, NJ: Barnes & Noble, 1985), 174–198.

7. J. Paul Hunter in *Occasional Form,* 209.

8. Henry Fielding, *Amelia.* Edited by Martin Battestin, with a textual introduction by Fredson Bowers (Middletown, CT: Wesleyan University Press, 1983), 46–47.

9. Ibid., 170.

10. Ibid., 208.

11. The portrait of Mrs. James renders impossible "a confident and coherent picture of [her] character," Campbell argues, and underscores the unsteadiness of the narrator. But this implies an omniscience in the earlier narrators that is not there. It seems to me at least as plausible to suggest that Mrs. James lives so thoroughly in the thrall of her circumstances that her behavior takes its bearings from what is to her present advantage. The narrator's shifting commentary documents this fact, rather than his own unsteadiness. Campbell evinces much more comfort with Booth's vacillation between past and future masculine roles (213), but these seem if anything more contradictory than Mrs. James's consistent self-interest.

12. Ibid., 342–343.

13. Several of Fielding's best readers would seem to disagree, but their observations on this dimension of *Amelia* clearly measure the novel in terms of *Tom Jones.* Alter regards the shift from narrator to character as symptomatic of "this whole didactic weakness in *Amelia,*" which results in "a damaging effect on some of the characterization, particularly in the two exemplary figures of the novel, Dr. Harrison and Amelia" (*Fielding and the Nature of the Novel,* 161). For Rawson and Hunter it underscores the sheer difficulty of human action in the world of the novel. Rawson writes, "For the characters in *Amelia* [the 'art of life'] is hard, uphill work, often unsupported by displays of authorial confidence. The author is now a subdued presence . . ." (*The Augustan Ideal Under Stress,* 131). Hunter remarks that Fielding's portrayal of powerlessness "achieves at times a certain claustrophobic, smothering sense of frustration, panic, and doom," and that " . . . its portrait of virtue rewarded suggests a real trial" (*Occasional Form,* 195).

14. Spacks argues that, as a creation of the male fantasy for stable female characters, Amelia is only allowed utter fealty to her husband: "Fielding, characterizing his heroine by her total dedication to her husband, frees her from profound conflict" ("Female Changelessness," 279). In the course of the novel, however, Amelia doubts her husband and her faith, and bitterly

laments her circumstances. The portrait is not merely or simply idealized: Amelia is heroic, but her suffering has real dimension. Her saintliness is complex: there is, for example, a real, if not fully developed, distinction between her being and her acting in the novel.

15. Ibid., 166–167.
16. Ibid., 167.
17. Battestin, "The Problem of *Amelia*," regards this as Amelia's intuitive recognition of Booth's theory that the passions rule our behavior, and concludes that "Amelia herself is the embodiment of the ethical system in the novel" (640). This seems, however, to invest one character in *Amelia* with moral authority, when in fact Fielding's last novel differs from its predecessors precisely in its insistence on the playing out of alternative, at times even contradictory views. On this point Rawson nicely captures the effect of Amelia's expostulations for the novel as a whole: "There is more pressing conviction in those recurrent exclamations of Amelia . . . than in any ultimate resolution of her troubles. This is true even though Amelia's statements are either qualified in context, or known by the reader to rest partly on an inaccurate analysis of the situation, because the grinding actuality of the Booths' predicament overwhelms finer discriminations" (*Augustan Ideal Under Stress*, 70–71).
18. Ibid., 307.
19. Ibid., 316.
20. Ibid., 316. Rawson describes the "pained recoil" of *Amelia*'s narrator in such scenes, and the cumulative sense, both in Amelia's pronouncements and in the narrator's hand-wringing over what to say, of a "violated faith in the fitnesses of an ordered world" (*Augustan Ideal Under Stress*, 75).
21. Ibid., 490–491.
22. The character in *Amelia* who most closely parallels Allworthy, that is, who marries native virtue with fortune, is Colonel James. This is itself a telling barometer for the distance Fielding has traveled in his decisions about how to depict the world to the best advantage for his meaning.
23. Ibid., 100–101.
24. Ibid., 136–137.
25. Ibid., 139.
26. One example among many of Amelia's adoption of Harrison's attitude is this statement, from one of her discussions with Mrs. Ellison on Amelia's superiority to her husband: "'Alas! my dear Mrs. *Ellison*,' answered *Amelia*, 'do you think Happiness and a Crown so closely united? How many miserable Women have lain in the Arms of Kings?—Indeed, Mrs. *Ellison*, if I had all the Merit you compliment me with, I should think it all fully rewarded with such a Man as I thank Heaven hath fallen to my Lot; nor would I, upon my Soul, exchange that Lot with any queen in the Universe'" (ibid., 239).
27. Ibid., 376–377.
28. Ibid., 372.
29. Ibid., 517.

30. Ibid., 522.
31. Ibid., 528.
32. Claims that Harrison is Fielding's spokesman in the novel range from Battestin, "The Problem of *Amelia*," and Dircks, *Henry Fielding*, to Scheuermann, "Man Not Providence," and Osland, "Fielding's *Amelia:* Problem Child or Problem Reader?"
33. Martin Battestin sees these conflicts unresolved because he reads the presence of providence and its human analogue prudence in the earlier novels much more strongly and unambiguously. In my judgment, the seeds of *Amelia* are sown precisely in the ending of *Tom Jones*. Campbell in *Natural Masques* (228) also ultimately sees disjunction, but she distinguishes her work from Battestin by its emphasis on the connection between problems in narration and changing social structures of class and gender. Yet in the end she must highlight Booth's conversion to an "unconflicted" Christianity via his discarding of the classics for Barrow's sermons—a nice irony that underscores the pervasively theological nature of the novels.

Chapter 5

1. In this respect Fielding is the practitioner par excellence of Mikhail Bakhtin's theory that the novel absorbs and assimilates other genres. See *The Dialogical Imagination,* ed. Michael Holquist, trans. Caryl Emerson and Michael Holquist (Austin: University of Texas Press, 1981), especially chapter one, "Epic and Novel." Fielding figures somewhat prominently in Bakhtin's typologized lists, once in the service of a claim that would appear to be at odds with my argument (on *Tom Jones* and Richardson's introduction of "an alien force" into "the classic family novel," 232). These are brief and unelaborated, however, and Fielding is decidedly a Bakhtinian literary figure.
2. Fielding's ideal reader would not be William Law, who to the best of my knowledge stands alone among eighteenth-century writers in betraying no misgivings about such apparently deleterious divine interpositions. Turning directly to Genesis 22 in *The Case Against Reason* to argue that faithful obedience is in fact a suprarational proposition, Law coolly observes that we shall all die when God ordains it, and argues that this fact of life's ending overwhelms consideration of the means. The instance of God's directive to Abraham is thus neither more nor less than yet another, albeit more explicit, declaration of a common divine activity.
3. The phrase is Wayne Booth's (*The Rhetoric of Fiction,* 217).

Bibliography

Abrams, M. H. *A Glossary of Literary Terms*. 3rd ed. New York: Holt, Rinehart & Winston, 1971.

———. *The Mirror and the Lamp: Romantic Theory and the Critical Tradition*. New York: Oxford University Press, 1953.

Adler, Doris. "The Half-Life of Tate in *King Lear*." *Kenyon Review* 7 (1985): 52–56.

Alter, Robert. *Fielding and the Nature of the Novel*. Cambridge: Harvard University Press, 1968.

Augustine, *Confessions*. Trans. by Henry Chadwick. New York: Oxford University Press, 1991.

Battestin, Martin. *The Moral Basis of Fielding's Art*. Middletown, CT: Wesleyan University Press, 1959.

———. "The Problem of *Amelia:* Hume, Barrow, and the Conversion of Captain Booth." *English Literary History* 41 (1974): 613–648.

———. *The Providence of Wit: Aspects of Form in Augustan Literature and the Arts*. Oxford: Clarendon Press, 1974.

Beardslee, John W. *Reformed Dogmatics*. Grand Rapids, MI: Baker Book House, 1977.

Bond, Donald F., ed. *The Spectator*. With an introduction and notes by Donald F. Bond. Oxford: Clarendon Press, 1965.

Booth, Wayne. *The Rhetoric of Fiction*. 2nd ed. Chicago: University of Chicago Press, 1983.

Braudy, Leo. *Narrative Form in History and Fiction: Hume, Fielding, and Gibbon*. Princeton: Princeton University Press, 1970.

Brooks, Peter. *Reading for the Plot: Design and Intention in Narrative*. New York: Alfred A. Knopf, 1984.

Browning, John D., ed. *Satire in the Eighteenth Century*. New York: Garland, 1983.

Bulman, J. C., ed. *Shakespeare on Television: An Anthology of Essays and Reviews*. Hanover: University Press of New England, 1988.

Butler, Joseph. *The Analogy of Religion, Natural and Revealed, to the Constitution and Course of Nature*. Hartford, CT: Samuel G. Goodrich, 1819.

Byrne, Peter. *Natural Religion and the Nature of Religion: The Legacy of Deism*. New York: Routledge, 1989.

Campbell, Jill. *Natural Masques: Gender and Identity in Fielding's Novels and Plays* (Stanford, CA: Stanford University Press, 1995).

Chibka, Robert L. "Taking 'The Serious' Seriously: The Introductory Chapters of *Tom Jones.*" *The Eighteenth Century: Theory and Interpretation* 31 (1990): 23–45.

Clark, J. C. D. *English Society 1688–1832: Ideology, social structure and political practice during the ancien regime.* Cambridge, UK: Cambridge University Press, 1985.

Collier, Jeremy. *A defence of the Short View of the Profaneness and Immorality of the English Stage & c.; Being a Reply to Mr. congreve's Amendments, &c. And to the Vindiction of the author of The Relapse.* London, 1699.

Cope, Kevin L., ed. *Compendious Conversations: The Method of Dialogue in the Early Enlightenment.* Frankfurt: Peter Lang, 1992.

Cragg, Gerald R. *The Church and the Age of Reason.* New York: Penguin Books, 1970.

———. *Reason and Authority in the Eighteenth Century.* New York: Cambridge University Press, 1964.

Craig, William Lane. *The Historical Argument for the Resurrection of Jesus During the Deist Controversy,* Lewiston/Queenston: The Edwin Mellen Press, 1985.

Crane, R. S. "Suggestions Toward a Genealogy of the 'Man of Feeling.'" *English Literary History* 1 (1934): 205–230.

Crites, Stephen. "The Narrative Quality of Experience." *Journal of the American Academy of Religion* 39 (1971), 291–311.

Cunliffe, Christopher, ed. *Joseph Butler's Moral and Religious Thought: Tercentenary Essays.* Oxford: Clarendon Press, 1992.

Damrosch, Leopold. *God's Plot and Man's Stories: Studies in the Fictional Imagination from Milton to Fielding.* Chicago: University of Chicago Press, 1985.

Damrosch, Leo, ed. *The Profession of Eighteenth-Century Literature: Reflections on an Institution.* Madison: University of Wisconsin Press, 1992.

Danto, Arthur C. *Narration and Knowledge.* New York: Columbia University Press, 1985.

Davis, Lennard. *Factual Fictions: The Origins of the English Novel.* New York: Columbia University Press, 1983.

Digeon, Aurelien. *The Novels of Fielding.* New York: E.P. Dutton & Co., 1925.

Dircks, Richard. *Henry Fielding.* Boston: Twayne Publishers, 1983.

Dollimore, Jonathan. *Radical Tragedy: Religion, Ideology and Power in the Drama of Shakespeare and His Contemporaries.* Chicago: University of Chicago Press, 1984.

Evans, James E. "The World According to Paul: Comedy and Theology in *Joseph Andrews.*" *Ariel* 15 (1984): 45–56.

Farley, Benjamin Wirt. *The Providence of God.* Grand Rapids, MI: Baker Book House, 1988.

Fielding, Henry. *Amelia.* Edited by Martin C. Battestin, with a textual introduction by Fredson Bowers. Middletown, CT: Wesleyan University Press, 1983.

———. "Examples of the Interposition of Providence in the Detection and Punishment of Murder." London, 1752.

———. *The History of Tom Jones, A Foundling.* Edited by Fredson Bowers, with an introduction by Martin Battestin. Middletown, CT: Wesleyan University Press, 1975.

————. *Joseph Andrews.* Edited by Martin C. Battestin, with an introduction by Fredson Bowers. Middletown, CT: Wesleyan University Press, 1967.

————. *Tom Jones.* Edited by Sheridan Baker. New York: W.W. Norton & Co., 1973.

Frei, Hans W. *The Eclipse of Biblical Narrative: A Study in Eighteenth and Nineteenth Century Hermeneutics.* New Haven: Yale University Press, 1974.

Gerrish, B. A. *The Old Protestantism and the New: Essays on the Reformation Heritage.* Chicago: University of Chicago Press, 1982.

————. *Tradition and the Modern World: Reformed Theology in the Nineteenth Century.* Chicago: University of Chicago Press, 1978.

Gilkey, Langdon. *Naming the Whirlwind: The Renewal of God-Language.* Indianapolis and New York: The Bobbs-Merrill Co., 1969.

————. *Reaping the Whirlwind: A Christian Interpretation of History.* New York: Seabury Press, 1981.

Goldberg, Homer. *The Art of "Joseph Andrews."* Chicago: University of Chicago Press, 1969.

Goldberg, Michael. "God, Action, and Narrative: *Which* Narrative? *Which* Action? *Which* God?" *Journal of Religion* 68 (1988), 39–56.

Green, Clarence C. *The Neo-Classic Theory of Tragedy in England During the Eighteenth Century.* Cambridge: Harvard University Press, 1934.

Green, Garrett, ed. *Scriptural Authority and Narrative Interpretation.* Philadelphia: Fortress Press, 1987.

Greene, Donald. "Latitudinarianism and Sensibility: The Genealogy of the 'Man of Feeling' Reconsidered." *Modern Philology* 75 (1977): 159–183.

Grelle, Ole Peter, Jonathan I. Israel, and Nicholas Tyacke, eds. *From Persecution to Toleration: The Glorious Revolution and Religion in England.* Oxford: Clarendon Press, 1991.

Harrison, Bernard. *Henry Fielding's "Tom Jones": The Novelist as Moral Philosopher.* London: Chatto & Windus, 1975.

Harrison, Peter. *'Religion' and the Religions in the English Enlightenment.* Cambridge, UK: Cambridge University Press, 1990.

Hatfield, Glenn. *Henry Fielding and the Language of Irony.* Chicago: University of Chicago Press, 1968.

Hauerwas, Stanley and L. Gregory Jones, eds. *Why Narrative? Readings in Narrative Theology.* Grand Rapids, MI: William Eerdmans Publishing Co. 1989.

Heppe, Heinrich. *Reformed Dogmatics.* Rev. and ed. by Ernst Bizer, trans. by G. T. Thomson. Grand Rapids, MI: Baker Book House, 1978.

Hick, John. *Evil and the God of Love.* Rev. and ed. San Francisco: Harper and Row, 1977.

Hilles, Frederick W., ed. *The Age of Johnson: Essays Presented to Chauncey Brewster Tinker.* New Haven: Yale University Press, 1949.

Holquist, Michael. *The Dialogic Imagination: Four Essays by M. M. Bakhtin.* Austin: University of Texas Press,1981.

Hooker, E. N. *The Critical Works of John Dennis.* 2 vols. Baltimore: Johns Hopkins University Press, 1939.

Hudson, Nicholas. "Fielding's Hierarchy of Dialogue: 'Meta-Response' and the Reader of *Tom Jones.*" *Philological Quarterly* 68 (1989): 177–194.

Hume, David. *An Enquiry Concerning Human Understanding/A Letter from a Gentleman to his Friend in Edinburgh.* Ed. Eric Steinberg. Indianapolis: Hackett Publishing Co., 1977.

———. *Dialogues Concerning Natural Religion.* Ed. by Norman Kemp Smith. New York: Macmillan Publishing Co., 1947.

———. *Of the Standard of Taste and Other Essays.* Ed. John W. Lenz. Indianapolis: Bobbs-Merrill Co., 1965.

Hunter, J. Paul. *Before Novels: The Cultural Contexts of Eighteenth-Century English Fiction.* New York: W.W. Norton & Co., 1990.

———, and Martin Battestin. *Henry Fielding in His Time and Ours.* Introduction by Andrew Wright. Pasadena: Castle Press, 1987.

———. *Occasional Form: Henry Fielding and the Chains of Circumstance.* Baltimore: Johns Hopkins University Press, 1975.

Iser, Wolfgang. *The Implied Reader: Patterns of Communication in Prose Fiction from Bunyan to Beckett.* Baltimore: Johns Hopkins University Press, 1974.

Kalpakgian, Mitchell. *The Marvellous in Fielding's Novels.* Lanham, MD: University Press of America, 1981.

Kermode, Frank. *The Art of Telling.* Cambridge: Harvard University Press, 1983.

———. *The Sense of an Ending: Studies in the Theory of Fiction.* New York: Oxford University Press, 1966.

Klingle, Joan E. "Reconciling Johnson's Views on Poetic Justice." *Rocky Mountain Review of Language and Literature* 37 (1983): 195–205.

Knight, Charles A. "*Joseph Andrews* and the Failure of Authority." *Eighteenth-Century Fiction* 4 (1992): 109–124.

Langer, Suzanne K. *Feeling and Form: A theory of art developed from Philosophy in a New Key.* New York: Charles Scribner's Sons, 1953.

Law, William. *The Case of Reason, or Natural Religion, Fairly and Fully Stated. In answer to a Book, entitled, Christianity as Old as the Creation.* vol. 2 of *The Works of William Law.* London: Printed for J. Richardson, 1762 and reprinted for G. Moreton, 1892.

Lechler, Gotthard Victor. *Geschichte des Englischen Deismus.* Stuttgart und Tübingen: J. G. Cottascher Verlag, 1841.

Leith, John, ed. *Creeds of the Churches.* 3rd ed. Atlanta: John Knox Press, 1982.

Locke, John. *An Essay concerning Human Understanding.* Ed. Peter H. Nidditch. Oxford: Clarendon Press, 1975.

Lovejoy, Arthur O. *Essays in the History of Ideas.* Baltimore: Johns Hopkins University Press, 1948.

Lynch, James J. *Henry Fielding and the Heliodoran Novel.* Cranbury, NJ: Associated University Presses, 1986.

———. "Moral Sense and the Narrator of *Tom Jones.*" *Studies in English Literature* 25 (1985): 599 614.

Mackey, Louis. *Peregrinations of the Word* (Ann Arbor: University of Michigan Press, 1997).

Manuel, Frank. *The Changing of the Gods.* Hanover: University Press of New England, 1983.

Marsden, Jean, ed. *The Appropriation of Shakespeare: Post-Renaissance Reconstructions of the Works and the Myth.* New York: Harvester Wheatsheaf, 1991.

McCrea, Brian. "Rewriting *Pamela:* Social Change and Religious Faith in *Joseph Andrews.*" *Studies in the Novel* 16 (1984): 137–149.

McKeon, Michael. *The Origins of the English Novel 1600–1740.* Baltimore: Johns Hopkins University Press, 1987.

McNeill, John T., ed. *Calvin: Institutes of the Christian Religion.* 2 vols. Trans. and indexed by Ford Lewis Battles. Philadelphia: Westminster Press, 1960.

Michaelson, Patricia Howell. "*The Wrongs of Woman* as a Feminist *Amelia.*" *Journal of Narrative Technique* 21 (1991): 250–261.

Miller, Henry Knight. *Henry Fielding's "Tom Jones" and the Romance Tradition.* Victoria: University of Victoria Press, 1976.

Nichols, James and William Nichols. Trans. *The Works of James Arminius.* 3 vols. Intro. by Carl Bangs. Grand Rapids, MI: Baker Book House, 1986.

Nussbaum, Martha C. *The Fragility of Goodness: Luck and Ethics in Greek Tragedy.* Cambridge, UK: Cambridge University Press, 1986.

Orr, John. *English Deism: Its Roots and Its Fruits.* Grand Rapids, MI: Wm. B. Eerdmans Publishing Company, 1934.

Osland, Dianne. "Fielding's *Amelia:* Problem Child or Problem Reader?" *Journal of Narrative Technique* 10 (1980): 56–67.

———. "Tied Back to Back: The Discourse between the Poet and Player and the Exhortations of Parson Adams in *Joseph Andrews.*" *Journal of Narrative Technique* 12 (1982): 191–200.

Paine, Thomas. *The Age of Reason.* Intro. by Philip S. Foner. Secaucus, NJ: Citadel Press, 1974.

Paulson, Ronald. *Satire and the Novel in Eighteenth-Century England.* New Haven: Yale University Press, 1967.

———, and Thomas Lockwood, eds. *Henry Fielding: The Critical Heritage.* New York: Barnes & Noble, 1969.

Pegis, Anton C. *Introduction to St. Thomas Aquinas.* New York: Random House, 1945.

Pelikan, Jaroslav. *The Christian Tradition: A History of the Development of Doctrine.* 5 vols. Chicago: University of Chicago Press, 1971–1987.

Perl, Jeffrey M. "Anagogic Surfaces: How to Read *Joseph Andrews.*" *The Eighteenth Century: Theory and Interpretation* 22 (1981): 249–270.

Preston, John. *The Created Self: The Reader's Role in Eighteenth-Century Fiction.* London: Heinemann Educational Books, 1970.

Preus, Samuel. "Secularizing Divination: Spiritual Biography and the Invention of the Novel." *Journal of the American Academy of Religion* 59 (1991), 441–466.

Quinlan, M. A. *Poetic Justice in the Drama: The History of an Ethical Principle in Literary Criticism.* Notre Dame, IN: Notre Dame University Press, 1912.

Rawson, C. J. *Henry Fielding.* New York: Humanities Press, 1968.

———. *Henry Fielding and the Augustan Ideal Under Stress.* London: Routledge & Kegan Paul, 1972.

————. *Order from Confusion Sprung: Studies in Eighteenth-Century Literature from Swift to Cowper.* London: George Allen & Unwin, 1985.

Ribble, Frederick G. "Aristotle and the 'Prudence' Theme of *Tom Jones.*" *Eighteenth-Century Studies* 15 (1981): 26–47.

————and Anne G. Ribble, *Fielding's Library: An Annotated Catalogue.* Charlottesville: Bibliographical Society of the University of Virginia, 1996.

Richetti, John. "Voice and Gender in Eighteenth-Century Fiction: Haywood to Burney." *Studies in the Novel* 19 (1987): 263–272.

Ricoeur, Paul. *Time and Narrative* (vol. 1). Trans. Kathleen McLaughlin and David Pellauer. Chicago: University of Chicago Press, 1984.

Rogers, Katharine. "Sensitive Feminism *versus* Conventional Sympathy: Richardson and Fielding on Women." *Novel* 9 (1976): 256–270.

Rothstein, Eric. *Systems of Order and Inquiry in Late Eighteenth-Century Fiction.* Berkeley: University of California Press, 1975.

Rupp, Gordon. *Religion in England 1688–1791.* Oxford: Clarendon Press, 1986.

Sacks, Sheldon. *Fiction and the Shape of Belief.* Berkeley and Los Angeles: University of California Press, 1964.

Scheuermann, Mona. "Man Not Providence: Fielding's *Amelia* as a Novel of Social Criticism." *Forum for Modern Language Studies* 20 (1984): 106–123.

Schneider, Aaron. "Hearts and Minds in *Joseph Andrews:* Parson Adams and a War of Ideas." *Philological Quarterly* 66 (1987): 367–389.

Schofield, Mary Anne. "Exploring the Woman Question: A Reading of Fielding's *Amelia.*" *Ariel: A Review of International English Literature* 15 (1985): 45–57.

Shakespeare, William. *King Lear.* Ed. David Bevington. Toronto: Bantam Books, 1980.

Sherbo, Arthur, ed. *Johnson on Shakespeare.* With an introduction by Bertrand H. Bronson. The Yale Edition of the Works of Samuel Johnson. New Haven: Yale University Press, 1968.

Shershow, Scott Cutler. "'Higlety, Piglety, Right or Wrong': Providence and Poetic Justice in Rymer, Dryden, and Tate." *Restoration Studies in English Literary Culture 1660–1700* 15 (1991): 17–26.

Simpson, K. G., ed. *Henry Fielding: Justice Observed.* London and Totowa, NJ: Barnes & Noble, 1985.

Singh, Amrik. "The Argument on Poetic Justice (Addison *versus* Dennis)." *Indian Journal of English Studies* 3 (1962): 61–77.

Smallwood, Angela. *Fielding and the Woman Question.* New York: St. Martin's Press, 1989.

Spacks, Patricia Meyer. "Female Changelessness; Or, What Do Women Want?" *Studies in the Novel* 19 (1987): 273–283.

Stephen, Sir Leslie. *History of English Thought in the Eighteenth Century.* 2 vols. New York: Peter Smith, 1949.

Sternberg, Meir. *Expositional Modes and Temporal Ordering in Fiction.* Baltimore: Johns Hopkins University Press, 1978.

Sullivan, Robert E. *John Toland and the Deist Controversy: A Study in Adaptations.* Cambridge, MA: Harvard University Press, 1982.

Tate, Nahum. *The History of King Lear.* Ed. James Black. Lincoln: University of Nebraska Press, 1975.

Taylor, Charles. *Sources of the Self: The Making of the Modern Identity.* Cambridge: Harvard University Press, 1989.

Taylor, Mark. *Erring: A Postmodern A/Theology.* Chicago: University of Chicago Press, 1984.

Thornbury, E. M. *Henry Fielding's Theory of the Comic Prose Epic.* New York: Russell and Russell, 1966.

Toland, John. *Christianity Not Mysterious.* Faksimile-Neudruck der Erstausgabe London 1696 mit einter Einleitung von Gunter Gawlick und einem textkritischen Anhang. Stuttgart-Bad Cannstatt: Friedrich Frommann Verlag [Gunther Holzboog], 1964.

Tyre, Richard. "Versions of Poetic Justice in the Early Eighteenth Century." *Studies in Philology* 54 (1957): 29–44.

Van Boheemen, Christine. *The Novel as Family Romance: Language, Gender, and Authority from Fielding to Joyce.* Ithaca: Cornell University Press, 1987.

Vance, Eugene. *Mervelous Signals.* Lincoln: University of Nebraska Press, 1986.

Varey, Simon. *Henry Fielding.* New York: Cambridge University Press, 1986.

Wanko, Cheryl. "Characterization and the Reader's Quandary in Fielding's *Amelia.*" *Journal of English and Germanic Philology* 90 (1991): 505–523.

Watt, Ian. *The Rise of the Novel: Studies in Defoe, Richardson and Fielding.* Berkeley: University of California Press, 1957.

Weinsheimer, Joel C. *Eighteenth-Century Hermeneutics: Philosophy of Interpretation in England from Locke to Burke.* New Haven: Yale University Press, 1993.

West, Rebecca. *The Court and the Castle: A Study of the Interactions of Political and Religious Ideas in Imaginative Literature.* London: Macmillan & Co., 1958.

Willey, Basil. *The Eighteenth Century Background: Studies on the Idea of Nature in the Thought of the Period.* Boston: Beacon Press, 1961.

Williams, Aubrey. *An Approach to Congreve.* New Haven: Yale University Press, 1979.

———. "Interpositions of Providence and the Design of Fielding's Novels." *South Atlantic Quarterly* 70 (1971): 265–286.

Zach, Wolfgang. *Poetic Justice: Theorie und Geschichte einer literarischen Doktrin: Begriff—Idee—Komoedienkonzeption.* Tübingen: Max Niemeyer Verlag, 1986.

Zimansky, Curt A., ed. *The Critical Works of Thomas Rymer.* New Haven: Yale University Press, 1956.

Ziolkowski, Eric J. *The Sanctification of Don Quixote: From Hidalgo to Priest.* University Park: Penn State University Press, 1991

Index

Abraham, 36, 37, 43, 123, 124, 125, 126
"absolute man," 16
Addison, Joseph, 22, 24, 29, 30, 31, 32, 47, 49, 92, 118
agency, divine (supernatural), 15
    human, xii, xiv, 77, 78, 79, 83, 88, 79
allegory, 15, 40
Alter, Robert, 7, 17, 92
Amelia, xiii, xvi, 3, 5, 7, 8, 9, 11, 17, 18, 22, 51, 52, 55, 84, 87, 89, 91, 92, 93, 94, 95, 96, 97, 98, 99, 100, 101, 103, 105, 107, 108, 110, 112, 113, 114, 115, 118, 119, 120, 121, 123
Aquinas, xiii, xiv
Aristotle, 26, 58, 59, 68, 78, 111
Arminius, xiv
Arnold, Matthew, 23
atheism, atheists, 37, 38,48
atonement, xiv, 42
Augustine, xiv, xv, xvi, 1, 2, 3, 13, 18, 19, 52, 119, 120, 121, 126, 127, 128
    Confessions, xiv, 1, 52, 119

Barth, Karl, 16
Battestin, Martin, 8, 9, 10, 17, 18
beauty, xi, 29, 68
Beckett, Samuel, 127
    Waiting for Godot, 127
Bible, 14, 15, 36, 37, 66
    biblical hermeneutics, approaches to biblical narrative, 14, 15, 16, 41

Gospels, 126
    See also Scriptures
Braudy, Leo, 9, 10, 12, 18
Butler, Joseph, 22, 23, 44, 46, 47, 48, 49, 81, 92, 119, 128
    The Analogy of Religion, 44, 45, 92
Byrne, 33

Calvin, John, xiv, xv
chance, accident, fate, xii, xiv, xvi, 3, 10, 17, 18, 84
    See also fatalism, fortune, wheel of fortune
Christ/Jesus/Son, 35, 36, 41, 42, 46
Christian piety, 45
Christianity, Christians, xi, 7, 8, 9, 13, 14, 17, 22, 23, 24, 25, 26, 31, 32, 33, 34, 46, 48, 49, 61, 62, 78, 80, 84, 93, 108, 112, 113, 114, 119, 124, 128
    Christian apologetics, 32
    reasonableness of, 34, 35, 36, 38, 41, 44 (of God)
    See also reason
Church, xi
Church of England, xi, 67, 68
Coleridge, Samuel Taylor, 5
Collier, Jeremy, 22, 24, 25, 26, 32
comedy/comic, 26, 82, 85, 115, 124
Confucius, 42
Congreve, William, 21, 25
conversion, 119–121
created order/natural order, 25, 49, 118, 122, 123, 127,

creation, created world, xiii, 4, 5, 18,
    22, 23, 33, 39, 40, 47, 48, 49,
    80, 117, 118, 122, 123, 125
criminal biography, 12
critical faith/covenant of critical faith,
    74, 88
    See also readerly faith

deconstruction, 6
Defoe, Daniel, 11, 12
deism, deists, deism controversy, xiii, 4,
    9, 22, 32, 37, 43, 44, 48, 49,
    51, 67, 80, 81, 87, 88, 92, 118,
    123
Dennis, John, 22, 24, 29, 30, 31, 32,
    47, 92, 118
denouement, xvi, 23, 25, 31, 32, 83,
    84
    in *King Lear* (Shakespeare's or
        Tate's), 27, 28, 29, 31, 118
design, human plans, see *agency, human*
    divine, see *divine providence*
devil, 85, 86
divine justice, 45
divine plan, design/providential order,
    9, 10, 52, 53, 60, 67, 85, 86,
    87, 88, 89, 91, 107, 122
    See also divine providence
divine power, 43
divine providence (intervention),
    supernatural interposition xiii,
    xiv, xv, xvi, 1, 2, 3, 4, 5, 8, 9,
    10, 12, 13, 17, 18, 21, 22, 23,
    24, 25, 30, 31, 32, 33, 36, 37,
    39, 40, 43, 44, 45, 46, 47, 49,
    51, 52, 53, 60, 62, 64, 65, 66,
    67, 72, 74, 76, 77, 78, 80, 83,
    84, 85, 86, 87, 88, 89, 91, 92,
    93, 101, 102, 103, 107, 111,
    112, 113, 114, 115, 117, 118,
    119, 120, 121, 122, 123, 125,
    126, 127, 128
divine reason. *See* reason, divine

empiricism, 12, 13, 122

Enlightenment, xiii, 16, 126
eschatology, eschaton, xiii, 4, 5, 18, 23,
    33, 49, 86, 122, 123, 127
Eubulus, 21, 22
Euripides, 24, 25
evil, xiv, xv, 4, 5, 8, 19, 22, 23, 29, 30,
    39, 42, 47, 48, 49, 51, 52, 53,
    62, 64, 65, 66, 67, 68, 74, 75,
    80, 81, 85, 86, 87, 88, 89, 91,
    92, 93, 97, 98, 99, 100, 101,
    102, 103, 104, 105, 107, 111,
    112, 113, 114, 118, 122, 123
    three dimensions of evil in *Amelia*,
        120
    three kinds of evil in the novels of
        Fielding, xv, xvi.
    See also incursions of evil

faith, xiv, 1, 7, 22, 30, 36, 38, 41, 42,
    73, 74, 77, 79, 82, 83, 88, 115,
    127
    and understanding, rationality, 36,
        38
    See also readerly faith
fall, fallenness, 16, 19, 52, 120
family, family life, xvi
    See also marriage
fatalism, fate, xii, 45, 18
    See also chance
Faulkner, William, 2, 3, 18, 19, 126,
    127
Feuerbach, Ludwig Andreas, 127
Fielding, Henry
    action in the novels of, 57, 59,
        72–78, 83, 98
    against a background of polemics,
        22
    characterization in the novels of,
        54
    as Christian, 7, 8, 17
    conflict of/relation between
        literature and religion, 8, 10
        See also literature and religion
    (didactic) role of narrator in, 54, 73,
        119

displacement of divine design, language of in *Amelia,* 91, 92, 93, 97, 102, 103, 107, 113
distance from romance, 13
and ethics/morality, 8, 9
evil in the novels of/conflict of evil and providence in the novels of, 51, 53, 62, 65, 74, 85, 100, 101
See also evil, incursions of evil
"Examples of the Interposition . . . ," 21, 51
historical context of narrative art, 118
historical method, 57
hypocrisy in, 63
"Interpositions . . . ," 22, 84
modernity of, 114
narrative art, xii, xiii, xvii, 3, 16, 17, 18, 22, 51, 54, 55, 57, 58, 59, 60, 67, 72, 73, 74, 75, 84, 91, 93, 114, 115, 117, 127, 128
narrative as (credible/reliable) history, 58, 79, 87, 99
narrative commentary, 9, 12, 13, 52, 53, 67, 68, 69, 70, 71, 72, 73, 75, 82, 83, 87, 95, 98, 99, 101, 105, 127
narrative didacticism, intrusiveness, controlling interest, authority, xiii, 4, 6, 10, 52, 54, 68, 70, 71, 73, 98, 119
as narrative theologian, 6, 19, 128
narrator as historian, 16, 58, 77
playfulness in the writings of F./of narrator, 82- 85
principled diffidence in, *see principled diffidence*
psychology in/Fielding as psychologist, 7, 54, 91, 121
reception of, 6
reliability of narrator, 57, 73, 74
religion as fundamental/unavoidable in Fielding's novels, 17, 18

religion in, xii, 6, 7, 8, 10, 11, 13, 17
rhetoric of embellishment in the novels of, 57
and social realism, 7, 8
(social) realism in, 7, 8
and theological orientation/religious sensibility, xvii, 16, 118, 123, 127
verisimilitude (realism) in the novels of, 12, 13, 15, 16, 54, 57, 58, 71, 72, 73, 75, 79, 80, 87, 89, 97, 98
historical credibility, 77
possibility, 77, 78, 79, 84
probability, 77, 79, 84
conservation of character, 77, 84
Yahweh, Fielding's narrator as, 126
final judgment, Day of Judgment, xiii, 19, 22, 25, 47, 48, 49, 51, 64, 81, 86, 87, 92, 93, 101, 104, 107, 108, 109, 112, 113, 118, 119, 122, 127
forgiveness, 47
"formal realism," 11, 12, 13, 16, 87
F/fortune, 3, 27, 46, 77, 81, 94, 104
freedom, free activity of humans, free will, liberty, xiii, xiv, 40, 45
See also human will
Frei, Hans, 14, 15, 16, 17, 87
The Eclipse of Biblical Narrative, 14, 15, 16
on *Tom Jones,* 15
on narrative realism, 15

Garrick, David, 28
Genesis, 14
as "realistic narrative," 14
Chapter 22, 63, 123, 124, 126
Gibbon, Edward, 10
God, xiii, xiv, xv, 1, 2, 3, 23, 31, 35, 36, 37, 38, 39, 43, 44, 46, 52, 55, 64, 103, 119, 120, 121, 123, 125, 126, 127, 128
activity in the world, *see divine providence*

goodness, beneficence, and
    perfection, xv, 23, 39, 40, 42,
    117
    faith in, *See* faith
the good, natural good, xi, 53
goodness, 4, 23, 29, 40, 51, 63, 75, 77,
    97, 103, 104, 109, 111, 127
    of the created order, 23
    See also virtue

happiness, (happy ending), 3, 5, 17,
    30, 31, 38, 39, 41, 42, 45, 46,
    47, 48, 49, 52, 63, 65, 73, 77,
    80, 81, 82, 83, 84, 86, 87, 88,
    94, 108, 110, 115, 117, 122,
    123
    as a state of pleasure, 31
Harrison, 33
hatred, 44
hermeneutics
    See also biblical hermeneutics
Hick, John, xv
historical realism, 17
"History," concept of in eighteenth-
    century writing, 9, 10, 16
    See also history, the historical
history, the historical, 12, 13, 15, 16,
    21, 25, 33, 37, 57, 67, 77, 78,
    79, 80, 83, 84, 86, 87, 88, 89,
    99
    biblical narrative as, 14
    See also "History"
history, vs. providence, 12
The History of Tom Jones, xi, xiii, xv, xvi,
    3, 5, 7, 8, 9, 10, 12, 13, 15, 17,
    18, 21, 51, 52, 53, 54, 55, 66,
    67, 68, 71, 72, 73, 74, 75, 76,
    77, 78, 79, 82, 83, 84, 85, 86,
    87, 88, 89, 91, 92, 93, 95, 96,
    97, 98, 100, 101, 103, 109,
    112, 113, 115, 117, 119, 120,
    121, 122, 123, 124, 125, 126
Holy Spirit, 46
Homer, 55, 78, 111
    The Iliad, 111

honor, xi
Horace, 26, 54
    translation of *The Odyssey,* 54
hubris, 43
human immortality, 30
human judgment, limits of, 74, 75
human knowledge, 55, 126, 127
human mortality, 30
human nature/character, xii, 30, 54, 60,
    71, 73, 74, 77, 79, 86, 98
human psychology, 54
    See also Fielding, psychology in
human will, xiii, xiv
    See also agency
Hume, David, xii, 10, 48, 49, 119, 122
    *Dialogue Concerning Natural
        Religion,* 48
    *An Enquiry Concerning Human
        Understanding,* 48, 49, 119
Hunter, J. Paul, 5, 92

incredible, the, 79
    See also marvelous
incursions (intrusions) of evil, xiv, 65,
    67, 85, 86, 87, 88
    See also evil
infidelity, 93, 120, 121
Isaac, 36, 37, 123, 124, 126
Islam, xi

Jefferson, Thomas, 126
John, Archbishop, 34
Johnson, Ben, 5
Johnson, Samuel, 24, 28, 29, 31, 32,
    118
Joseph Andrews, xiii, xv, 3, 5, 7, 10, 22,
    51, 52, 53, 54, 55, 57, 58, 59,
    60, 62, 64, 65, 66, 67, 68, 87,
    89, 93, 94, 95, 112, 115, 117,
    119, 121, 122, 123, 124, 125
Judaism, xi
    anti-Jewish sentiment, 48
    in relation to Christianity, 48
justice, 28, 29, 30, 47
    See also divine justice

Kermode, Frank, 17, 72

language, 41
latitudinarianism, 8, 9
Law, William, xii, 22, 23, 32, 42, 43,
    44, 49, 119, 128
    The Case of Reason, 42, 44
Leland, John, 48
literature and religion, 4, 6, 8, 10, 14
    See also Fielding, conflict of/relation
        between literature and religion
Locke, John, 33
London, xvi, 21, 22
love, 44, 54, 70, 73, 76, 77, 79, 88,
    103
Luke, Gospel of, 35
lust, 62
    See also vice

Mandeville, Bernard, xii
marriage, marital union, 58, 62, 66, 80,
    81, 88, 94, 99, 100, 101, 108,
    117, 118, 120, 121, 123
marvelous, the, 12, 13, 16, 72, 77, 78,
    79, 80, 83, 87, 88, 89
    See also incredible
Mary, 35, 37
Matthew, Gospel of, 62
McKeon, Michael, 12, 13, 14, 16, 18,
    23
Middleton, Conyers, 35
Milton, John, 52
    Paradise Lost, 52
mimesis, 29, 31, 59
miracles, miraculous activity, 35, 37,
    48, 49
miraculous, the, 14, 14
misery, 31, 45, 46, 81, 82, 104, 122,
    123
morality, moral obligation,
    (culpability), xii, xvi, 8, 40, 41,
    42, 43, 58, 80, 89, 91, 100,
    120, 124
Morgan, Thomas, 48, 119
    The Moral Philosopher, 119

mystery, 36, 42, 44
myth, 15

narrating providence, xiv, 1, 17
    See also Fielding, narrative art
narrative, xii, xiv, 1, 2, 3, 4, 5, 6, 19
    in study of religion, 6, 14
    Biblical, 14
    See also Fielding, narrative art
    See also retrospection
narrative commentary,
    See Fielding, narrative commentary
narrative realism, 15, 16
narrative theology, xvi, 6, 14, 49
    See also Fielding, theological
        orientation
narratorial authority
    See Fielding, narrative didacticism,
        etc.
natural history, 21
nature/natural world/"natural" order of
    the world, 25, 39, 40, 42, 49,
    118, 122,123, 125, 127
natural religion, 38, 42, 46, 119
necessity, 45, 84
novel
    role of religion in, 11
    See also "rise of the novel"

patience, 62
Paul, 41
Plato, 25, 66, 68
Plautus, 26
poetic justice, xiii, 4, 22, 23, 24, 25,
    26, 28, 29, 30, 31, 32, 33, 44,
    47, 49, 51, 88, 92, 123
Pope, Alexander, 117
possibility of narrative, 77, 78, 79
predestination, xiv
(principled) diffidence, xvi, 3, 4, 5 (9),
    17, 18, 51, 54, 121
probability of narrative, 77, 78, 79
providential narrative, xvii, 126
    See also narrating providence
prudence, 8, 9, 76, 77, 88, 89, 106

Rawson, C. J., 92
reader-response criticism, 54
readerly contempt, 79
readerly faith, 77, 88
    See also critical faith
readers' judgment, 54, 73, 74, 75
    see also sagacious reader
reason, rational capacities, 23, 31, 34,
    35, 36, 37, 38, 39, 40, 41, 42,
    43, 44, 45, 47, 48, 67, 80, 124
    authority/power of, 41, 43
    conflict with temptation, 45
    divine, 43, 44
    enhanced by education, 44
    and happiness, 39
Reformation, 13
religion, xi, xii, 6, 7, 9, 31, 32, 42, 67,
    68, 69
    and art, 31
    Christianity as true religion, 48
        See also Christianity
    and human happiness, 42
    and literature, *See also* literature and
        religion and Fielding, literature
        and religion
    rational/reasonable religion/relation
        to reason, 32, 41, 43
        See also reason
    revealed, 40, 46
    and stories, 14
    theology/theological controversy in
        the eighteenth century, 6, 33
    see also deism
    study of, 6
    vs. honor, xi
retrospection, retrospective
    commentary/narrative, xii, xiii,
    xiv, xv, xvi, 2, 3, 4, 19, 52, 55,
    58, 74, 75, 76, 84, 85, 87, 88,
    89, 115, 128
revelation (divine) (revealed truth), 26,
    32, 34, 35, 36, 38, 39, 42, 46,
    47, 67, 80
    reasonableness of, 36, 38
Richardson, Samuel, 11, 12, 91
    Clarissa, 91

    Pamela, 91
rise of the novel, 6, 10, 11
romance (genre), 12, 13, 79
Rymer, Thomas, 24, 25, 28, 29
    on "poetic justice," 24, 25

sagacious reader/sagacity, 4, 54, 58, 59,
    60, 61, 62, 66, 71, 72, 73, 75,
    77, 79, 85, 86, 91, 95, 96, 99,
    113, 120
salvation, xiv
Scriptures/Holy Scriptures, 25, 26, 34,
    35, 36, 37, 40, 46, 47, 123
    New Testament/Old Testament, 36,
        37, 46
    Old Testament prophecies, 41
    Scriptural authority, 41
    See also Bible, Genesis, Genesis 22
Second Coming, 41
Seneca, 61, 66
sense of ending, 51, 84, 112, 121, 122,
    123, 126
sense of the story, 14
sex, 120
Shakespeare, 26, 27, 28, 29, 124
    King Lear, 24, 26, 27, 28, 29, 32,
    124
Sherlock, Thomas, Bishop of London,
    21
sin, 16
skepticism, 4, 12, 13, 122, 127
Smith, Adam, 38
Sophocles, 5, 24, 25, 83, 84
    Oedipus Rex, 83, 84
souls, 25
South, Robert, 34
The Spectator, 29, 30
spiritual autobiography, 12
Sullivan, Robert, 32
Synoptic Gospels, 14
    as "realistic narrative," 14

Tate, Nahum, 24, 26, 27, 32, 118, 124
    on "poetic justice," 24
    The History of King Lear, 26, 27, 28,
    29, 30, 31, 32, 118, 124

temptation, 45, 121
See also reason, conflict with
temptation
Terence, 26
theodicy, xiv, 23, 42, 101
Tillotson, 34
Tindal, Matthew, 22, 23, 32, 33, 38,
39, 40, 41, 42, 43, 45, 47, 48,
49, 80, 118
Christianity As Old As the Creation,
38, 42
Toland, John, 22, 23, 32, 33, 34, 35,
36, 37, 38, 41, 43, 44, 45, 47,
48, 80, 118, 124
Christianity Not Mysterious, 33, 34,
35, 36, 124
Tom Jones, xi
tragedy/tragic, 26, 28, 29, 30, 31, 82,
83, 85, 115, 118, 124
transubstantiation, 34
travel narrative, 12

understanding, 1, 36, 48

vice, wickedness, 16, 24, 26, 28, 30,
44, 46, 47, 48, 51, 66, 79, 80,
81, 84, 122, 123
Virgil, 55
virtue (goodness), xi, 9, 12, 16, 24, 26,
27, 28, 29, 44, 45, 46, 47, 48,
51, 68, 69, 71, 75, 76, 77, 79,
80, 81, 87, 88, 89, 103, 107,
122, 127
See also goodness
Voltaire, 53, 64, 126
Candide, 53

Watt, Ian, 11, 12, 13, 14, 16, 18,
87
on Sophia Western and Tom Jones,
12
The Rise of the Novel, 11
Wesley, John, xii, xiv
wheel of fortune, 7, 8, 17
See also fortune, chance
Wilde, Oscar, 5
wishful thinking, 127